THE
LONELY
QUEST

The Evolution of Presidential Leadership

Robert Rienow
and
Leona Train Rienow

FOLLETT PUBLISHING COMPANY

Chicago New York

Library of Congress Catalog Card Number: 66-16601

Manufactured in the United States of America

First Printing

Designed by Patrick J. Birch

FOLLETT PUBLISHING COMPANY
1010 West Washington Boulevard
Chicago, Illinois 60607

To the memory of
FRANK
the most loyal of friends,
the strongest support in bad times,
the most joyful companion in good.

Preface

Every naturalist knows that when the forests are decimated, the timber wolves perish; that when the swamps are drained, the waterfowl decline. A few concerned people are even aware that, routed by bulldozers and pesticides, the American eagle has begun its slow but ineluctable flight into eternity. An altered habitat is death to its denizens.

But few of us have realized that the great majority of our Presidents of the past could not have thrived, either, in a forest of radio and television transmitting towers. Today's President is a new creature with startingly different talents from his forerunners, and with a greatly enhanced and more dangerous role. Technology and environmental change have transformed the Presidency into a power complex never dreamed of, and into an agency of upheaval that has tremendous overtones for the future.

The Presidency, for all the long years of American history right up to the present day, has towered on the political horizon. But the "President of all the people," the titular leader, the ceremonial head, hungered for greater closeness and understanding with the populace. Now at last he has reached the people and adds the authority of a direct and continuing mandate to his role. This, then, is the story of that restless, lonely seeking, a tracing of presidential leadership from its very beginnings.

It is also a study of the incredible changes that have come about in our government because of the new intimacy and of what they may portend. For as we embrace the new "instant democracy" we hazard many things. One is the loss of the President as the President of all the people, the symbol of our national unity—the only stabilizing and centralizing influence this democracy possesses. This is his "kingship," his unifying role and his international image. Will the President, descending to commonalty, cultivating political support mainly in the cities as he now *must* do, be forced to forfeit his royal image?

Many things have happened to the image of the President since George Washington accepted the three stilted huzzahs of the populace with a stiff bow, re-entered the legislative chambers, and stood there fumbling before the Senate with his inaugural speech, "agitated and embarrassed more than ever he was by leveled cannon or pointed musket, [who] trembled, and several times could scarce make out to read." How did the diffident, unsure, circumscribed leader of the eighteenth and nineteenth centuries evolve into the polished, free-wheeling, confident Chief Executive of today? And how did the awe-struck, almost inarticulate mass that was the people evolve into the uninhibited mob that today fights to reach the President's person to touch, embrace, even manhandle him?

The story of the nineteenth-century Presidents is a story of frustration, crushed spirit, and despair. Some of these shackled men were unambitious and quiescent; a handful of them lashed out violently against their bars. It is to this handful that we give attention, for they are the men who have helped narrow the chasm between the leader and the populace. Because the dialogue of the nineteenth century was confined almost entirely to election campaigns, we have concentrated on them, particularly on those most significant in bringing the President and the people into closer understanding.

Throughout the study we sensed in the earlier Presidents a strong yearning to become what the twentieth century has at last made possible. The father-leader is now a political reality. Congress, courts, and corporations fade into the background before the potentials of such a power alliance. We have arrived at a milestone in our government, and it demands recognition.

But the dialogue between the President and the people, pursued with such anguish of frustration over the decades and but so recently realized, is in real danger of distortion —by the very technology that brought it about. And is it possible to reconcile the President's kingship (at which only the uninformed will scoff) with his new role as "President of the cities"?

On the other side of the ledger, the possibility of great good in the new intimacy is so awesome as to raise a fever in the most torpid mind.

What is the compromise?

Acknowledgments

One of the bonuses in the writing of a volume such as this is the stimulating association it affords with scholars in the field. Our long participation in conservation has provided us with a similarly challenging friendship with outstanding specialists in the fascinating field of ecology. In the following pages the reader will see how we have borrowed the conception of environmental relationships and influences from the natural sciences and applied them to the political field. We can scarcely acknowledge all the persons who contributed to this exercise in cross-pollination (which might be christened "ecopolitics").

We are heavily indebted to Dr. Hugh M. Flick, historian

and Associate Commissioner of Education of New York State, who not only read the manuscript and identified its controversy, but rekindled our enthusiasm. The long hours spent over this manuscript by our editor, Donald J. Davidson, are greatly appreciated.

To the fraternity of friendly librarians who staff the New York State Library and the State University of New York Library, who have helped and shown constant interest, we owe a continuing obligation.

Our dedication page marks the major tragedy that befell our household while this book was being written. In the death of Frank Fraser we lost a friend who vigilantly protected our creative moments from interruption; his role was shared and continues to be filled by his widow Gertrude. Our thanks must go, too, to our meticulous research assistant, Miss Florence L. Powell.

We pray that our part in this undertaking matches the skill and dedication of those who have helped us. If, in spite of care and diligence, a foundling fact has been misplaced, we ask that it be returned to our doorstep.

Contents

xiii

Contents

Part I

The Eighteenth-Century Pattern:
The Hero-God President

One

One Stubborn Man

"Get Wilson!" shouted the mob as, to the ragged beat of drums, the militia began its maudlin march from Burns's Tavern in Philadelphia to the home of James Wilson, signer of the Declaration of Independence, gentleman, and fervent patriot.

For days in this fall of 1779 militiamen had been congregating at Paddy Burns's Tavern on Tenth Street "full of dark threats and mutterings" against well-to-do Philadelphians who had been suspected of profiteering, price fixing, and speculating in western lands.

And with the lifting of each mug of October's nut-brown ale the grievances and grumblings had increased.

For the Revolution, directed against the British overlords, was nonetheless infused with strong resentment against those whom Thomas Jefferson had called the pseudo aristocrats among the colonists. In every state, not least Pennsylvania, there existed a seething demand for social change. Many of these boisterous fellows were German recruits, poorly trained and more poorly disciplined; all were restless with the restlessness and quick angers of wartime. And weapons in hand have a way of sparking a bravado never felt when the hand is on the plow.

"Let's get some of these fancy nabobs. . . . Who lives hereabouts? Speak up! Who can we go after?" Men mounted tables and droned through the lists of wrongs, lists that became longer and more colorful as the hours passed. "I ask you, how much British gold is behind these so-called Republicans? All these Easterners are speculators, rascals. . . ."

"Didn't Tom Paine say Wilson was a partner in the Foreign Commercial Company? Then there's Robert Morris—"

"You take Morris! *I'll* take James Wilson!"

"Get Wilson!" rose the cries. "Get Wilson!"

The frontiersmen against the commercial Easterners, radical defenders of the state constitution against the advocates of a new and more forward-looking constitution for Pennsylvania, sometimes hungry and always suspicious farmers against businessmen who, it was whispered, were speculating in wartime in public moneys and in foodstuffs. Had not their Commander in Chief, George Washington, himself indicted the profiteers when he said, "Such a dearth of public spirit and want of virtue, such stockjobbing and fertility in all the low arts to obtain advantage of one kind or another . . . I never saw before, and I pray God I may never be a witness to again! . . . Such a dirty mercenary spirit pervades the whole that I should not be at all surprised at any disaster that may happen."

But Dr. Benjamin Rush, noted physician, scholar, and signer of the Declaration of Independence, had shrugged off the accusations that were flying about with an impatient sigh: the current money instability and price fluctuations would "corrupt a community of angels." Who could regulate them? Certainly the defenders of Pennsylvania's constitution—the "Constitutionalists"—were making such efforts in their frequent rump sessions, with wild futility. In Rush's unvarnished medical phraseology, such local, bootless stabs at control did as much good as "a violent puke given to a man in the last stages of consumption." And where there was price instability men would take advantage of it, would they not? But how to explain all this to an unthinking, restless, and increasingly intoxicated mob?

Charles Page Smith, in *James Wilson, Founding Father,* recounts what followed on that memorable October day. As the mob got its blood up, names were bandied about with more and more fervor. What of Delaney? What of Nesbitt? There was something of a choice. The haranguers against Robert Morris shouted these names down. Then someone remembered: hadn't James Wilson, that stubborn Scot, stood in court and defended those two Quakers, those *Tory lovers,* Carlisle and Roberts, who were later executed for hobnobbing with the British? Besides, Wilson's home was close at hand. A roar went up. Wilson it would be!

There was a rush toward the door. These angry farmers

5

did not pause to recollect that war cannot be pursued without money, lots of it, and that quite possibly their wages, such as they were, were at that moment being paid by the funds raised by men such as Morris and Wilson, who knew how to manipulate prices to divert a small trickle of gold into Washington's depleted war chest. If, as someone has remarked, the tongue, the pen, and the sword of the Revolution were all Virginian (Henry, Jefferson, and Washington), the purse was largely Pennsylvanian.

As for land speculation, even their beloved General dealt vastly in land—33,000 acres of it, in fact. But the General was a soldier who had had two horses shot from under him and four bullet holes in his cloak. There were no whispers about Washington's apprehending a shipment of tea or sugar in transit. Washington did not defend traitors. Joseph Nathan Kane related in his small handbook, *Facts About the Presidents,* that when Thomas Hickey, one of the General's own bodyguard, was court-martialed for conspiracy and condemned to hang in the Bowery before twenty thousand approving citizens, the General merely said he hoped that it would "be a warning to every soldier in the Army to avoid those crimes and all other, so disgraceful to the character of a soldier and pernicious to his country, whose pay he receives and bread he eats."

So it was "Get Wilson!" The shouts became so loud that friends of the wealthy lawyer heard them and came to warn him, persuading him to appeal urgently to the Pennsylvania Assembly for protection. But assemblies are notoriously slow to move; quickly the harassed patriot sent his wife Rachel, late in her fourth pregnancy, to the home of

Robert Morris, their close friend, and braced himself to defend his home against the attack he now knew could not be forestalled.

Happily the Wilson home was a stout brick house with double walls and recessed windows; this day it bristled with the muskets of as courageous a little band as ever had faced a redcoat brigade. Within the fortress were the besieged man's relatives and loyal friends: Colonel Stephen Chambers of the militia, Captain Campbell, an invalided Continental officer, and several other heroes and officers who had seen battle against the British. There was also Wilson's law apprentice, the financier Robert Morris, a druggist named Delaney, a doctor friend and his brother, Sam Morris, and General John Mifflin, who at once took command of the defenders, examined their weapons, and proceeded to march them in military formation up and down before the brick citadel. The druggist was sent running to Carpenter's Hall "to cram his pockets with powder and bullets" for the siege. The oncoming mob was now but three blocks away.

With Delaney's return the small but stouthearted band fell back to the "fort" and at once barricaded the first-floor doors and windows. As the drunken militiamen and hangers-on surged into Walnut Street, two Continental officers stepped forth to halt them. But the mob rushed at the officers, jabbing crazily at them with bayonets, and broke into a run toward the house. They surged into the yard yelling curses that brought Captain Campbell to the window. "Move on! You fools! What are you doing? I order you, move on!" he shouted. His answer was a musket shot, and he fell, mortally wounded.

Shock and horror gripped the defenders; rifle fire blazed

from every window; the siege had begun in earnest. As the shots burst forth, the disorganized crowd scuttled for shelter. But they left five bodies sprawled on the cobblestones in puddles of blood.

Sobered now, but still determined, the militiamen regrouped. They sent a few of their number to the fort for crowbars and a fieldpiece. General Mifflin, hazarding his life, appeared at an upper window to plead with the mob to disperse; his only answer was catcalls and shot that splintered the glass above him. Out came the General's two pistols, and more of the mob went down. But even as he fired, the ominous sound of sledges against the rear door told the defenders that time was running out. They rushed for the stairs, and as the back door came crashing in, they loosed a withering volley. The invaders wavered, but before they retreated, firing blindly, Captain Chambers was dragged from the stairs and bayonetted. And before the invaders could reform behind the newly arrived fieldpiece, with which they expected to demolish the house and all in it, the City Troop of Light Horse, "knee buttons unfastened and boots unlaced," came dashing in to restore order.

The arrival of the city forces was the fresh wind that dispersed the last fogs of intoxication from the minds of the unruly militiamen; they vanished like wraiths, but not before twenty-seven stragglers had been roughly clapped into the State House prison. Fourteen bodies lay on the stones; within the house were one dead and three wounded. When at last General Benedict Arnold, military commandant of Philadelphia, came steaming up on his horse, he encountered only the wilted, relieved little battalion; and the towering, heavy-set Wilson was lumbering about his ravaged home peering ruefully over the thick-lensed glasses perched on his nose.

Wilson had been stubborn and foolhardy enough to withstand the assault, but he was not witless enough to linger in Philadelphia and invite another such attack. For that very day the Germantown militia rushed the jail in attempts to release their incarcerated fellows; and the burial of the "poor unfortunates" who had expired on the cobblestones was scheduled for the next day.

Bowing to these "Circumstances Not Calculated to Allay the Passions of Men in a Ferment," as Morris expressed it, Wilson reluctantly fled from the city. For two interminable weeks he sat at the Morrises' country estate in a fidgety gloom, composing long missives of indignation and defense to the various authorities, absentmindedly drinking the tepid tea and munching the indifferent victuals produced by the Morrises' manservant.

But by the nineteenth of October he could endure his exile no longer. He was never a man to turn his back on action. Soon he was back in Philadelphia, busy again with his campaign against the Pennsylvania constitution, as determined and fervent as ever. "The single legislature is the incubus of despotism," he had said, and he would fight the Constitutionalists to the end to reform the outmoded constitution, cost what it might. But he could not understand why his countrymen, the men of the woods and frontiers, so misinterpreted his motives. "I have no motives—" he mumbled to himself, gazing through the shattered glass while his servants loosened the tacks in the blood-spattered carpeting of the stairwell and worked to repair the broken door, "no interest . . . but the liberty and happiness of the State of Pennsylvania. . . ." God was his judge.

The assault had settled down to a series of court orders, hearings, posted bail, and legal entanglements. Then suddenly the crisis, the small "war within a war," dissipated entirely at the tremendous news of the arrival of the French fleet off Georgia! Fie now on petty disturbances, inflamed tempers, and such mundane considerations as the price of tea and bread. There was a war *nearly won,* they said—no, *won,* said some! And discontented militiamen looking for a brawl were soon forgotten, just as it is always infinitely easier to forget a shameful incident in one's life than a proud one.

Thus terminated the most perilous and shaking experience in the life of James Wilson, Founding Father, a man dedicated in every act to the cause of freedom and to the new nation. It is recounted here because of a strange anomaly: this man who was almost lynched by a mob, who was forced to seek refuge from the intolerance and violence of the people, turned out to be the foremost proponent of the wisdom of the will of the common people. Always the outstanding champion of popular rule in government, he declared, in 1776, that the raising of troops was "an Honour . . . cloathed . . . with the sacred Authority of the People, from WHOM ALL LEGITIMATE AUTHORITY proceeds." The attack on his life by Hamilton's "common-rabble"—this taste of mob rule—made Wilson waver not one whit; indeed, it seems to have cemented his conviction.

Had James Wilson been of a different temperament— had he been a trifle less stubborn or, perhaps, a little less forgiving—the entire history of American government might have been altered. For it was James Wilson who insisted in the Constitutional Convention so strongly and consistently on the popular election of the President of the United States that he weakened the opposition (even though indirectly), swayed Madison (and one or two others), and converted the most strategically placed man

in the Convention, former New Yorker but now Pennsylvanian Gouverneur Morris. From Wilson's plan came a
brilliant compromise, the electoral college. And popular
election was an outgrowth of the altered plan. In effect the
plan, by wresting the choice of President from the machi-
nations of the Congress, threw open the office to a man of
will and opinion instead of a puppet of provincial interests.
Thus it changed the entire potential of American presidential history. It gave the President to the people.

Two

The Drafting of the Pattern

How, after the assault upon him, could James Wilson continue to believe of human beings that "our instincts are no other than the oracles of eternal wisdom; our conscience is the voice of God within us"? Yet he did. Whether high-born or lowborn, propertied or propertyless, every citizen of the Republic was sooner or later impelled to heed these admonitions of conscience to fulfill his "upright role"—or so Wilson sincerely believed.

That he dared utter such sentiments before the young nation's Constitutional Convention, sitting in the big red-brick State House in Philadelphia in that eventful spring and summer of 1787, is amazing. Certainly here was a

gathering of idealists such as had never before come together under one roof, men sneered at as "visionaries" over
the rest of the world. Edgar DeWitt Jones, nineteenth-
century preacher-historian, said, "Whoever ventures into a
study of American history ventures into a veritable field of
the cloth of gold. It would seem that when the American
Revolution was in the offing, and during that period and
immediately afterwards, we had men to match the
mountains."

Yet, strangely enough, this Constitutional Convention,
meeting in the same quarters where the Declaration of Independence was signed and where Washington was sworn
in as Commander in Chief of the army (later to return to
lay the twenty-four flags of Yorktown at the feet of the
Continental Congress), was also an assemblage of practical,
and practiced, politicians. If they were not exactly the
"obscure, pettifogging attorneys, bankrupt shopkeepers,
outlawed smugglers" that the Tory New York *Gazette*
labeled them, they possessed much hard common sense and
toughness. In spite of their diverse visions of a utopian
government, in spite of their impassioned provincialism,
they were still able to cut their way through the maze of dis-
unity, disorganization, and distrust—John Fiske's "critical
period" of the seventeen-eighties—to bring forth a virile
federal Constitution that has endured as a model for the
world.

In fact, this body of visionaries (who actually believed
they might succeed with a republic, a government without
a king!) was well peppered with democratic doubters and
cynics to whom any thought of unalloyed governance by
the illiterate, unwashed masses was anathema. (Perhaps,
conceded Hamilton with distaste, the people "intend" to

13

do right—but let us understand that they are inept, incapable, fickle.) Constantly these men reminded each other of the "wild, popular passions" which had been exhibited so shockingly in the recent incident known as "Shays's Rebellion."

Indeed, the memory of Shays's Rebellion lay like a dark cloud at the back of the mind of every delegate at the Convention. This Massachusetts insurrection, in which small property holders sought more equitable taxation for the poor, relief for debtors, reform of the courts, and greater enfranchisement, lasted from August 1786 to February 1787. It had been a pitiful strike, hopeless from the beginning, but it had greatly alarmed the country, so recently freed from war. The conservatives saw the outbreak of a few dissidents as indicative of the temper of the whole people. From the opening day of the Constitutional Convention the fresh memory of this untidy event haunted the deliberations. Thus it took courage for any member to espouse too ardently the cause of the people.

Yet James Wilson, who had personally known mob violence, seems to have been the delegate to show least fear of the people. He entered upon his duties as delegate with a plea for direct election by the people of both houses of Congress and of the executive as well, and he ended his duties in the same frame of mind. In the buzz and excitement of those first few days, Wilson's suggestions were either not heard, or were quickly forgotten. They never struck home. And had he foreseen the violent uproar that was later to erupt when the issue of popular election of Congress came to a vote, he might have been less buoyant. Indeed, in that embroilment between the big states and the little states George Mason was to wish himself dead, William Paterson

14

to cry out for adjournment of the entire Convention as an utter failure, and men were to thunder, "We will never confederate!" This issue was to send the delegates all but at one another's throats and cause John Rutledge of South Carolina to groan in despair, "I see no hope." And many were to agree with him.

All this, however, was in the future. In the initial weeks of deliberations, in the glorious month of June, the delegates' hearts were hopeful and their visions soared. And presently James Wilson, his first snub forgotten, rose to expound on his idea of a President, a single executive, of popular election, with warm and heartfelt words.

He was astounded at the reception. Someone muttered, but loud enough, "He wants to impose on us a *King!*" Roger Sherman jumped to his feet. An executive *independent of the legislature and responsible only to the people?* "This is the very essence of Tyranny!" he shouted. Delegate Randolph of Virginia rose, his cheeks inflamed, to declare that such an executive was "the foetus of monarchy." Wilson had indeed touched a raw nerve.

For the moment he was subdued. He sank to his seat. The issue was quickly shelved with the other fundamental issues that had been only touched upon; the business of the Convention went on. Yet the Pennsylvanian, although startled, had by no means been deterred from his goal. As he sat bemused at his table under the many-paned windows while the oratory droned on and the blue smoke of York County stogies swirled about him, his mind was busier than ever. He was set upon evolving an ingenious plan that would accomplish his purpose despite the prejudices he had encountered.

To make the Chief Magistrate of the nation dependent

on the legislature was intolerable. Yet the present temper of the convention pointed in that very direction. Such a move must be circumvented—at all costs. But how? These men would never stomach the election of the Chief by the populace in its raw, pure form. There must be—no, not a subterfuge, certainly—but some sort of palliative. . . . Was there an answer?

While trudging home that evening, his gold-rimmed spectacles drooping on his nose, his downcast eyes clouded with thought, James Wilson began to give form to his plan. At home, seated before his library of political jurisprudence, before the ghostly presences of Montesquieu, Locke, Vattel, Burlamaqui, Burch, and Reid, he let his fertile mind wander. At length he took up his quill.

He decided he had a workable plan, a plan that might make acceptable the election of the President by the people themselves. First, the fact that the people were electing the executive must be masked, its directness and offensive suggestion of mob rule lined out. Second, the arrangement must be quickly acceptable to the small states, so fearful of subjugation by the others. Yet the plan must bypass the legislature, with its conspiracies, corruptions, ambitions, and cabals. James Wilson's proposal was to set up a temporary, independent body, elected by the people, to elect the Chief. He called this body the "electoral college."

On the next day Wilson presented his plan as enthusiastically as he could. Stares and sniffs greeted it, and it was almost immediately voted down, only Pennsylvania and a somewhat hesitant Maryland supporting it. Crushed, the cause of the popularly elected executive was soon forgotten again by all but Wilson as a fierce squabble began between the large states and the small states. Only when this controversy was resolved on July 17 (with the establishment of popular representation for the House and geographical representation for the Senate), and when both the weather and the delegates' tempers had had an opportunity to cool, did the issue of the executive again take forestage.

The thinking of the delegates was now quite clear. The President of the people, their only protector, was to be bound to the national legislature like a trussed-up papoose to do with as it saw fit. In anger Wilson stood up to demand whether they would make the President nothing more than a hapless buffer between the intrigues of the legislature and the people? Nor did he wince when even democratic George Mason of Virginia sarcastically remarked that it would be "as unnatural to refer the proper character for Chief Magistrate to the People, as it would be to refer a trial of colours to a blind man."

Just as another George III was discerned hiding behind every proposition for a strong executive, so every proposal for giving the choice of President to the people evoked the specter of mob rule. Again the members rose to remind the delegates of Shays's rebellion, to bolster the general conviction that the people were an ignorant, passionate lot to whom democracy must be parceled out like sweetmeats to children, with forebearance and firm restraint. They hardly gave ear to Wilson's compromise; they concentrated on the *idea* of popular election. In the hubbub, Elbridge Gerry's suggestion that the President be selected by the governors of the states was shouted down. But to what avail?

At length Wilson's Pennsylvania colleague, brilliant, peg-legged Gouverneur Morris, with his cosmopolitan airs and the manner of a dandy, stopped in his interminable thumping to announce that he was ready to accept and to fight for a popularly elected President. It was a maxim in political science, he pointed out, that a republican form of government was not adaptable to a large country "because the energy of the Executive Magistracy cannot reach the extreme parts of it. Our Country is an extensive one. We must either then *renounce* the blessings of the Union, or provide an Executive with sufficient vigor to *pervade every part of it.*"

This logic gained the attention of the assembly. "One great object of the Executive is to control the Legislature," continued the practical Pennsylvanian. "The Legislature will continually seek to aggrandise and perpetuate themselves; and will seize those critical moments produced by war, invasion and convulsion for that purpose. It is necessary then that the Executive Magistrate should be the *guardian of the people,* even of the lower classes, *against Legislative tyranny,* against the Great and Wealthy who in the course of things will necessarily compose the Legislative body. . . ."

Then Morris concluded with convincing logic: "If he is to be the Guardian of the people, *let him be appointed by the people!*" It was not that Morris shared Wilson's unquenchable faith in human nature; Morris saw the President only as a balance against the Legislature, a position needing popular election for support. But eagerly, now that he had the ears of the delegates, Wilson pressed his advantage: The President must be akin to the populace, not removed from them; truly he needed "the *mind*—or *sense*—of the people at large." If, he repeated, the President were not a free man, who would guard against legislative dominion or tyranny—as dire a threat as any tyranny of a king? To this Gouverneur Morris added, with telling effect, "I see no way to make the Executive independent of the Legislature but either to give him his office for life—or make him eligible by the people."

The delegates were confused, wavering. Then James Madison got to his feet to offer his support of popular election. Yet in the minds of all lingered the thoughtful words of John Adams: "But who are the people? . . . If by the people is meant the whole body of a great nation, it should never be forgotten, that they can never act, consult, or reason together, because they cannot march five hundred miles, nor spare the time, nor find a space to meet; and therefore, the proposition, that they are the best keepers of their own liberties, is not true. They are the worst conceivable; they are no keepers at all. . . ." Nor could the delegates help the ill-disguised shudder that ran over them when Wilson cheerfully pleaded the "wisdom" and the "virtue" of the populace. So engrossed were they with the *principle* of popular election that Wilson's clever compromise seems to have made no impression at all.

On Thursday, July 26, nine states present and voting, the convention voted six states to three that the President of the United States be elected by the national legislature! A month later the harried delegates threw all the unresolved issues, details, and minutiae into a barrel of Unfinished Parts, handed it with a sigh to the Committee on Remaining Matters, and prepared to tackle the tough problem of ratification of the Constitution. The stubborn Scot had been utterly beaten down.

Fortuitously, the chairman of the Committee on Remaining Matters was Gouverneur Morris. Retiring to the quiet and unmolested confines of his closet, he opened the Unfinished Parts and proceeded, after some fumbling, to

19

draw forth a painstakingly written, erudite paper speckled with the names of Aristotle, Cicero, Hooker, Reid, and Locke. Buried in the classical references was a proposition he faintly remembered, and wished desperately to recall, some sort of fanciful plan—but perhaps there was something in it that would salvage for the people a semblance of control over their Chief Magistrate. At length Morris found it and drew it forth from the welter of papers and studied it. James Wilson had penned (among much else): ". . . that the states be divided into districts; and that persons qualified to vote in each district for members of the first branch of the national Legislature elect . . . members for their respective districts *to be electors of the Executive magistracy.* . . ." (Emphasis ours.)

Morris read the provisions again under his breath, his lace cuff brushing the manuscript as his finger moved across it, evaluating every word. Here was the core of a viable scheme to avoid selection of the executive by the Congress. The people of the nation would elect *electors to choose their Chief*, a sort of second Congress, as it were. The idea of a second Congress, or special elective body, the delegates might swallow.

But instantly he realized the boldness with which the state legislatures had been bypassed; never in a thousand years would this plan pass a convention whose distrust of the people so overwhelmingly exceeded its distrust of the lawmaking bodies themselves. Yet there was something here, a germ, a hope, a potential. . . .

The ultimate wording of Wilson's proposal of an electoral college was this: "Each State shall appoint, *in such manner as the legislature thereof may direct,* a number of electors, equal to the whole number of Senators and Representatives to which the State may be entitled in the Congress; but no Senator or Representative, or person holding an office of trust or profit under the United States, shall be appointed an elector." (Emphasis ours.)

It was a compromise within a compromise. It had bypassed the arbitrary choice of the President by the Congress, indeed. This "electoral college" idea not only freed the President from the Congress. It also avoided direct election by the "unpredictable multitude." James Wilson, that die-hard, would bitterly chide Morris that it was not popular election at all, since it did not specifically declare (as Wilson had suggested) that the *qualified voters in each state* should elect the presidential electors.

Instead, "each State shall appoint, in such manner as the legislature thereof may direct," that *state's* electors. Here, to the canny Morris, was the means to secure the plan's acceptance. However, each state could make its choice of electors as democratic and representative of the people's will or as undemocratic and unrepresentative *as it pleased.* Moreover, if representation were weighted in the electoral college just as it was in the Congress, it would quite neatly avoid any more large-state, small-state bickerings and battles. In this plan the Congress, the national legislature, would have no part in the choice of the Chief—this was the vital consideration. Now let the people—the voters of each state—fight it out as to how much influence they would have in choosing the electors! This was the best the convention could do for them.

Morris' sagacity was vindicated by such stunning acceptance that both he and Wilson were amazed. The plan was quickly and almost routinely passed, and once and for all the notion of having Congress pick the Chief was scrapped. The delegates, fretted with delays and haunted by the specter of complete failure, proved only too willing to push off the touchy issue of the degree of popular participation on the states themselves.

In fact, in the desperate and often bitter campaign for ratification of the Constitution which followed, none of the vitriol of the debates seemed to spill over on the method of choosing a President. Alexander Hamilton could aver in the *Federalist* (No. 68) that "the mode of the appointment of the Chief Magistrate of the United States is almost the only part of the system of any consequence which has escaped without some censure, or which has received the slightest mark of approbation from its opponents."

Little did that generation understand the rare potential of the post they were creating by removing the formidable barrier of the national legislature from between the President and the people. Nor did they envision the evolution of the plan as popular suffrage broadened to blot out the authority of the state legislatures themselves, nor the growing intoxication that such an unimpeded view of the President was to engender in the common rabble.

An evolution of the Presidency was farthest from the Founding Fathers' thoughts. They conceived of the "Chief Magistracy" as a place to ensconce heroes, not to make them. Every time the word "President" was mentioned, the delegates' eyes wandered to the austere and revered George Washington, the President of the Convention, as he stood sedately framed by the Greek pillars and the two great fireplaces, like a niched god. One doesn't debate how many horses Apollo should have on his chariot.

Three

The Hero-God Emerges

From the moment that Charles Thomson, Esq., emissary of the Senate, appeared like a royal herald on the broad steps of Mount Vernon, armed with a flowery plea that George Washington "sacrifice domestic ease and private enjoyment" to accept the Presidency of the United States, an aura of regal dignity enveloped the office. The red carpet treatment was at once adopted as a matter of course. By congressional resolve, five Representatives and three Senators waited on the President-elect at Elizabethtown, New Jersey, with a splendidly festooned barge to escort the Father of His Country to the Presidency of the new nation.

Through the description left by the Secretary of the

United Netherlands legation we may relive the sparkling and historic scene. The colorful barge bearing Washington was rowed ceremoniously across the river by thirteen dashing pilots arrayed in dazzling white. On all sides luxurious sloops and a multitude of smaller vessels, crammed with festively attired citizens, gave escort or speckled the river as far as the eye could see. A Spanish packet anchored in the harbor fired a signal shot and magically dressed itself in the flags of all nations. Thirteen guns boomed over the water. The fort at the Battery echoed and re-echoed the salute.

Alighting at the foot of Wall Street, Washington was received with deference and full military honors by Governor George Clinton of New York, the mayor of the city, troops, bands, and an assortment of officials all dressed in their church finery. A parade formed from Queen Street to the Franklin house headed by a troop of horse, artillery and Legion members, off-duty military officers in uniform, the President's Guard composed of Grenadiers of the First Regiment, followed by the President and Governor, their suites, the principal officers of the state, the mayor of New York City, the clergy, merchants, and just plain paraders!

Yet for all the excitement there was a hushed and awed air about the proceedings. In Washington's reception wherever he appears there is the germ of a role of strong leadership. There is also more than a hint of a yearning for an intimacy with this hero-god. But though the yearning was already there, the people touched him only with their eyes.

Nonetheless, the Congress appeared concerned about the relationship of the new President to the people. The inauguration would take place in the Senate Chamber, but "to the end that the oath of office may be administered to the President in the most public manner and that the great-est number of the people of the United States, and with-out distinction, may be witnesses to the solemnity, . . . the oath [would] be administered in the outer gallery adjoin-ing the Senate Chamber." This was formalized conde-scension to the great American public, and yet properly aloof. There on the balcony, *above* the people, the Presi-dent, his hand on a Masonic Bible, took the oath. Yet he wore, that festive day, no satin vestments of royal purple, but a "complete suit of Homespun Cloathes; the cloth . . . of a fine fabric, and as handsomely finished, as any Euro-pean superfine cloth," jingoistically recorded the *U.S. Chronicle* of May 21, 1789. The fireworks display at the State House, climaxed by thirteen skyrockets, conferred on the occasion a kind of tribal approbation, and the brilliantly illuminated homes of the French and Spanish ambassadors added the royal bow.

The inaugural address, delivered in the Senate Chamber, was directed, significantly enough, only to "Fellow Citi-zens of the Senate and House of Representatives." An appeal to make the Republic work, it was not addressed to the people nor declaimed to them from the gallery: what had the common folk to do with that? Yet the new Presi-dent's "distrustful scrutiny" into his own personal qualifi-cations, and his further announcement that, as he had taken no pay as a military leader, so he would continue to "renounce every pecuniary compensation" as President, were bruited around the country and added to the popular acclaim.

So now, with the hero-god installed, how was the Con-gress to properly answer the inaugural address? The re-sponse, insisted the self-conscious members of the Senate,

25

must be precisely right. Having prayed on the subject at some length in St. Paul's chapel, the Senators climbed the long flight of stairs to their secret chambers and went into a prolonged tussle over the nature of their response. It would set the tone for all future relations with the President; it would be a historic milestone!

First, they must thank the President for rescuing the nation "from anarchy and confusion." No, indeed, they would *not*. Such an admission would "fix a stain upon the annals of America." A warm debate followed. Well, then they might say, "Rescued us from impending evils over us." "Tautological!" snapped Oliver Elsworth, in disgust. For lack of a better, the phrase carried. The President, they must now assert, would "bring dignity and splendor" to the government. *"Splendor?"* echoed several voices in querulous disagreement. Did this not imply "all the faulty finery, brilliant scenes, and expensive trappings of royal government"? "Then we shall use the word 'responsibility'...." But here John Adams, who had a passion for pomp and grandeur, was obdurate; the word "splendor" was retained, to his great comfort.

And how proper these words seemed when, at the appointed time, the Senators, headed by the ceremony-loving Adams, made their stately, self-conscious way to the President's abode. There they beheld at one end of a spacious room from which all furniture had been removed, erect before the glowing fireplace, "a tall and superb figure, clad in a suit of black velvet with black silk stockings and silver buckles. [It is not recorded that this outfit was made this side of the Atlantic.] His hair, white with powder, is gathered behind in a silk bag. He wears yellow gloves and holds a cocked hat with a cockade and plume. A sword, with hilt of polished steel and sheath of white leather, further relieve the somber magnificence of the President's form," as Parton, in *The Life of Aaron Burr*, so graphically described him. (This was, by the way, the sword that the "cold" and unexpressive Washington was to will to his nephew, adjuring him to unsheath it only in defense of his country and then to die with it in his hand rather than ever to relinquish it.)

In reverent but embarrassing silence the Senators formed a stiff semicircle around His Excellency, and John Adams, his hands trembling with the portentous precedent of the moment, read, somewhat haltingly, the Senate's carefully phrased response.

There is no implication here or elsewhere that the President wanted to put on airs. But all his precedents were royal. What was expected of him? Better to err in dignity than in commonness! By living up to his titular role he honored the Republic. He gave no thought to the cultivation of public support or to the getting of votes. His demeanor was conscious image-building, but of a sort intended to personify the virtues, importance, and, especially, the stability of the new nation. Let the ambassadors of France and Spain take note.

Although the opposition press was later to castigate the President as "frail . . . a spoiled child, a despot, an anemic imitation of the English kings," as John Tebbel quotes them, and though the majority of newspapers throughout the young nation effused over the Chief's virtues—neither friend nor enemy attempted the familiarity common today. One cannot imagine a headline about "Washy," "Georgie," or even "G.W."

Indeed, when the democratic House of Representatives

addressed the President without "annexing any styles or titles" other than "The President of the United States," the Senate debated the insolence with some vigor and acrimony. Vice-President Adams and others, including Richard Henry Lee (whom William Maclay refers to as "the high priest in all this idolatrous business"), wished Washington to be addressed as "His Highness, President of the United States and Protector of Their Liberties." "What," they demanded, "will the common people of foreign countries, what will the sailors and soldiers say, 'George Washington, President of the United States'? They will despise him to all eternity!" At length Washington's feelings about the matter, not verbally expressed, but quite obvious nonetheless, seem to have decided the matter; the humbler—or rather, the less pretentious—title survived. "We can have nothing to fear from him," reluctantly admitted the sour Maclay, recorder of the minutes of the First Senate; then, as if to rectify his slip, he added quickly, ". . . but much from the *precedents* which he may establish."

Washington himself feared desperately that he might be considered above advice, or "supercilious and secluded," as he expressed it; yet he was also understandably fearful of being regarded as having "too free intercourse and too much familiarity." For the President, pontificates dyspeptic Maclay, "to suffer himself to be run down, on the one hand, by a crowd of visitants so as to engross his time, would never do, as it would render the doing of business impracticable; but, on the other hand, for him to be seen only in public on stated times, like an Eastern Lama, would be equally offensive." There should not be too much hospitality, of this Washington was certain. Else wouldn't the President of the United States lose his dignity and be considered no better than a "maitre-d'hotel"?

Yet to secure official support for his program (to se-
duce the Senators, sniffed Maclay), the President enter-
tained lavishly at dinner. "It was a great dinner—all in the
taste of high life," penned the recorder of one such event.
"I consider it as a part of my duty as a Senator to submit to
it. . . ." Washington brought a kind of gloomy charm to
these events, which might well consist of twelve or thirteen
courses, followed by as many formal and quickly gulped
toasts—all in an atmosphere of severe propriety and serious
demeanor in which Maclay could find no happy face, no
"ray of convivial sunshine" to counteract the President's
"settled aspect of melancholy." A jolly picture to leave to
posterity! Yet perhaps one can expect no more cheery view
when filtered through the waves of acute bilious in-
digestion.

Washington's position was certainly difficult. He had to
establish himself in relation to the government he headed.
It was inconceivable that his relations with the masses of
Americans should be closer. In the first place, most of them
did not matter, politically, and in the second, they could not
be mobilized readily, if at all. But Washington, superb ad-
ministrator, courted the good will of legislative leaders,
acutely aware that excessive sectionalism, if permitted to
develop, might shatter the whole fabric of the new nation.

After the ruckus with Great Britain over the impress-
ment of American seamen and other offenses, when the
President, instead of taking the opportunity to embrace
the degenerating French Revolution, actually sent John Jay
to England to negotiate a peace with the bitter enemy,
Washington's popular glory came under eclipse. On one
occasion, according to David Cushman Coyle, in *The
Ordeal of the Presidency,* tens of thousands of rioters raged
through the streets of Philadelphia, cursing the President

and threatening to drag him from his chambers and initiate a revolution. Wrote the cowardly critic "Valerius": "Your voice may have been heard when it called to virtue and glory, but it will be lost in the tempest of popular fury, whenever it shall speak the language of lawless ambition. The American People, Sir, *will look to death* the man who assumes the character of an usurper."

Thus, while the people longed for a strong protector, loud-mouthed dissenters among them roundly lashed the President for every show of authority. As for Jay, when it was rumored that he had actually kissed the Queen's hand, thus "prostrating the sovereignty of the people at the feet of Majesty!" the cry went up that the "groveling" emissary "richly deserved to have his lips blistered to the bone."

Washington was not only the target of foul and violent abuse; he was assailed for every petty foible and mannerism. Even his bowing was "formal and stiff," resembling that of the Court of St. James's—incontestable proof that the President was actually a monarchist at heart. Ruefully, Washington responded that it might have been more charitable to ascribe his stiffness to age rather than to monarchical aspirations.

Nonetheless, this truly great man, for all his "cold heart" and stiff knees, never lost the "idolatrous worship" of the common throng, nor surrendered his faith in their integrity. He seemed to be drawn to the people in a strange and ineluctable way. As the Secretary of the Netherlands, an eyewitness, described it, "The rush of the people to see their beloved General Washington was amazing, and their delight and joy were truly universal and cordial." Could it be expected that such love would not spark a response in that military breast?

President Washington made several attempts to come closer to the people. Hardly understanding why he should put himself to such torture, the President of the United States felt impelled to make a presidential tour through the New England states. The journey occupied the entire month between October 15 and November 13, 1789. He traveled in a fine coach accompanied by his aide-de-camp Major William Jackson, his private secretary Tobias Leer, six servants, nine horses, and a rumbling luggage wagon. But travel in those days, even in the finest coach, seated on a hard board over an "intolerable bad" road cluttered with all manner of stones large and small, was a killing ordeal.

Washington was no Boswell, but his *Diary* of the years 1789–91 reveals that he was as solicitous a leader as the American people have ever had. The diary itself is as laconic and unemotional as a military report, but Washington notes that the "immensely stoney" roads were "trying to wheels and carriages" and that he was forced to stop over for days when the horses went lame. (He made no mention of his own condition; probably the horses were merely an excuse.) His greatest interest was the condition of the people, and the state of their manufactures and especially of their farms: "I find by conversing with the farmers along the road, that a medium crop of wheat to the acre is about 15 bushels—of corn, 20, of oats, the same."

At Kings-Bridge, the President of the people worried lest, in spite of their large size, the legs of the hogs "were rather too long." He insisted upon lodging at taverns or upon paying tavern rates for all accommodations lest he be said to have slighted the hospitality of some gentlemen, as would have been the case had he journeyed as an honored guest. Upon entering the hamlets he would often be stopped by the welcoming committee for "odes and songs" in his honor, which pleased him much.

The President did not summon the fortitude for another such adventure until April 7, 1791, when he set forth on a tour of the southern states. From Mount Vernon he traveled northward through Philadelphia, thence south to Virginia and the Carolinas, into Georgia and back to Mount Vernon—1,887 backbreaking miles in all, keeping him on the road for two months and six days! Fatigued though he might be, the President, when he reached the land of southern belles, could still count: his diary takes on a bit of sparkle as he writes of the "very elegant dancing Assembly—At which were 256 elegantly dressed and handsome ladies," and of the concert next day at the Exchange in Charleston "at wch there were at least 400 ladies the number & appearance of wch exceeded any thing of the kind I had ever seen."

But Charleston was a rare oasis; most of the southern journey was undertaken in either a deluge of rain or a swirling sea of dust from which, as he briefly observes, he "suffered very much." Indeed, he underwent such misery that, on one occasion, "finding that parties of Horse, & a number of other Gentlemen were intending to attend me part of the way to day, I caused their enquiries respecting the time of my setting out, to be answered that, I should endeavor to do it before eight o'clock; but I did it a little after five, by which means I avoided the inconveniences above mentioned."

Canny though he proved himself to be in both war and peace, the Father of His Country was able to avoid but few other "inconveniences" on his southern tour. Earnestly he observed the condition of the land and the people: he recorded the state of the defenses, cannon, militia, census evasion (the people, when summoned to the green to be counted, ran, instead, to hide, fearing that to be counted was to be taxed). He took painstaking note of the crops of rice, tobacco, and corn, the appearance of the houses and the harbors, and the number of ships. Many a subsequent President, with all the advantages of high speed and luxurious means of travel, has demonstrated less solicitude and interest in the people.

Washington's diary abounds with references to the places at which he breakfasted, luncheoned, and dined. No doubt he consumed the best the taverns afforded: cock a' leeky, pork pies, haunch of mutton, hotch-potch, Indian pudding. No doubt he sipped a bowl of flipp with rhum to ease his aching back when the day's ordeal was over. He never complained except to mention that this or that tavern "was a very indifferent one," and his appreciation of cordial reception and generous hospitality was earnest.

On both his journeys Washington met many city officials, army officers, and other dignitaries. The people saw him, but seldom heard him; he did not emerge from his carriage to shake hands or fraternize. Yet when, on December 13, 1799, two years after he had left the Presidency, Washington took the "quinsey" or "Crupe," and died within twenty-four hours, the mourning of the people was deep.

That the Presidency had as yet developed no popular roots was evidenced when John Adams, the aristocratic revolutionary, was elevated to the office. Sensitive that he had garnered but three electoral votes more than Jefferson, President Adams established no powerful support, much less sought affinity with the common throng of whom, ac-

33

cording to Charles Beard, he had acquired a deathly fear. When he warned that "democracy never lasts long. It soon wastes, exhausts, and murders itself," he seems concerned lest its unfortunate demise occur during his own administration.

Yet Adams was a strong and principled man. Although "by temper and conviction . . . unfitted to quell a popular tumult," or to spark any measurable love in the public breast, he strove manfully to make himself available. He traveled from state to state to attend banquets in his honor, and tried not to notice the lack of enthusiasm of the populace.

Of one such embarrassment a Republican paper wrote, not without bias, that the sole paraders consisted of militiamen, with naval officers and collectors of the excise bringing up the rear: "No gaping multitudes rent the air with shouts. No martial music disturbed the quiet of the scene. A funeral could not have been more decorous. Two or three constables, to be sure, attended at his Highness's door, and sought to make some disturbance. 'Huzza!' cried they as his Highness mounted the steps. But all was still as death. 'Huzza!' again shouted the constables, 'won't you huzza for the President?' Thereupon some boys cried 'Huzza!' and the President went in and shut the door."

By 1797 the Republicans and the fomenters of war with France were burning Adams' effigy all along the seaboard; prominent political figures, including even Hamilton, vilified him cruelly, and as Adams saw his Federalist party founder under the new wave of Republicanism, he had no way to turn.

He never thought to turn to the people for support. They were "far, far away." In 1787, speaking of the independent yeomanry, Adams had observed that "living chiefly by agriculture, in small numbers, sprinkled over large tracts of land, they are not subject to those panics and transports, those contagions of madness and folly, which are seen in countries where large numbers live in small places, in daily fear of perishing for want. We know, therefore, that the people can live and increase under almost any kind of government, or *without any government at all.*" What need had the independent American yeoman, who made his own laws and his own way, of a father-leader? What could he ever mean to them?

It is true that Adams had spoken out in favor of a strong executive as a protector of the people against the legislature. Executive power in the hands of the assembly would corrupt "as rust corrupts iron, as arsenic poisons the human body; and when the legislature is corrupted, the people are undone." But all this might be a development of the future; right now, President Adams stood alone, and he felt that the people did not care in the least.

"Adams' monumental service to his country while President was his averting of war with France," says Maxim E. Armbruster in *The Presidents of the United States, a New Appraisal,* and Adams himself agreed with this judgment. President Adams kept his head as one provocation followed another, while hotheads assailed him in vulgar and brutal terms—just as they had assailed Washington when he resisted the break with England. Adams' service, too, was great.

The far-flung citizenry had blindly worshiped Washington, who had faced British lead and risked the noose, but Adams was no such hero. And the effort of trying to live up to the hero-god pattern was more of a strain than he

35

could endure. In old age, pondering his past, he wrote to Jefferson that his administration would, "like Pope's Woman, have no Character at all. The impious Idolatry to Washington, destroyed all Character."

In the broad sweep of American history, President Jefferson is identified with all that is democratic. An extremely poor speaker, he could not rouse a crowd, and the people in general had no communication with him except through his numerous letters, which were published everywhere and which his enemies called "intrigues." Yet he was a master politician (it was he who introduced the presidential custom of handshaking!). Even during Washington's administration Jefferson's political clubs, called "Democratic Societies," were sprouting throughout the countryside, preparing the way for the tremendous groundswell for Jefferson and Burr in 1800. In that year the Republicans took over not only the Presidency, but also both houses of Congress.

The Republicans had mercilessly lambasted President Adams, but the desperate Federalists were no more sparing of Jefferson. Who was this dilettante who, since his retirement to Monticello after having served as Secretary of State, spent his time "impaling butterflies" and building an "Epicurean side-board and other Gim-Krackery" such as the "Whirligig Chair," which had the "miraculous quality of allowing the person seated in it to turn his head, without moving his tail"? Was *he* to be President of the United States?

When such ridicule failed to impress the public, which was rapidly responding to the democratic swell, his enemies produced the following description: "Tom Jefferson ... a mean-spirited, low-lived fellow, the son of a half-breed

Indian squaw, sired by a Virginia mullatto father . . . raised wholly on hoe-cake made of coarse-ground Southern corn, bacon and hominy, with an occasional change of fricasseed bullfrog." If this menu was damning in Rhode Island, it certainly was not in the South.

When the outcome of the election became fairly certain, Jefferson had occasion to call on Adams at Philadelphia on another matter. Adams, in the words of Jefferson, was "very sensibly affected, and accosted me with these words: 'Well, I understand that you are to beat me in this contest, and I will only say that I will be as faithful a subject as any you will have.' 'Mr. Adams,' said I, 'this is no personal contest between you and me. Two systems of principles . . . divide our fellow citizens into two parties. With one of these you concur, and I with the other. . . . Were we both to die today, tomorrow two other names would be in the place of ours, without any change in the motion of the machinery. Its motion is from its principle, not from you or myself.' "

This explanation is hardly acceptable; the opposing "systems of principles" were the very lifeblood of each of these men. Adams was in no way reconciled. Unable to face what he in anguish of soul termed "the dissolution of the Republic," he arose before dawn on that Inauguration Day of 1801 and quietly slipped out of town. Peremptorily, in six separate letters sent by different routes, he summoned his son home from his position of Minister to Prussia to save him the indignity of dismissal by the new President. Even to the day of death the rivalry between Adams and Jefferson persisted. Though when, dying, Adams murmured in envy, "Jefferson still survives," he had no way of knowing that on that very morning of July 4, 1826, his friendly antagonist had himself slipped into the long sleep.

Jefferson was a powerful President, but he repeatedly affirmed that the Presidency was the "direct gift of the people," and that he had more confidence in the "natural integrity and discretion of the people" than had Washington himself. (Nonetheless, he quickly added that Washington would "spend his last drop of blood" to give the new republic a chance.) He sought no power for its own sake; "power is not alluring to pure minds," he declared earnestly, "and is not with them, the primary principle of contest." Had it been but a power contest, he would long ago have bowed out to be with "family, farm, friends, and books." Charles Beard calls Jefferson the "most-civilized man ever called to the Presidency."

But the program Jefferson advanced in the interests of the common man, he promoted as a manager of legislators and as a legislative party leader. He used the office of President to buttress his legislative managers. He was an organization expert who appeared *before* the day when a President could tap the sentiments of the people directly.

Democratic philosopher that he was, Jefferson could heartily adjure that no one should be frightened by "the alarms of the timid or the croakings of wealth against the ascendancy of the people." Yet he did nothing to enable these special people, the yeomanry, to express their opinions in the decision-making in the new White House he now occupied.

"Murder, robbery, rape, adultery, and incest" would dominate the nation if the democratic Jefferson was elected, declared one righteous orator. "The air will be rent with the cries of distress, the soil soaked with blood, and the nation black with crimes." But for Tom Jefferson the nation was willing to take the chance.

After his retirement the adoration of the public (whom he had often spoken for, but never to) became evident. Thousands of pilgrims journeyed to his temple, Monticello, and literally "ate him out of house and home." He died in poverty; and the Monticello that he had so loved, even his large collection of fine books, had to be auctioned to pay the debts. So did the people repay him—with too much love.

Although Jefferson had had to reach for the people through their representatives, he had never ceased to proclaim, "Let every man who fights or pays" vote to elect the President. Unfortunately, most of the male citizens—by direction of the individual states, which defined the suffrage as they saw fit—were quite unable to vote at all.

Part II

The Struggle in the Nineteenth-Century: The People Cannot Reach Him

Four

But the People Cannot Vote

The American Revolution not only heralded the freedom of a nation but marked that nation's commitment to the equality of men. Chilton Williamson, in his definitive study, *American Suffrage,* says, "In retrospect it is clear that they [the changes in suffrage made during the Revolution] committed the country to a democratic suffrage. Those opposed to the commitment fought a series of delaying actions almost down to the Civil War, all of which failed." Indeed, this long-range commitment took twenty-five years to broaden and a century really to consolidate. For a long period the citizenry's right to vote was so limited that this

43

fact in itself erected an unscalable wall between the people and their President.

Revolutionary dicta and fine phrases to the contrary, most eminent minds in the years after the establishment of the Republic opposed the expansion of universal suffrage in every phase. Even Gouverneur Morris, Founding Father, whose last-minute reconstruction of James Wilson's dream had insured that the people would eventually choose their President, did not want the "popular" franchise to be too "popular." In fact, he said, "Life and liberty might be the first consideration of savages, but in civilized countries property was the principal object of Society," and hence of voting requirements.

We find more evidence of this attitude in the eighth article of the impeachment proceedings taken against Supreme Court Justice Samuel Chase in 1802: the distinguished jurist was charged with exciting a grand jury against electoral reform in Maryland by referring to such reform as "mobocratic rule." In the same year the Connecticut Supreme Court contrarily found Seth Wetmore guilty of sedition and fined him $100 because he advocated "equal representation which we fought for in the Revolution and universal suffrage"!

For decades after the Revolution most of the states clung to their strict property qualifications for the vote. Significant suffrage reform was pushed vigorously in only six states: Vermont, New Hampshire, New Jersey, Pennsylvania, Georgia, and Maryland.

At the Virginia Ratification Convention in 1788 the proud-spirited John Randolph, in whose veins flowed the blood of Pocahontas, opposed a broader suffrage: "A rat hole," he said, "will let in the ocean!" The aristocrat was shocked at the inference that the Revolution had carried America to such unspeakable lengths. "Shall we enfranchise *paupers?*" he asked scornfully. Flushed with indignation, he continued, "See that ragged fellow staggering out of a grogshop and see that slattern who has gone to reclaim him. . . . he is free from all concern for his family because he has voted for a patriarchal system of education for his children. . . . he can now spend his money on whiskey!"

But the Constitution of the United States held every man, rich or poor, to have equal democratic rights. Where, then, was the inspiration, the authoritative text, for the Forefathers who so stubbornly fought *against* the doctrine of men's equal right to the franchise?

Experts claim that the impetus behind this rearguard action was the publication in America, in 1771, of the *Commentaries* of the famous British jurist William Blackstone. The *Commentaries* was a kind of political odds sheet on voting, and the odds on property qualifications were high. Blackstone had written, "The true reason of requiring any qualification with regard to property in voters is to exclude such persons as are in so mean a situation as to be esteemed to have no will of their own."

Certainly Blackstone's argument was an intensely practical one. If one were to be a good voter, one could be beholden to no one. Since rural tenants were beholden to landlords and urban mechanics to their employers, what independence of will could they display? When the farmer or workman stepped forth at the polls to proclaim his vote, he faced a battery of eyes—not only of the candidates or electors, but also of his landlord or employer.

Colonial experience bore out Blackstone's fears. In a classic case in Virginia a man of means who was defeated as a candidate for the assembly took vengeance on those who refused to support him; he foreclosed on thirty-three men who owed him money. To a man, they lost their property, and a number of them went to debtor's prison. This proved that "beholden" men could maintain no independence of conscience without reprisal, did it not?

Now in Massachusetts, in Connecticut, in New York, in Virginia—even in the western states where presumably a man was a man—opponents of universal suffrage were damming up the movement with pages from Blackstone's *Commentaries*. What of England's rotten boroughs and the corruption of buying the votes of the unpropertied? The opponents of equal suffrage had powerful facts on their side.

So universal suffrage came to America slowly and with much pain. And the people's inability to participate in the selection of the President made James Madison, James Monroe, and John Quincy Adams somewhat less than popular choices. (In the election of 1828 fewer than 356,000 votes were cast by a total population of 9,638,453.) The authority of these early Presidents, then, did not derive from a clear-cut mandate. Too many people in too many states were without the vote, and apparently without any hope of ever getting it.

True, compared with Europe, or, indeed, with any other part of the world, the drive for universal suffrage in the infant nation—for the right of the common man to take part in the election of the Chief Executive—was exceptional. When a candidate for the Illinois legislature, A. Lincoln, declared in 1830, "I go for admitting to the right of suffrage all who pay taxes or bear arms, by no means excluding females," he was, by European standards, not only a boorish demagogue but an anarchist of sorts.

Europeans considered the suffrage movement a lunatic vagary. But although American thinking outpaced the rest of the world, it was still a fight, fiery and bitter.

The pressure for votes for the unpropertied came to a powerful climax in the fall of 1821 when a brilliant constitutional convention gathered in Albany, New York, on the steep hillsides of the Hudson River, to reconsider the terms on which men could come to the polls. At that time in New York, as in a number of other states, notably Rhode Island, only freeholders (owners of real property) might cast a ballot. But by generously interpreting "freeholder" as including "leaseholder," it was estimated in 1821, 38 per cent of the adult males could vote for the governor and for members of the state senate.

Dissatisfaction with the limited franchise in New York was widespread. Thirty-one members of the convention had been born in Connecticut, and seven in Massachusetts, where the privilege of voting had been more widely extended. But over this New York convention there also hovered the spirit of Blackstone seeking out a spokesman against the brash artisans and laborers, carters and tenant farmers, weavers and militiamen who were demanding their say in the selection of their leaders.

The spokesman was soon found in the person of the awesomely learned, distinguished Chancellor of the State of New York, James Kent, an intellectual giant who rose at five in the morning to devote two hours to the study of Latin and two more to Greek (breakfasting in between) before proceeding on his daily study and practice of the law. Men without number have saluted the "purity of motive" of this "true and ardent lover of his country and its institutions."

There he stood, aggressive, the bushy white side thatch

framing a bald pate, the stern eyes burning like those of an inquisitor, the large mouth firmly clamped shut as though some devastating legal pronouncement had just been enunciated, the kind that leaves the opponent in shards. In somber frock coat, striped vest, and billowed tie, stiff-necked and erect, Kent began to speak, and the chamber was hushed in respect. These were not the words of a demagogue, but of a man who has been called the "Father of American Jurisprudence."

Appropriately, Kent first noted the great progress of the country. He projected that growth into the future, a future of the masses. "We are no longer to remain plain and simple republics of farmers. We are fast becoming a great nation, with great commerce, manufactures, population, wealth, luxuries, and *with the vices and miseries they engender.*" To illustrate the miseries of greatness he added that "one-seventh of the population of Paris at this day subsists on charity. . . ."

Now the Blackstone he had studied so diligently found application. Think, he adjured his listeners. Do we want to submit our future to *such masses?* "The tendency of universal suffrage is to jeopardize the rights of property and the principles of liberty. . . . there is a constant tendency in the poor to covet and to share the plunder of the rich; in the debtor to relax or avoid the obligations of contract; in the indolent and profligate to cast the whole burthen of society upon the industrious and the virtuous; and there is a tendency in ambitious and wicked men to inflame those combustible materials. . . ."

But for all Kent's sincerity, his oratory in defense of the propertied had a hollow ring. Daniel Tompkins bent over and scribbled a note: "Elegant epitaph prepared for the old constitution!" Some heads shook sadly and eyes were cast down, but the Chancellor was not through. "I hope, sir," he continued, emphasizing each word, "we shall not carry desolation through all the departments of the fabric erected by our fathers! I hope we shall not put forward to the world a new constitution, as will meet with the scorn of the wise and the tears of the patriot!"

It was indeed an elegant epitaph on the old order, but, significantly, it was not written during the Revolution but almost half a century later. Kent's polemic was the culmination of a long and acrimonious battle against the new suffrage movement, the keystone of true democracy.

Rebuttal was quick. Peter R. Livingston rose: "But we are asked, what evidence we have that the people want this extension of suffrage? Sir, 74,000 witnesses testified last spring, that they wanted it! Meetings and resolutions, public prints, and conversation have united to require it!" And Jacob Radcliff of New York City added, with some sting, "Property will always carry with it an influence sufficient for its own protection."

Nor were the advocates of an extended suffrage wanting in their own emotional oratory. "And whom do you find in your armies in time of war?" blazed Livingston. "The miser? The monied Shylock? The speculator? No sir, it is the poor and hardy soldier who spills his blood in defense of his country; the veteran to whom you allow the privilege to fight, but not the vote. If there is value in the right of suffrage, or reliance to be placed upon our fellow citizens in time of war, where, I ask, is the justice of withholding that right in times of peace and safety?"

Livingston, however, was voted down. Chancellor Kent and his backers continued to harp on "the immensity of consequences" of this "new, untried, and bold experiment" to "annihilate all distinction." And although they seem to have carried the day, they lost the war, for they succeeded only in delaying universal suffrage in New York until 1826. Said Kent on that date, sorrowfully, "... our posterity will have occasion to deplore, in sackcloth and ashes, the delusions of this day!"

No matter; there was no turning back. There was the first weak flexing of the common man's muscles when the *Workingman's Advocate* of New York darkly printed, on May 7, 1829: "Be warned ... that it is a dangerous thing to sneer at universal suffrage in this republican country." Throughout the nation the idea of universal suffrage was slowly gaining recognition.

Scholars took pains to note that the voters were far from the elite pictured by the people's advocates, that in Massachusetts the change in suffrage was actually in a reactionary direction, that qualifications were intricate and varied in different states, that some states found the populace stolidly indifferent as to whether it voted or no. The important point was not that the American masses were rushing to the banners, but that, as Chancellor Kent put it, "If the proposition ... had been offered ten years ago, instead of the complacency with which it is now received, it would have struck the people with astonishment and terror." At last the people were beginning to think for themselves— to place the promises of the Constitution and Bill of Rights alongside their own importance—and to wonder.

And along with the growing ferment for extension of the suffrage was the ferment over the choice of presidential electors. Neither you nor I—nobody—has a *constitutional* right to vote for the electors who choose the President of the United States. The Founding Fathers did not intend that a presidential constituency be created. They held no opinion that a dialogue between the people and the President was desirable, or any idea that it would ever be possible. Nor did they believe communications would ever be such that the voters at large could come to an agreement of any effective kind to produce a winning candidate.

If you cast a vote for the lower house of your state legislature, you have a *constitutional* right to vote for a representative in Congress. But whether you have a right to cast a ballot for a presidential elector is *wholly up to your state legislature to decide*. Indeed, when Judge Jedediah Peck had the effrontery to propose to the New York Assembly in 1800 that the people (that is, the limited property holders who could vote) should choose their electors by district (James Wilson's original idea), he was shouted down by cries of "Unconstitutional!" What nonsense was this? Did not the Constitution declare that *each state* should elect its electors? The state must act as a corporate body through its legislators. The people directly had no voice.

In the first three presidential elections (1788, 1792, and 1796), the electors were chosen mainly by the state legislatures, without fanfare. Constitutionally, there is absolutely nothing but the citizens' indignation to prevent the state legislatures' assuming that power once again. Indeed, they not only have the authority to choose presidential electors, and without consulting anyone, but they can vest that authority, apparently, in anyone they please—"a board of bank directors, a turnpike corporation—or a synagogue," marveled Representative Henry R. Storrs of New York in 1826.

Although legislatures went to no such extremes at the beginning of the nineteenth century, and certainly would not dare to today, the system was wholly unstable. For a long time some state legislatures monopolized the privilege; some allowed the electorate (by temporary sufferance, it was understood) to choose electors by single districts; some others went so far as to choose a general ticket for electors state-wide.

In 1824, for example, twelve states voted by general ticket, six selected their electors directly by the legislature, four provided for electoral districts, and two had a mixture of districts and general ticket. This was quite a change in thinking since 1800, but, significantly, the states still maintained the upper hand; the part the people played was a privilege that might be rescinded at any time. Such was the mix-up, one scholar commented, that the outcome of presidential elections was determined nearly as much "by the devices used as by the sense of the people."

In fact, the electorate was pulled around by the nose to suit the rascally purposes of the legislatures. In Massachusetts the electors were never chosen by the same system twice in succession until 1828! And in the other states the constant and whimsical shifting of methods of electoral choice in order to make an advantage for the legislature's favorite candidate was one of the milder scandals of the age. In 1800 a "spartan Band" of thirteen Federalists in the Pennsylvania State Senate stood stoutly forth to oppose "to the death" both the twelve Jefferson senators and an overwhelmingly Jeffersonian Assembly. "If the state does not vote Federalist—it shall not vote at all!" was their cry. It almost didn't. Only at the price of an indefensible "deal" which divided the electors between the parties and gave the odd one to the Assembly was Pennsylvania counted in that presidential election!

Again, in 1812, the North Carolina legislature, on the pretext that some ten thousand of its citizens were abroad in military service, relieved voters of the task of choosing electors and boldly cast the ballots as it pleased—to secure the state to Madison. In that same year, according to Lucius Wilmerding in his carefully documented *Electoral College,* the legislature of New Jersey cavalierly tossed the long-standing general election law out the window to insure that its eight votes would go to DeWitt Clinton. And when the voters of Maryland gave signs that they wanted John Quincy Adams in 1824, a quick shift to the district system cleverly cut his strength to three out of eleven votes.

So at this point in history, although the mass of people and their President sensed a strong attraction one for the other, they were separated by a chasm across which they might wave at each other in wordless endearment. (In 1800 only one person out of 33,000 [or 120,000 out of 4,000,000] was eligible to vote, and the *majority* of electors was arbitrarily picked by state legislatures—a practice not to be wholly discarded until after the Civil War.) So the populace, in large part voteless, duped, bullied, and canceled out by their legislatures, mouthed the lofty phrases of the Constitution—and bided their time.

But if the people were sheep, the President himself was a goat. Perhaps the Founding Fathers had not intended that the President be subordinate to the Congress, but that was how it was working out. Only with the beaming nod of the congressional leaders could a man hope for nomination to the chieftainship. Thus, after Jefferson left the White House, there followed a series of gifted and honorable men, but men who were being rewarded for their endeavors on behalf of the young Republic, rather than men with popular appeal or great leadership. President Madison, to whom fame came when historians pondered his carefully inscribed records, his philosophy, and his ideals, saw America's future largely as a conflict between the property holders and the indigent masses. And the Presidency came to Monroe, wrote Charles Beard, through the influence of Jefferson and Madison and considerable maneuvering— "not because he awakened great popular enthusiasm."

As for John Quincy Adams, that dour and high-minded Puritan, he was a minority President and, according to David Cushman Coyle, "temperamentally unable to fit into the requirements of President." An idealist who lacked "the common arts of the politician," he could attract no enthusiastic following, nor even win support to his program. Stunned by the rough blows he received from the Congress, he gratefully retired to his home district. His neighbors, understanding him and loving him for his integrity and worth, returned him to the House of Representatives, where he served for the rest of his life. There, in innumerable orations, in a voice that was "half tremble, half shriek," he pursued his high-minded goals and gained greatness at last as "Old Man Eloquence," the most revered member of the assembly, until he fell dead at his desk.

The congressional conventions, in folksy fashion, had chosen the Presidents before 1800, but from then on the congressional caucus chose the presidential candidates. Simultaneously, parties became dominant and the great American party war began.

Two parties—Hamilton's Federalists and Jefferson's Republicans (later Democrats)—reared their gangling (but sharp-toothed) heads. "Adams and Pinckney," declared the Federalists in 1800, and since both the President and the Vice-President were elected by the same ballot, hoped in their conniving hearts that the order might, in the election, be reversed. The Republicans, at their congressional caucus at Philadelphia, raised aloft the banners of Jefferson of Virginia and Aaron Burr of New York, enunciated the first national platform ever drawn up by a political party, and set forth on a vigorous campaign that set the callow young nation back on its heels. Shock and resentment countered raucous delight—according to one's political affiliation.

When the ballots of the 276 electors were counted, Jefferson and Burr had each received 73 votes. John Adams was third with 65 votes; Charles Pinckney received 64, and John Jay of New York was honored with a single vote. Inasmuch as Jefferson and Burr were tied for the Presidency, the House of Representatives had to decide which of these powerful figures should become the nation's Chief.

Since both men were of the same party, this was no party contest, but it took seven days and thirty-six ballots for Thomas Jefferson, author of the Declaration of Independence, to defeat Aaron Burr. However, a lesson had been learned. Out of this election came the Twelfth Amendment to the Constitution, and from then on the electors voted *separately* for President and Vice-President.

But out of it had also come the congressional caucus, a snare and a trap from which no independent presidential leadership could possibly arise. In the long sweep of history the most significant thing that may be said of this period in which Representatives and Senators took it upon themselves to present the nation with its Presidents is that the caucus stunted the Presidency and forestalled its growth.

The Constitution had made no provision for the nomination of presidential candidates, presumably because the individual electors were to arrive at personal choices, a simple matter in the elections when Washington was the unanimously supported candidate. Then in 1796 the Federalist members of Congress met in secret conclave to name their presidential and vice-presidential candidates. The Republicans did likewise. Both followed the same practice in 1800. Thereafter the Federalist decline left the Republicans almost alone and in control. They held a congressional caucus from then until 1824, over the increasing protests of those who saw this process for what it was—a political predation, a pre-emption of the choice of the Chief Executive.

In 1816 the Federalist party completely collapsed, and President Monroe (a Democrat-Republican) had only token opposition in 1820. There was then no catalyst of outside political competition, no opposing party to bring solidarity in the remaining party's ranks. The election of 1824 was a fiasco. Five strong contenders leaped to the starting line for Monroe's vacated chieftainship: John Quincy Adams, Henry Clay, John C. Calhoun, Andrew Jackson, and William H. Crawford. This election was the death knell of the caucus, "this engine that manufactured Presidents," as Jackson dubbed it. When the caucus met and, with decimated and discredited numbers, nominated Crawford, for him it was the kiss of death.

The state legislatures revolted. Tennessee rose with an angry shout and a banner that read "Old Hickory Forever!" At Philadelphia a rigged convention was all set to confirm the nomination of Calhoun. As the delegates prepared to vote, some bewhiskered farmer in the last row impulsively rose to his feet and stammered: "I nominate General Jackson!" It was like the bursting of a dam. The entire room broke into uncontrollable shouts of acclamation and supported Jackson in a landslide.

When the votes of the electoral college were counted, Jackson had 99, Adams 84, Crawford 41, and Clay 37. But no man had received the requisite majority, so once more the House of Representatives found the choice of a President dumped in its lap.

What followed is one of the most dramatic incidents in our history. Clay, being fourth, was out of the running, and Crawford was on his deathbed. Adams had the pledges of twelve of the twenty-four states *for the first ballot*—just one short of a majority. It was evident to the Adams men that if the ballot went beyond the first, Adams was lost. Maryland had promised to defect to Jackson on the second ballot, and other states would follow suit on the third. It was "Adams in One, or Nothing Won!"

Clay, if he could not be President, would be President-maker. Now the plots, conspiracies, and counterplots thickened. Pennsylvania militiamen muttered that, if Jackson did not win, they would storm the Capitol and take it for him. Adams supporters whispered to DeWitt Clinton that he might become minister to Great Britain if Adams were elected, and other Adams supporters whispered the same promise to Daniel Webster. Between the deep sea, represented by Adams, and the devil, represented by Jackson, the spirits of the representatives writhed, but they found no escape.

As the New York delegation was being polled, pious, vacillating General Stephen Van Rensselaer of the old New York family of landed gentry (historians have described him as old and senile; actually he was fifty-nine) dropped his head on his arm to ask his duty of God.

The General had faithfully promised Martin Van Buren he would *not* vote the first round so that Van Buren might hold intact seventeen of New York's caucus votes for future bargaining. If the good General voted for Adams on the first New York balloting (as both Clay and Webster had been frantically urging him to do), then the tie in the New York delegation would be broken, and New York's one vote would go on the first general ballot to Adams. But if New York's vote went to Adams, the election itself would go to Adams!

So the gentleman prayed. When he removed his hands from his eyes, they chanced to fall upon a discarded Adams ballot which lay at his feet on the floor. He stooped, picked up the ballot, and placed it in the box. Thus a rich and vacillating landowner from the upper Hudson elected the President of the United States.

"Treachery! Treachery! Damnable falsehood!" stormed Congressman Cobb of Georgia. Jackson's personal followers were even more expressive. With inflamed faces they shouted, "Assassins! Perfidious blackguards! Cheat!" "The cards were packed," said Randolph of Roanoke between his teeth. Someone mentioned Van Rensselaer. "The poor, miserable wretch!" said Cobb.

Certainly, Henry Clay was made Secretary of State. Things went back to normal. But the real casualty of this 1824 campaign was not Andrew Jackson, the ignorant backwoods presumptive, but "King Caucus" himself. He had been deposed forever. One more hurdle between the people and the President had been eliminated.

Five

The Search for a
Father-Leader

With cannon booming over the swampy, mud-rutted city of Washington on that March 4, 1829, the horde of variegated, weather-beaten humanity awaited the carriage of their hero, Andrew Jackson. He was staying at Gadsby's hotel, and the sea of faces surged at its door. All of a sudden a great roaring cheer rolled up, beginning at Gadsby's and billowing all the way to Capitol Hill. Their man had not failed them. There was no carriage.

Slender, gray, erect, with deeply lined face, General Jackson emerged from the hotel. Bands, military attendants, even the dancing homage of the cavalry escort—all these had been quietly dismissed beforehand. The General and his small entourage were picking their way through the jostling crowd, *walking* up the hill to his inauguration as President of the United States. "True greatness!" breathed the onlookers. "A common man!" they exulted. "True greatness needs no pomp." To Francis Scott Key the moment was "sublime."

The tumult in the capital city was in great part, of course, born of greed and a taste for plunder such as has always been let loose when the palace doors of the elite have been smashed. But from the time of John Adams at the turn of the century there had been evident a popular yearning for a popular leader in the White House. The revered Washington, whom the people had regarded with worshipful awe, was gone. And the men who had followed him had been able to trace their origins to nothing better than a congressional caucus and a ratification by an electoral elite; even the democratic Jefferson, born an aristocrat, could not truthfully identify himself with the masses. Jackson was born poor, and he shouted it.

That Andrew Jackson was a "popular" President, emotionally, cannot be denied. That he was a "popular" President from the angle of widespread voting participation can hardly be claimed. True enough, the total of popular votes had increased from a meager 356,038 in the election of 1824 to a total of 1,155,350 in the election of 1828, while the general population of the nation had advanced approximately 16 per cent. This was a threefold increase, and the number of eligible voters was slowly growing yearly as the property restrictions fell before the axe of public demand. Historians generally acclaim the election of 1828 as the first in which the popular vote became an important factor in the selection of presidential electors.

However, this great increase for Jackson was due only in part to the relaxation of requirements for voting; in larger share it was the consequence of a fuller response of those who were already eligible to vote. The excitement attendant on the previous election and the opening of the choice of electors to the direct vote at the public polls—these were the elements mainly at work. Jackson's men interpreted the large vote not only as a general uprising for their idol, but as a public sign of approval for the battering down of "King Caucus" and the take-over of the nomination by the people.

Nonetheless, the ferment for broader franchise was working over the nation, and although every state but South Carolina had provided for popular election of presidential electors by 1832, property restrictions, depriving many citizens of the vote, lingered on here and there for generations —indeed, far into the nineteenth century.

But General Jackson, although the great majority of the citizens were unable to vote for him, was popular in a deeply emotional way that had little to do with election totals. This tough and wiry commoner of a hundred duels and brawls, who bore Jesse Benton's bullet in his arm and Dickinson's lead close to his heart, whose only college had been the battlefield and the frontier, whose constant slogan was "the people's right," was involved with the people. They understood him. In his six years on the Supreme Court of Tennessee he had never made a move or written a decision, but Jackson knew what to do when a cruel father cut off his child's ears and then hid. He left the bench, caught the man, brought him to court, tried and branded him—all within twenty-four hours! This was the people's kind of justice. Jackson was their man.

Who cared that he could not spell? *Could they?* De Tocqueville called him "a man of violent temper and mediocre talents" raised to the Presidency by a victory of ordinary achievement (Battle of New Orleans), and which "could only be remembered in a country where battles are rare." De Tocqueville—who was he?

Nor had the people winced when the President of the United States, John Quincy Adams, had failed to attend the inauguration because he was afraid to face the impassioned man who had sworn to "show no mercy" to the slanderers of his wife. There was more to this man's appeal than one fortuitous battle, and a man of passionate utterances was to be admired, not censured. What if some people considered him crazy because he took public offices and then threw them away almost at once? Weren't the "silver-forked" gentry against him? The class that, as Thomas Benton described it in *Thirty Years in the Senate,* ". . . hugged their gentilities, genealogies, conservatisms, and all the other antiquated and effeminating nonsense of which Europe itself is beginning to be ashamed and to toss off as a tawdry and ragged cloak," hated Jackson. This was commendation enough for the frontiersman and the farmer.

"Washington and Brandywine, LaFayette and Yorktown, Jackson and New Orleans," they muttered in the taverns. And after a glass or two, Napoleon, Alexander, and Julius Caesar entered into the comparisons, always to Jackson's credit. Truly, the people were hungry for a father-protector.

Born March 15, 1767 in Waxhaw, South Carolina, son of a farmer who died the very month of his birth, Andrew Jackson dallied with law, served as delegate to the Tennessee State Constitutional Convention, as a member of the House of Representatives (one year), and as a Senator (for another year). Then he served six years as a judge of the Supreme Court of Tennessee, after which he entered on a military career that encompassed the defeat of the Creek and Seminole Indians and of the British at New Orleans. Briefly, from March 10 to July 18, 1821, he was governor of Florida, and briefly, from March 4, 1823, to October 14, 1825, he tried the U. S. Senate, from which he resigned.

But General Jackson had been haranguing about injustices suffered by the people for some time before the Senate offered him its inimitable sounding board. Tennessee's newspapers had been building up their hero as presidential timber while they had been viciously attacking "King Caucus." Jackson was persuaded to make the "sacrifice" of ousting the incumbent Senator, Colonel Williams (a caucus man), in the cause against "King Caucus." After writing a namby-pamby protest, the General "submitted with good grace" and left for Washington.

It was the wisest thing he ever did. All Washington society awaited a glimpse of this "ugly, strong oak out in the swamp"; to the surprise of many he was discovered in the Senate to be a gentleman! When Secretary of State Adams gave him a dinner, everyone who was anyone was on hand to watch the crude and unlettered backwoodsman slurp his soup and eat with his fingers. Their astonishment, says A. S. Colyard, was great when they discovered that "his manners were as polished as anyone's at the table" (whatever that may be worth).

But the "polished gentleman" had no polished tongue. As the presidential boom waxed, the Senator's pronouncements grew louder and more caustic, and they were echoed, now, by newspapers over the land. "Should the people suffer themselves to be dictated to by designing demagogues who carry on everything by intrigue and management, they cannot expect to see their present happy government perpetuated," he wrote a friend (for publication). "It must sink under the scenes of corruption . . . if the people do not assume their rights of *choosing a President for themselves.*"

His protests against "God's will" became fainter. "If I ever fill *that office* it must be with the free choice of the people. I can then say that I am President of the nation, and my acts shall comport with that character," he declared.

The General may claim another precedent beside that of discrediting "King Caucus": there is proof that he initiated the political practice of baby-kissing. In a letter to Major William B. Lewis on February 22, 1824, he discussed his possible candidacy with his usual reluctant ardor, and ended: ". . . kiss the babes for me." By August 13, 1824, according to Colyard, the General was speaking of himself in the third person, like a demigod. "The General nor his friends will never adopt the course of intrigue. . . . Their cause . . . is the people's cause. . . ."

Although the General was speaking and behaving in the typical manner of all presidential aspirants, the communication with the people was as yet one-sided. The General spoke; the people listened. But they had little means of response except the response of the anointed on election day.

For a man to receive one and one-half times as many popular votes as a rival, and then to have this rival become President instead, was profoundly shocking to the American credo. When, in 1824, with Jackson lacking a majority of all electoral votes cast, Clay's followers in the House threw their support to Adams and made him President, it signaled the angry kickoff for Jackson's 1828 campaign. The rage of the South was met head-on by an unprecedented mudslinging campaign in the North. Never had a candidate aroused such passionate partisanship. If Jackson was the "man of the common people," there were some equally "common" people on the other side.

One Thomas Arnold, called by Marquis James, in *Andrew Jackson, Portrait,* "an obscure politician," slandered Jackson mercilessly, and the target of most of the abuse was Jackson's irregular marriage to a grass widow before her divorce decree had been granted. Wrote Arnold: "A vote for him would be a vote to sanction the code whereby if a man should fancy his neighbor's pretty wife . . . he has nothing to do but to take a pistol in one hand, a horse whip in another and . . . possess her. . . . General Jackson has admitted that he boarded at the house of old Mrs. Donelson, and that Roberts became jealous of him, but he omits . . . that one day Roberts surprised General Jackson and his wife exchanging most delicious kisses . . . and that on the trip to Natchez with Colonel Stark they slept under the same blanket."

There was a great deal more of this. General Jackson, short-tempered and quick to take offense at best, was slowly going mad at this abuse of the woman he loved. He well understood that an aspirant to the Presidency dare not fight a duel; but he fondled his pistols lovingly. He was caught in a fatal web. He scribbled hasty letters of denunciation; he tore them up in a burst of angry tears. He paced and stormed. It was then his backers came to him with a proposal: "Let's defile Mrs. Adams . . . as having had premarital relations. . . ." Responded Old Hickory with enforced calm: "I never war against females."

But against the rare appeal of Jackson, the feeling of strength and protection and understanding that he gave the people, no weapons of slander or even of truth could prevail. Not even full-page pictures of coffins of the various militiamen Jackson had ordered shot, with heart-rending stories of their wives and nine children, had much effect.

The voters could ignore the scandalous shafts and elect Jackson to the Presidency, but they could not deflect the barbs from their mark. A few weeks later Rachel Jackson died, cut to the heart.

In nine weeks Jackson would be sworn in as President of the United States, the goal of his entire restless life. But now he retired into the Hermitage, his home, refusing callers and answering none of the avalanche of letters and good wishes. Those close friends who were admitted discovered him sitting staring at the picture of his wife, weeping un-ashamedly while all about him was strewn the disarray of packing. The President of the United States was a heart-broken man, haggard, aging, and now extremely bitter. Rumors of his death swept the nation.

But only his heart was dead; his body would present it-self in Washington for the inauguration. Dressed in heavy mourning, he began the toilsome journey. As the word went on before him, he was again badgered and harassed on every side, and from the moment the coach jolted to a stop at the hamlets along the route, not by his enemies but by the loving people. They swarmed about him at the inns, clodhoppers from the cornfields, their boots thick with spring mud, occupants of city flophouses looking for a handout, political hopefuls, local politicians, greedy vultures, and adoring followers, one and all they pressed upon his defenseless person all the way to his hotel at every stop.

The General had been encouraging all this. He had identified himself so closely with the common folk that he could not now in good grace protect himself from the onslaughts. On a Pittsburgh-bound packet his fellow travelers on the boat were revolted by the "brutal familiarity" to which they saw him exposed. Jackson could thank God when, in Maryland, he suddenly was spirited away from the scheduled route that was to have swept him to a tremendous Washington welcome and taken into the private carriage of John Henry Eaton, his old friend, to be driven to the Major's private apartments at Gadsby's four hours before the cannon were to signal the new President's entry into the city.

But although the great army of cormorants who posed as "the people" had been foiled at the coach stop, they were not long in laying siege not only to the hotel, but to the Capitol, and to every public building in the city. "It was like the inundation of the northern barbarians into Rome," wrote Colyard. "Strange faces filled every public place. . . . They swarmed, especially in the lobbies of the House, an expectant host, a sort of Praetorian band, which, having borne in upon their shields their idolized leader, claimed the reward of the hard-fought contest."

Never had Washington, accustomed to chaos and excitement, witnessed such a sight. Twenty-four hours a day audience-seekers crammed the lobby, stairways, corridors, and public rooms of the hotel, "pressing and jostling until nervous persons feared for the safety of the building." Such an array of fringe-area Americana had never met the cold Washington eye!

Coonskinned, buckskinned, hand-loomed, and leathern-aproned they came; pioneers, plainsmen, keelboaters, and politicians; editors, adventurers, immigrants, and cormorants. They clotted street corners, traveled from bar to bar, mounted soap boxes, held up the carriages, and almost brought about a whiskey famine. They cut their hair in imitation of their leader; they slept on billiard tables or in alleys; they mobbed the entrance to Gadsby's, parting ranks grumblingly only to permit passage of the carriages of certain members of the upper crust who, it now appeared, also believed themselves members of the race of "common men."

All this for some eleven thousand offices directly (or indirectly) within the gift of the President. The cry was for a "clean sweep"—each one hoping to be brought in on the backlash.

How General Jackson and his entourage ever walked to the Capitol on his inauguration day is unknown; somehow he managed to press his way through the sea of humanity, scale a wall behind the Capitol, enter a basement door, and reach at last the Senate Chamber, where Anne Royall, a newspaperwoman of the day, was waiting to describe what she saw.

The Committee on Arrangements had constructed a platform in the East Portico so that this President of the common man might take his oath in the sight of all; as it turned out the ceremony was visible to no one except the handful in contact with his person. The foreign ministers, arrayed in their gold lace and decorations, arrived to swell the Senate; next came the Justices of the Supreme Court in their long silk robes. The appearance of the General was a shock. He wore mourning clothes, and he leaned on a cane; his hair, which had been black, was all but white; his face was a ghastly color.

Anne Royall, "by hard squeezing," slipped out to the portico before the oath had been administered to all the new Senators, and there the sight baffled description. "Not only every seat, but every inch of the platform was crowded, by men, women, and children. These had forced the guards, and taken possession. I was shoved and pushed from one place to another, squeezed, and betrampled; and at length wedged up, about an inch from the door. . . . How the President, the Judges, Foreign Ministers, and Senators, etc. got out of the Senate Chamber, I am at a loss to divine; for I saw nothing of the President but the top of his head. The chairs, intended for the Honorables, were filled with women, standing on them, and the whole appeared one mass of solid people . . . nor did I hear one word of the President's address; much less did I hear him take the oath."

No one heard the President's speech, though those at his side said the pages trembled as he turned them. What did he say to his people? History finds it of mediocre content; the people cared not one solitary whit.

Anne Royall fled from the portico and hid herself in a Senate room where she might look out and see the President after he had taken the oath. At the booming of the cannon the crowd came thundering down the steps and President Jackson appeared, bareheaded, "leaning upon two gentlemen, one on each side," who were literally holding him up. The shouting was ear-splitting. "The earth was literally, covered with people . . . the square, the Avenue, all was now all motion." She ends, ". . . if ever I am caught in such another crowd, while I live, it will be an accident."

It was now necessary, if the new President was to reach the White House for the reception, that he mount a horse, and thus he slowly traveled down Pennsylvania Avenue, the mob closing in at the horse's hooves. A stately reception, the tables laden with cake and ice cream and orange punch, had been laid for the possessors of tickets, as was the custom. Tickets to the reception for the "elect"? Hadn't the General himself said that the "elect" were the "sovereign common people"?

Through the gates in the wake of the horse swept the uncontrollable mob, tickets of admission soon thrown to the chill March wind. The scene that ensued has been too often described to dwell upon it here, but its implications are such that it must be briefly brought into focus.

True enough, Jefferson's common-man followers had soiled the White House satins at his inauguration. But nothing like this had ever been witnessed before. The pack of humanity was so dense that women fainted to right and left, dishes and antiques were broken, tables turned over, clothes ripped, "one-hundred-and-fifty dollar chairs were profaned by the feet of clodhoppers," as Marquis James puts it, their brocaded silks ruined. Gold spoons were snatched at and the food consumed in one gulp (it is not said how many spoons were missing at day's end).

Official guests escaped through windows; but not until President Jackson collapsed from exhaustion did the strongest men lock arms to encircle him and permit his slipping out the back way to his hotel. Nonetheless, the spree at the White House continued until some resourceful functionary emptied the ravaged building by placing great tubs of punch on the White House lawn.

Certainly only a few in this multitude were vultures. Many of them were the curious, the jubilant, the adoring. But these latter departed for their homes quickly, while the vultures lingered on, hounding the President, crying for a "cleaning of the Augean stables," organizing under leaders, grumbling at delays in the rewards they anticipated, until finally expenses took their toll, and they, too, were forced to leave the city. "If I had a tit for every one of these pigs to suck at they would still be my friends," said the rueful President as he watched the bedraggled retreat of the disappointed.

Truly the coming of Jackson heralded a new relationship between the people and the President; his Presidency furnished an emotional outlet such as they had never known. The people yearned for a strong chieftain, perhaps even a "tyrant"—as Jackson soon came to be called by his congressional enemies. Here, then, for the first time in American history, was a President whom the people could approach, touch, importune, and even maul, the first President they felt they owned. It was a heady experience.

But when they left Washington over the thawing spring roads of gumbo corduroy, jogging and bumping slowly back to their farms twenty or fifty or a hundred miles away, suddenly they were as far from him as they had ever been, and he was lost to them once more.

Jackson in his first administration tried hard to "clean the stables," but his efforts in this direction have been grossly exaggerated and were too cautious to please any of his loudest backers. His cabinet list was greeted sarcastically

71

as "the Millenium of the Minnows," and his friends shook
their heads and apologized that "the old man" was out of
his mind with grief. They may have been right. "Late in
the night I retire to my chamber . . . deprived of all hope of
happiness this side of the grave and often wish myself at
the Hermitage there to spend the remnant of my days and
drop a daily tear on the tomb of my beloved wife," he said.

It was William L. Marcy, an old associate of Van Buren's,
who coined "To the Victors belong the spoils." Jackson,
the old soldier with the severed viscera that broke from the
breastbone when he stumbled, who at intervals must bleed
himself in the arm while a servant held him erect, knew
something of wounds, albeit his most troublesome were the
result of private battles. When his followers urged that
he remove from an Albany postmastership an old soldier
who had ardently supported Adams, Jackson leaped to his
feet, threw away his pipe, and shouted: "By the Eternal!
I will not remove the old man. Do you know that he carries
a pound of British lead in his body?"

He did uncover some truly unsavory situations among
public servants—pilfering, the illegal use of the frank, the
use of bankruptcy to avoid legal debts, "expense accounts"
that could not be explained, defaulters, and eighty-seven
jailbirds in good civil service jobs. He highhandedly removed the public treasury from the Bank of the United
States and vetoed the bill that would maintain the high
prices on public lands, declaring that, rather than recharter
the bank, "I would cut my right arm from my body . . . I
would rather undergo the torture of ten Spanish inquisi-
tions. . . ."

Yet in all that he did, he was utterly convinced that he
acted for the people. (To Clay it appeared that Jackson
was a bit confused as to the distinction between the people

and *himself*.) "Sir, the currency of the country is in dreadful situation." "Sir," responds the President, "you keep one-sided company. Andrew Jackson has fifty letters from persons of all parties daily on this subject." "Sir, the people—" "The people! The people, sir, *are with me.*"

Perhaps "the people" did not understand the bank bill or the land bill, but when certain of the President's enemies waylaid him and the Vice-President in the dark streets one night, and Jackson said, "Get behind me, Mr. Van Buren," and then clicked the snuff can in his pocket like a pistol and frightened the attackers off—the people heard. "There were brave men among them," said Jackson, "but no man likes to be killed in the dark." All this the people—when at length it came to their ears—avidly drank in.

This most explosive and colorful of all Presidents faced a formidable galaxy of brilliant men in the Senate: Webster, Clay, Calhoun, Wright, Frelinghuysen, Benton, Southard, Clayton, Rives, Tyler, Preston, Forsyth, and Poindexter, to name a few. Of the members of Jackson's Congress, five became President, five Vice-President, three Secretary of State, and twenty-five had been, or were to be, governors of states.

Jackson consistently carried a majority of the House, which was popularly elected, but took a continual lacing in the Senate, which was elected by the state legislatures and was far removed from the people. This body censured the President as a "tyrant," and most of the members agreed with Jesse Benton, who, according to Marquis James, called Jackson a "bloodthirsty ... dishonest, incompetent; mediocre politician, cock-fighter, horse-racer, gambler, brawler and participant in shady deals, a military chieftain whose renown rests on the deeds of his subordinates."

Senator Clay's formal resolution of censure of the President was passed on March 28, 1834. It charged, among many other things, "that the President, in the late executive proceedings relating to the revenue, has assumed upon himself authority and power not conferred by the Constitution and laws, but in derogation of both." This resolution, which was carried by a vote of 26 to 20, was received by Jackson as an outrage that must be expunged at any cost.

The President found a confederate in Senator Thomas Benton, Jesse's brother. It took Senator Benton three years of unremitting effort to get that censure resolution expunged, for the Senate is not quick to retract or apologize.

Benton understood it would never do so of its own volition. So, with great patience, he started his campaign. He went to the public at large and reached it in every way at his command. He delivered thirty major speeches on the subject. He made a national scandal of the issue and whipped up a rising flood of public indignation. The people then took it to their legislatures with determination, demanding that the Senate retract. This was done when, on the election of Jackson's protégé, Martin Van Buren, in 1836, a Jacksonian Senate finally came into power.

The resolution was retracted; but nothing would satisfy Jackson short of a dramatic midnight session where, before his defeated enemies and crowded galleries, black lines were ceremoniously drawn around the resolve in the manuscript journal and the words "Expunged by order of the Senate this 16th day of January, 1837," scrawled across the face.

So ended eight years of ceaseless fighting between the President and the removed-from-the-people Senate. And even more than Senator Benton, it was the critics of the Jacksonian conception of the Presidency who had advertised it among the people. "I look upon Jackson," Chancellor James Kent declared in 1834, "as a detestable, ignorant, reckless . . . tyrant. . . . This American elective monarchy frightens me. The experiment, with its foundations laid on universal suffrage and our unfettered press, is of too violent a nature for our excitable people." Universal suffrage? An unfettered press? An ignorant, reckless tyrant? The excitable people approved them all!

But the lordly Senators, though forced by public clamor to expunge their censure, did so in a pyrotechnic thunder never heard before or since in those marble halls. "Proceed, then," said Senator Calhoun acidly, "and like other skillful executioners, do it quickly, and when you have perpetrated it go home *to the people* and tell them what glorious things you have achieved for our common country. Tell them you have exterminated one of the brightest and purest lights that ever burned at the altar of civil liberty; . . . silenced one of the noblest batteries that ever thundered in defense of the Constitution, and bravely spiked the cannon; tell them that henceforward no matter what daring and outrageous act any President may perform, you have forever hermetically sealed the mouth of the Senate. . . !" Frenzied and ashen, he sat down, while Webster rose to indulge in "epithets, vituperative, coarse language never before heard in the U. S. Senate."

The day and the night had worn away. The expungers, mightily fortified by a mammoth supper of cold ham, turkeys, beef, pickles, wines, and mugs of hot coffee which they had stored in their committee room, jovially confident in the new Jacksonian majority, proceeded with a flourish to their "damnable deed." In years to come, despite the warnings delivered to the crowded lobbies and galleries that night, the Senate was to torment, bind, castigate, and belittle the President again and again; such was its independence. But this night the public had tasted something quite new to them: they had had a whiff of the power of public opinion. They would never forget it.

Corwin and Koenig, in *The Presidency Today*, consider that the Jackson administration accomplished little other than negative. "When he left office he left behind him a political vacuum that a resuscitated Congress presently filled in, thanks to the manipulations of the slavery interest, and continued to fill until the outbreak of the Civil War."

Yet Jackson's impact on the relationship of the American people to their President had been great. True, Jackson scarcely formulated a program. But the people in that day and age understood little of what was going on or what was needed; what they wanted was a strong leader who would do the deciding (and acting) for them. Said one Senator, "The people believed in Jackson as the Turks in their prophet." Whether what he did was proper, or even good, did not seem to matter as much as the fact that he strove mightily *to be* right, and the populace felt this striving, and was reassured.

William Cullen Bryant believed that Jackson was precisely the man for the hour, and Marquis James that Jackson knew the people did not want to rule, but to be ruled. He used a majority or he went ahead anyhow and made himself the majority pro tem. If he did not always provide a government *of* the people, he provided one *for* them. He lived by sheer nerve. He never hesitated to throw his entire political life into the ring for any cause, great or small. He could with equal fervor champion a small cold lamb on a stormy night (which he brought in to his fireside), the indigent son of Daniel Boone (whose financial distress he relieved), or the savagely attacked wife of his Secretary of War (whom he stuck by through one of the most sensational scandals in American history).

In everything that Jackson did, he identified himself with the people. His first Annual Message to Congress called for direct election of the President by the people. His seventh Annual Message (December 7, 1835) spoke of the people as "the great source of authority." The role he cut out for himself was oracular. His self-righteous insistence that *he* was the voice of the people brought down on his head both vicious condemnation and ardent, unreasoning worship.

Nothing, nothing whatever seemed to diminish the popularity of Jackson. His prestige suffered hardly at all from the torrent of insults. The people's hero, fighter of nearly a hundred duels and brawls, was infallible. Certainly he was shallow, constantly embroiled in personal vendettas. And the Senate was right to challenge his overbearing attitude, to try to preserve what it could of the balance of power. Jackson pushed an evolution of his office beyond the capacity of any successor to sustain. A hundred years would elapse before any Chief Executive could bolster these presumptions of authority with something more than the assertion that he was anointed.

But Jackson had to settle for the only kind of leadership he could offer a frontier people. That his leadership was not vastly wise is less significant than that it was *strong*. Because of this the people were prepared to forgive him anything.

Thomas Benton describes the day that "Old Hickory" took his leave of the people. His man, Martin Van Buren, had been elected, and the tall President and the dandified little President-elect came out onto the portico for the oath-taking. "For once," wrote Benton, "the rising sun was eclipsed by the setting sun." The presidential oath was taken in a great hush, "as if at a funeral." Then the General slowly made his way down the broad steps to the carriage and grays that awaited to take him away from the White House and out of the people's lives forever. The people looked on the rigidly erect figure whose shock of iron-gray hair defied the breeze. Uncovered, he bowed. Then he entered his carriage. There arose from the assembled crowd a cry as if of pain, a great aching cry "such as power never commanded, nor man in power received . . . the acclaim of posterity breaking from the bosoms of contemporaries. . . . I felt an emotion which had never passed through me before," wrote Senator Benton years later.

The carriage moved slowly away. "All I desire, before God," Andrew Jackson had said, "is to leave to the people a government devoid of pomp and special favors, a government such as is due the genius of the plain people of America." Instead, he left them with a void—and with a vision that would plague them forever.

Six

All That Thunder and
No Reign

In the 1840 campaign General William Henry Harrison's followers outthundered even Jackson's, but it was largely trumped-up thunder. There was also another difference. General Jackson's public had wildly worshiped its hero, but the great mass of them was voteless. Political frustration had added a threatening, almost bellicose undercurrent to their roars of acclamation. During the 1840 campaign it is doubtful whether the spontaneous enthusiasm was as much for the new hero as for the newly discovered power of the vote.

Adroit as General Jackson had been at feeling the public pulse without benefit of a dialogue—it was a sixth sense with him—he misfired completely when he personally chose Martin Van Buren to succeed him. Van Buren, unexcelled as a political manager, had no empathy with the people at large; he lived in a different world, a world of political mazes, deals, and trades, a tangle of intrigue. Yet Jackson, beholden to Van Buren for his own election, loved the conniver well and, as was his custom, effectively blinded himself to the public image of his protégé.

Certainly Van Buren's humiliation at the hands of a resentful, peevishly self-assertive Senate had something to do with his triumph in the election of 1836; for if Jackson misfired, the Senate of 1831 backfired. As Edward Stanwood describes the result, in *A History of the Presidency*, the gloating Jackson was able to witness "the glorious scene of Mr. Van Buren, once rejected by the Senate, sworn into office by Chief Justice Taney, also being rejected by the factious Senate."

The story of Van Buren's leap to the Presidency is a fascinating study in its irony.

In the spring of 1831 Van Buren resigned from the office of Secretary of State to take a recess appointment to the Court of St. James's. George Haynes relates, in *The Senate of the United States*, how the Senate leaders, Clay, Webster, and Calhoun (all presidential aspirants), conspired to recall him from his post in London, where he had already established himself when the Senate convened in December. "Senatorial condemnation," they believed, "would be political death" to the superpolitician. "It will kill him, Sir, kill him dead. He will never kick, Sir, never kick," Thomas Benton quotes Calhoun in his reminiscences. "This rejection," continues Haynes, "made Van Buren first a martyr, then Vice-President, and later President of the

United States." If this is oversimplification, the recall did get Van Buren (so safely put away) back into the Senate's hair and in line for what followed.

But Van Buren was no puppet of fate, for he was one of the most competent politicians who ever lived. An ardent disciple of Aaron Burr, he had presided at the funeral of King Caucus in 1828, and then he had thrown himself into a vigorous campaign to organize all the poorly-knit local and state gatherings of the Democratic-Republican party into a national nominating convention of party delegates, a massive federal pyramid of power composed of "wheels within wheels," as Matthew Josephson has described it, easily adaptable to political manipulation—particularly by Van Buren. He became an unrivaled expert at vote-seining and at managing the burgeoning and naïve electorate. Thus when he had so cleverly managed Jackson's campaign of 1828, what was more natural than for the General to assume that his ardent supporter had earned his own place in the presidential sun?

Van Buren, born in the log cabin of a farmer-tavern-keeper, apprenticed himself for seven years to the village attorney, entered law practice in debt, and retired from it at forty with a fortune of $200,000, according to George Stimpson in *A Book About American Politics*. He was called the "Little Magician" and the "Red Fox of Kinderhook," and because he was small and dandified, and wore tailored surtouts, fashionable hats, and fawn-colored gloves, unkind critics remarked that only his red and gray whiskers assured them that here was a man. Was he the natural son af Aaron Burr, who used to frequent his father's tavern in the years just preceding his birth? It is more important that Burr inculcated in Van Buren the art of politics, and with such effectiveness that he changed American history.

Martin Van Buren is famous (or notorious if you like) for establishing and heading the "Albany Regency," a political machine that controlled the Democratic party in New York State from around 1820 until 1850. His career is significant because he was intermediate between two highly emotional periods in the approach of the President and the people toward an understanding. His importance is a negative one: when he looked out beyond his White House windows over the roofs and hamlets of America, he saw not people but numbers.

The first President to be born under the Constitution, he managed, by the same political maneuvering that had raised him to the Presidency, to denigrate himself sadly by three successive attempts to regain the chair (in 1840, 1844, and 1848), receiving, on his fourth attempt, less than 11 per cent of the popular vote and not one electoral vote. His single administration, which was marked by the steady expansion of the suffrage and by the public choice of presidential electors, was stained by an act of perfidy that cancels out all else: on October 21, 1837, the Seminole chief Osceola was seized while under a flag of truce in Florida, and died shortly thereafter of heartbreak in an American prison while General Zachary Taylor decimated his people at Okeechobee Swamp.

Perhaps Van Buren did inherit the panic of 1837 from President Jackson's Specie Circular, which directed the Treasury to receive only gold and silver in the sale of public lands, as Joseph West Moore alleges in *The American Congress;* without doubt the advances in the direction of popular expression in the choice of President were great, as more and more voters participated in the nomination as well as in the election of their Chief; nonetheless, the people, as living, thinking human beings, rather than as voting units, seem never to have impinged upon Van Buren's consciousness. He had barred them from his vision, and they responded by rejecting him, not once, but three times. He could never be their hero; he could never touch their hearts.

But one was waiting in the wings who could be developed to fulfill this role.

On the rain-soaked day of February 21, 1840, the "Ohio State Convention of the Friends of Harrison and Tyler" convened at Columbus, a two-day mass demonstration of flamboyance, fervor, and demagoguery such as the nation had never witnessed, nor would ever witness again. From then until the election in November the whole country lived on the brink of mass hysteria; over a hundred silly campaign songs were written and sung; oceans of hard cider patriotically consumed; and pigs were barbecued in quantities that would feed whole counties at once. Harrison's election may be said to be the first to show the definite impact of the fast-broadening voting rights, and America, in celebration, got drunk on its own folklore.

The grand Columbus parade stretched out in the bone-chilling rain as far as the eye could see, band after band after band, each one brightly tootling its favorite campaign air, float after float with its display of frontier lore. There in soggy hunting shirts woodsmen gulped the fermented juice of unsprayed apples; trappers sat in mangy furs before log cabins and consumed corn bread and 'possum; Indians fell beneath the blows of brave General Harrison; canoes carried pretty maidens fluttering flags and kisses. Here was earthy, folksy America on parade, reeking of linsey-woolsey, cartwheel dollars, hodden gray, paddle boats, molasses, grits and cracklin's. The people (they had been told) were in the saddle at last: they could vote. And the Whigs were throwing all restraint to the winds in a gigantic spectacular as they sought to best Van Buren and place in his stead the "old soldier, the farmer, the lover of hard cider and of the people"—General William Henry Harrison.

> Old Tip, he wears a homespun coat—
> He has no ruffled shirt, shirt, shirt;
> But Mat he has the golden plate,
> And he's a little squirt, squirt, squirt.

A fair example of the poetic efforts that graced this national orgy of noise, ridicule, and commonness! "Farewell dear Van, you're not our man," sang the crowds as the carts and wagons rumbled past, spattering the onlookers with clods of Ohio gumbo.

"The iron-armed soldier, the true-hearted soldier, the gallant old soldier of Tippecanoe," chanted the hardy drinkers on the floats in reply. Yelps and impulsive screams rent the air. One observer recorded "Whoops!" "Ho!" "Hoorahhh!" "Tip and Tyler!" "Yip for Tip!" as bursting from the onlookers and paraders. "The voice of the people is indeed the voice of God," intoned the ranting orators. "To Save the Ship of State from Wreck; we'll place a Patriot on Her Deck," sang the throng.

One float depicted Diogenes giving Old Tip a hearty handshake at the door of his log cabin while the rays of his lantern illumined the General's honest proletarian face. There was no limit to the pathos. "Yonder goes a beautiful white horse," related one witness admiringly; ". . . on him are the empty military saddle and trappings of General Washington.... the horse is led by an old soldier of Washington's bodyguard ... followed by a number of old men of the Revolution, who gaze upon the vacant saddle of their dead Chief, and then turn to the picture of Harrison, cast their eyes over the multitude, and give a shout for 'Old Tippecanoe.' "

Such massive rallies took place all over the nation during that year of 1840. Triumphal arches adorned the streets of the big cities; buildings were so bedecked with American flags that the multitudes of ladies leaning from upper-story windows had difficulty in waving their white handkerchiefs; low roofs were shingled with human forms. "To great men's skirts he never hung, as Martin to brave Jackson's clung!" the people shouted; and little school children recited the immortal lines: "He invites them all into his cabin, But he has no time for them that's grabbin'."

The phenomenal events of this year have often been interpreted as a popular revolution, a spontaneous rising of the common people in which they exercised the privilege they had long sought, the vote, and placed in the President's chair a man of the people. Such is not strictly the case.

First, according to Arthur Charles Cole, in his informative *Whig Party in the South,* the Whigs, who sponsored Harrison, were not a people's party, but a party composed in great part of wealthy manufacturers, businessmen, and slave-owners. Knowing that they could never attract enough votes of the common folks to elect a President, they picked a candidate who, though by no means a "common man" or a log cabin dweller or a bona fide farmer, could masquerade as all three. Harrison was born in a Tidewater Virginia mansion of a slaveholding family; his familiarity with log cabins consisted (outside of military outposts) of a short period on his honeymoon spent in the five-room frontier log house of his wealthy father-in-law. But the General was indubitably a doughty fighter of the Indians, a strong arm, a father figure, and a protector—and this the Whigs exploited to the full.

So, shrewdly taking advantage of the political naïveté of the American public, the Whigs whooped up the General all over the nation—with so much noise, entertainment, and dust that nobody detected the humbug. The populace was busy raising log cabins in vacant lots, putting on country barbecues on "tables upwards of twelve thousand feet in length," maintaining open house for all wandering campaigners, and loudly singing while "martial music reverberated wildly through our highlands and valleys for many miles."

Indeed, the log-cabin-and-hard-cider battle cry found its origin in a Van Buren sneer. A Democratic journal had remarked with sarcasm that if the Democrats wanted to get rid of Harrison, all they would have to do was to hand him a $2,000-a-year pension, a log cabin, and a barrel of hard cider. Of course, to the hard-drinking common man and cabin-dwelling frontiersman, these were words of purest gold. "It is a contest between cabin and palace, between hard cider and champagne," effused the Whig press.

The excitement of the populace, once engendered, exceeded all Whig expectations. A wagon boy went on the stump for three months for the General, and a Buckeye blacksmith abandoned his trade to travel the vast distance to New York to harangue the vice-hardened city dwellers. A log cabin rose on Broadway. In Wheeling, Virginia, the people erected a pole 230 feet high to carry a flag in Harrison's honor while barrel after barrel of hard cider was cracked.

The "Locofocos"—as the Democrats of the North were generally known—were presented as effete. The fastidious President did not improve their reputation when he appeared at a rally in a snuff-colored coat, white trousers, lace-tipped cravat, yellow gloves, and morocco shoes. *"He* is no lion," said Dewitt Clinton cruelly, "but more of a fox or weasel." And Davey Crockett, to much laughter, pictured Van Buren as nothing more than a cunning political trickster: "He could take a piece of meat on one side of his mouth, a piece of bread on the other, and cabbage in the middle, and chew and swallow each severally while never mixing them together."

The General's political speeches were intended to say as little as possible in as long a time as possible. Harrison spent much time in boasting of his military exploits against the dwindling Indian tribes and in thumping his chest to show his unusual vitality and strength. He promised to promise nothing, other than that he would initiate no legislation and would not run for a second term. He paused at regular intervals for "Nine Cheers" and the thunderous response of "20,000 throats."

That Harrison had a genuine feeling for the populace, and that the populace came to have a genuine feeling for him, cannot be denied. After four years of the high-toned, distant Van Buren, the people hungered for a leader who would symbolize the decisiveness and power they had felt in Jackson. It is doubtful that, even if Harrison had been unmasked as the scion of an old aristocratic family, even if it had become known that he preferred featherbeds to straw, that he was a government place-seeker most of his life, that—if he dared—he would reach for a glass of imported whiskey rather than a mug of frontier cider, it would have affected the election at all. To the people Harrison was the tower of strength they were eternally seeking. Ironically, the effort to maintain this image spelled his doom.

To one who traveled about the country in rain and shine, who orated for hours in the vilest of weather and called upon the people to witness his hardiness (the Locofocos had tried to depict him as old and unfit because he had turned sixty-seven), the miserable storm on Inauguration Day, March 4, 1841, held no terrors. Casting aside his hat and throwing his great coat dramatically into the arms of an aide, the General mounted his white horse and rode slowly and unflinchingly along the route of the tedious inaugural parade. The people were in raptures at the sight of their "heart of oak."

Even this display was not enough. For nearly two hours the newly sworn President stood unprotected from the bitter weather as he read his inaugural address (whose 8,527 words make it the longest on record). Then, still half clad, he mounted his horse and led the parade of citizens, cider barrels, and log cabins to the White House. If he felt the chill in his bones that evening, he dared not mention it. Manfully he carried on. He attended three inaugural balls, the last the People's Tippecanoe Ball at Carusi's Saloon, where more than a thousand of the *hoi polloi* gladly paid ten dollars each to cheer him to the echo.

By March 27 the President could no longer hold himself erect. The pleurisy and high fever from which he had been suffering had become pneumonia. He was borne to his bed, and on Sunday morning, April 4, he followed to the grave his seven children who had died (he had fathered ten), literally a victim of his own hardiness. (Mrs. Harrison, who had been too ill to attend the inauguration, and who never saw the White House or her husband as President, lived on for twenty-three years after him, to a hale eighty-nine.)

The nation was stunned. But former President Jackson, stubborn old democrat that he was, welcomed Harrison's death as "the deed of a kind and overruling Providence."

This exuberant spectacle, then, was the fruit of suffrage liberation, and of it the Whigs took liberal advantage. Here and there remnants of property qualifications remained on the books, but newer passages conveying universal suffrage were constantly replacing them, and legislatures no longer dared pre-empt the right to choose electors. The tide of democracy had rolled in. Such, at least, was the belief in the aftermath of the Harrison campaign.

After the demise of the congressional caucus, a new if not wholly virtuous arrangement called a national convention had come into being, soon to be righteously removed to Baltimore where it was thought to be beyond the control of Congress (while still within messenger distance of the professional command post).

Was all this evidence of a new intimacy between the people and the President? Would the people, armed with their new right to select a Chief, find a protector and establish with him the close contact they seemed to yearn for? Were the voters and their Chief Executive at last to achieve political communion? Would the President now consider himself (contrary to Harrison's abnegation) the agent of a popular principal, as a man with a mandate, as a Moses to a lost tribe of commoners? Although Harrison had insisted that he would *"abridge* the power and influence of the National Executive," he had so effectively impressed upon his audiences his decisiveness and indomitable will that even those who understood the word did not take him seriously. What could "abridge"—whatever that was—this battle-hardened old warrior?

How he would have lived up to their hopes for a strong father-protector while at the same time honoring his own passionate promises of self-abnegation (drowned out, fortunately for him, by the bands and the shouts), no one now will ever know.

Seven

A Free People at Last
— But No Moses

It is something of a shock to observe, after Harrison's death, the long roster of self-effacing Presidents who occupied the White House in the years before the Civil War. Twice the populace had risen up in search of the kind of Chief who would give them a feeling of strength and security; each time the trophies on his shield and the battle scars on his body were what elected him. It is as if the people, at the death of their last hero, had been rebuked by Providence and were stunned into a long apathy. This is, of course, a romanticism; other factors rose up to deflect the movement of the President toward the people, and of them toward him.

For all the lackluster of the candidates of this era, the presidential campaign had established itself. And besides becoming an emotional outlet, as mentioned, it began to evidence other values. Robert Bendiner, in *White House Fever,* speaks of it this way: "Every four years the sovereign states of this country perform a collective act that quickens the cement of the Union, making the Georgian alive to the feelings of Oregonians and stimulating the New Yorker's awareness that beyond the Hudson lies more than Jersey City. If the making of Presidents served only to re-establish this sense of community, it would be worth all it costs in time, money, and folly. But the process does much more. In good part, it supplies the pomp and circumstance, the trappings and rituals, out of which a nation acquires tradition and continuity."

While today the presidential campaign may have exceeded all bounds of common sense and become a spectacle in extravagance, it does perform some services. In the years after Harrison's death the only occasion or event during which Americans for one moment thought as Americans, not as sectionalists, seemed to be the presidential election. This may seem paradoxical, but it is not. While sectional feelings were increased by these quadrennial crises of President-choosing, the consummation, the enthroning of the leader, was a unifying act, for all the various resentments the campaign might have inspired. For a short time the eyes of all the nation rested on the flag.

As for the outcome of these campaigns, we may make excuses for the lack of popularity of all the Presidents between Harrison and Lincoln; they are an ill-starred lot. Tyler, certainly, was foisted upon the people. A states' rights advocate, he accomplished little except the annexation of Texas, and that stirred up an antislavery storm. But the years of his administration were exciting. He narrowly escaped death aboard a warship when a gun exploded and killed most of the others in the presidential party; his entire cabinet, excepting Daniel Webster, resigned in a rage over policy; his first wife died, and he married a second, in the White House—as all the while he reared fifteen children. But he never "caught on" with the people. When he died at Richmond, Virginia, on January 18, 1862, the government made no announcement or proclamation of his death; his passing was ignored officially as well as popularly. Fifty years passed before Congress appropriated $10,000 to build him a monument.

James K. Polk, the dark-horse Democratic candidate who squeaked through to election on the coattails of New York's candidate for governor, Silas Wright, was not, of course, the political nonentity that the Whigs pretended. "Who is James K. Polk?" they asked sarcastically, and biased historians made a myth of his anonymity.

James K. Polk had been Speaker of the House and governor of Tennessee. A Jackson protégé (although none of the Jackson magic brushed off on him), he quickly forfeited his political support when, on taking office, he renounced any ambition to serve a second term.

Yet he controlled his ambitious subordinates and strove to attain the four goals he had set for his administration: tariff reform, re-establishment of the independent treasury system, settlement of the Oregon dispute, and the acquisition of California. By his accomplishments he deserves the "near-great" rating the historians have bestowed upon him.

But Polk was in no way in communion with the people.

He did nothing to deepen the popular roots of the Presidency. Normally—but more so in modern times—the effectiveness of a President is an outgrowth of his appeal to the people. And the measure of his accomplishment tends to coincide with the public's empathy for him. Polk, despite his administrative genius, was little appreciated. At the end of his only term, he said, "I am heartily rejoiced that my term is so near its close. I will soon cease to be a servant and become a sovereign."

Maxim Armbruster has called Polk's provoking of war with Mexico to gain California simply "old-fashioned depredation." But "Expansionist" Polk added eight hundred thousand square miles in all to the adolescent nation. He was not mourned, explains Armbruster, because he possessed none of the appealing qualities, such as humor, warmth, and imagination, so needed to stimulate the public. Had Polk possessed an empathy for the people, and shown it, this "near-great" of intrinsic worth and positive leadership might have attained true greatness.

The chief asset of Millard Fillmore, who succeeded Zachary Taylor in the White House, appears to have been a schoolteacher wife. Scandalized when she discovered that the White House did not possess a single book—not even a Bible—she set aside a large room and solicited $250 from the Congress to establish the first White House library. Although this act enhanced White House culture, it did nothing for her husband's popularity with the masses. Fillmore, handsome and genial, had probably been chosen as Vice-President in 1848 to somewhat balance General Taylor's unbenign looks and slovenly appearance. When, after succeeding Taylor, he became very humble and even besought the help of the Senate in his decisions and governing, he committed the irredeemable sin of presidential politics. And when he declined an honorary degree from Harvard because he was "unworthy," the American public believed him, and promptly forgot him.

As for Franklin Pierce, the magnetic, attractive lawyer from New Hampshire who exclaimed when nominated, "Gentlemen, you are looking at the most surprised man in the world," he might have been speaking for the public as well. Pierce was a general of some heroism and quite a bit of fame, but in the presidential race he was a very dark horse indeed. The Democrats had nominated him only after the four prominent candidates had deadlocked the convention. (His name was not even mentioned until the thirty-fifth ballot.) But the gay and charming Pierce never had a chance to charm the people. His four years in office drooped with heavy mourning. He had lost all three of his children before their teens, and his last son was killed in a train wreck only two months before the inauguration. As First Lady, Mrs. Pierce dressed always in black, and a funereal air pervaded the White House. The public sympathized—and turned away.

President Buchanan, although he exuded the glamor of bachelorhood, being true to his young love (his twenty-three-year-old sweetheart had unaccountably swallowed a lethal dose of laudanum in 1819), was able to evoke no tender response from the public. Certainly his inauguration was a production of extravagance. Models rose of the Goddess of Liberty, of battleships and historic scenes, and a $15,000 building was erected for the dancing. As if determined to convince themselves that Buchanan was the great man for whom they were waiting, the celebrating supper guests consumed 400 gallons of oysters, 60 saddles of mutton, untold quantities of venison, tongue, and ham, 500 quarts of chicken salad, 500 quarts of jellies, 12,000 quarts of ice cream, and a cake four feet high, not to mention $3,000 worth of wine! (Modern psychologists might call this compulsive eating to assuage frustration.)

But although James Buchanan had tried for the presidential nomination four times before succeeding, his heart was not in the task when he attained office. In 1859 he wrote his presidential swan song: "I am now in my sixty-ninth year and am heartily tired of my position as President. I shall leave it in the beginning of March 1861 . . . with much greater satisfaction than when entering on the duties of office." To the incoming Lincoln he said: "If you are as happy, my dear sir, on entering this house as I am on leaving it and returning home, you are the happiest man in the country."

We have left General Zachary Taylor to the last, because he was the one gentleman of the era with great potentials of popular appeal. "Old Zach," so unassuming he never wore a uniform unless he had to, or any decorations, who sat his horse sideways in a most unmilitary way, and who appeared before his troops in straw hat and checkered gingham coat, had all the ingredients, the folksy, lovable qualities, of the popular hero. The people knew that he had a drawerful of sparkling decorations if he wanted to wear them, that he had been too busy soldiering ever to have voted in his life. They loved him when he refused the letter that informed him of his nomination for the Presidency because postage was due. And when he pastured his faithful horse—the old war horse that had borne him through so many battles—right on the White House lawn, the symbolism (as well as genuine affection) touched the hearts of all who saw it.

Sadly, the people saw this brightest hope for a sympathetic approach between them and their Chief disappear. Taylor died after only a year and a half in office, aged sixty-five. One great thing he had accomplished, nonetheless. He created the Home Department, which was later to evolve into the Department of the Interior, guardian of America's resources in lands, waters, minerals, wildlife, and parks.

Yet beneath all the personal eccentricities and vicissitudes that hampered the foregoing Presidents from attaining understanding and greatness in their job lie the basic reasons for these presidential nonentities. The perilous times had closed in on them. Sectionalism, like a dark storm, had begun to lower so thickly over the nation that the smell of doom, like the smell of ozone after the lightning and before the torrent, was heavy in the air. The President, caught in the winds as a branch is caught, was buffeted between the earth and the sky. Always he must be for and against one half of his people. And the people turned from their uncertain Chief to seek the shelter of some other, closer authority that could guarantee the security of their little world, their own, sectional way of life.

Add to this unsettled state of presidential authority the incumbents' disclaimers of it and we understand their failure. Denial of authority and self-abnegation seemed to be the fashion for these ante-bellum Presidents. The public was in a mood to hiss when Millard Fillmore anointed himself with verbal ashes: ". . . both my respect for the

Legislature and my sense of propriety will restrain me from any attempt to control or influence your proceedings. With you (the Legislature) is the power, the honor, and the responsibility of the legislation of this country." These were the words of a weakling, not a god.

And as sectionalism came between the President and the people, Congress gained immeasurably in strength. Not that Congress needed strengthening! So prestigious was the Lower House that for sixteen years former President John Quincy Adams represented Plymouth there without denigration; so prestigious had the Senate become that the glitter of its great names caused this prewar period to be known forever after as the Senate's "Golden Age." Against this a self-effacing President had no chance at all.

Where, indeed, might you find the party leaders? When the Whigs were defeated in the off-year elections of 1842, it was Senator Henry Clay who resigned his post to rebuild the party's fortunes. When the country teetered on the very verge of war in 1850, and sectional antagonism flared over the complex issues that slavery evoked, the White House was strangely mute. When the Great Debate, the greatest of all time, on Clay's resolutions (a series of proposals for settling the differences between North and South) was in the legislative halls, Congress drew all eyes, not the White House.

And well it might! When in the history of man will such eloquence again resound, such brilliance be paraded, such passions find release? There in the intimacy of the Senate sat Calhoun, his piercing gaze undimmed though he was dying, the chin drawn back as though in indignation, the resplendent white pompadour tossing in anger like the flag of rebellion that it was, listening in tight-lipped silence while Senator James M. Mason read the paper Calhoun was too weak to enunciate. There paced Henry Clay, with his long-dished nose and voluminous brow, his deep-set eyes, never quiet, catching the light like restless water catches star-gleam. There, too, was William Seward, of the great nose and small pursed lips, his dark hair oiled to a shine and his neckcloth embedded with jewels. Davis, Chase, Benton, Cass, Douglas, and Foote—all helped elaborate what is now called the Compromise of 1850.

This, then, was the Congress that the lowering clouds of sectionalism and war further enhanced. Even the crisis of the Mexican War could add but little to the stature of the Presidency; because the President could not initiate the terms of acquisition of territory, Wilmot and Clay must do it for him. The nation could step forward together on "Fifty-Four Forty or Fight!" only to break apart again on whether the Oregon Territory should be slave or free. It could march arm in arm to the Pacific only to confront the same divisive issue when it got there. Slavery was an "either-or" question. Where was the middle ground in bleeding Kansas?

And the issue being hotly *sectional,* what security could a "President of all the people" offer anyone? Here, isolated in their sectional boundaries, with their sectional customs two centuries old, buttressed by their neighbors whom they sent to the national capital to represent them, they must find all the security they might! Even the centralizing effect of Manifest Destiny fell far short. And the President, daring nothing great, must resort for campaign material to matters as noncontroversial as a capacity for hard drink and the killing of Indians or Mexicans.

Thus, throughout these disquieting years, the people instinctively appealed to the Congress for a way out of their oppressive situations. The House was inundated with petitions; the gag resolution, which provided that these numerous "petitions, memorials, resolutions, propositions, or papers" be set aside without printing, notice, or action, gives clear evidence that the line of political communication, however unsatisfying, was by petition from people to Congress. When the issue of slavery complicated and almost frustrated the annexation of Texas, the channel of communication was by resolution of state legislatures to the *Senate* of the United States.

Could any President, no matter what his brilliance, decisiveness, and strength, have drawn the people to him in this hour of disintegration? The answer must be "no"; and our valuation of the "nonentities" who graced the White House must perforce be less harshly worded.

Certainly there were other forces which, in spite of the people's bright new toy, the vote, contributed to parochialism—forces less austere and terrifying, but nonetheless fundamental. The newly enfranchised electorate was largely illiterate, ignorant of political issues except the most obvious, and incapable of weighing national problems, much less following through to a reasoned solution. "Who will protect us from the Indians?" they asked. "When shall we have a new turnpike?" "Who is responsible for the fall in the price of hogs?"

Provincialism burns as fiercely today as it ever did. But today we are forced by the advance in communications to consider, however peevishly, our local concerns within the larger framework of the nation. In pre-Civil War days our forefathers were granted no such redemption. Even as the people's hope of finding a hero died, the flag-waving, torchlight parades, and general hullabaloo were an outlet, a release from provincialism, from the hard and brutal reality of their lives.

Moreover, there was yet no meaningful dialogue between the President and the people. The affinity that slumbered, the deep instinctive attraction that had existed from the beginning, was lost in the vast green spaces. The far-flung hamlets were connected only by frightfully impassable roads, the cities had no telephones or telegraph and few trains. The insurmountable difficulties of communication were everywhere. What rapport could be established in that day between the largely illiterate citizens of such a nation and a lonely man on the banks of the distant Potomac? Even had there been no burning, overriding issue of sectionalism, how could these two elements of the government even propose to exchange viewpoints?

Finally, for all the bands and parades, the role of the public in the choosing of the President was quite limited. The election, indeed, was less an election than a ratification. There were, of course, no primaries. The initial choice, then as now, rested with managed political conventions. But these conventions were little more than branches or arms of official congressional and administrative power groups. Barnstorming to build up a candidate's popularity, such as the Whigs had initiated for Harrison, was possible, but it took inhuman effort, money, brute endurance.

But what of Abraham Lincoln, who comes at the end of this period? What of this giant among giants who, in response to a heartfelt serenade by admiring crowds in 1864, said humbly, "I am thankful to God for this approval of the people. . . . I give thanks to the Almighty." In the echoing chambers of history Lincoln commends himself to us as the great commoner, the man of the people. He identified himself closely with their joys and sorrows, their hardships and hopes. Surely he bore a deep feeling for them, and they for him. How do we account for the greatness and popularity of Lincoln in this period of sinister forces and almost nonexistent communications?

In the first place, we must remember that Lincoln's dialogue with the people was extremely meager; he did not leave Springfield throughout the presidential campaign of 1860. It was the prearranged flutter of the white handkerchief of the otherwise unrenowned Burton Cook that set off the demonstration at the 1860 Republican convention—the first demonstration of its kind in history—and not the cries from the balcony. Charles Beard says Lincoln rose to greatness in a single act, and was fortuitously martyred to escape the "loss of majesty" that might have ensued. Armbruster says, rightly or wrongly, that Lincoln was "not of 'hero' material," and that only through the purest of accidents did he ever reach the Presidency at all. His nomination had been a quiet political deal made by bosses in the middle of the night in a hotel bedroom.

Moreover, Lincoln was a sectional President—and a *minority* President. And even within his own section he was hated as intensely as he came to be loved.

We have said that, as the nation rushed toward its doom, it was the environment, primarily, that minimized the President. With Lincoln this environment ends in the holocaust. Lincoln became a leader in the crisis, for a constitutional or military emergency always concentrates power in the Chief and draws all eyes away from the Congress to the leader. Lincoln was, certainly, a master politician. But he derived his support primarily from his role as Commander in Chief of the Army, and not from his Presidency of the nation. It was his victory as Commander in Chief that brought public adulation. And he was cut down before he could transpose his leadership to the political arena.

But for all this, there was greatness in Lincoln himself. Perhaps it did stem from "a single act"—but no other President had dared the agony of performing that single act! More likely, it was his perfect combination of courage, compassion, and simple plainness that drew to him during the war years (and especially following his martyrdom) such fanatic devotion. Certainly the "times were ripe"— but a coward will procrastinate whatever the times may be.

Lincoln drew not only the fiercest love but also the fiercest hate. He was, said some, "the criminal type," resembling a famous murderer of the day who terrified young maidens; but it was noticed, says Coyle, "that children liked to climb on his lap uninvited." He was known as the "original gorilla" and the "Big Baboon." He was said to preside at the slaughter by the freed Negroes of women and babies in their beds. His humor was ridiculed, scathingly criticized, and cruelly turned against him. His homeliness was paraded with vicious remarks. It seems evident now that his unfailing resort to a funny story or a quip may have been his only protection, thin-skinned as he was, against the torrent of insults, the only way he could divert the abuse with a modicum of gallantry, a measure of control.

In September 1864, *Harper's Weekly,* which had not hesitated to slander the "mole-eyed ignoramus, the swindler, monster, spavined, rail-splitting stallion," remarked with some awe that it was amazing, but the truth, that the people, in that strange psychic way of multitudes, saw through the abuse and was not moved; "the popular confidence in the unswerving fidelity and purity of purpose of the President has smiled the storm to scorn," it said. Rejoiced the *Spectator* of London: "Secure of their [the common people's] support, Mr. Lincoln can afford to disregard the clamor of city mobs and the apprehensions of the mercantile class."

The groundwork Lincoln had laid to unify the divided land was soon nullified by the Radical Republicans. Ironically, this man of compassion, in his tragic death, bequeathed to the dissilient forces of sectionalism the bloody shirt of his assassination to perpetuate their hate—and to deny him. The strength of the Congress, which had demeaned and intimidated Lincoln's predecessors (and which, in spite of the cries of "monarch, absolute despot, irresponsible and uncontrollable despot!" he had, as Commander in Chief, quickly surmounted), was not overcome; it had hardly been fazed. The power of the Congress closed in again on Lincoln's successors, more smothering than ever before.

For a limited, tumultuous period, a small part of the electorate, the rank and file, had come close to a strong leader. It had taken the exceptional condition of a devastating, fratricidal war to bring this about. The crisis signaled the breaking down of the barrier of space: communications, stimulated by the war, were beginning to burgeon. But the other barriers—a dominant Congress, public ignorance, and sectionalism—carried on. Sectionalism, in fact, was greatly aggravated.

Lincoln was so cruelly treated that he exclaimed, "I would rather be dead than, as President, thus abused in the house of my friends." And W. H. Lamon, in *Recollections of Abraham Lincoln,* quotes him as saying that "from my boyhood up my ambition was to be President. I am President of one part of this divided country at least; but look at me! I wish I had never been born!"

But Lincoln missed the worst, as though Fate were quietly withdrawing him to his niche in the hall of fame before his halo became tarnished. Speaking of the "subsidized gang of hirelings"—which is what he dubbed the Reconstruction Committee of Fifteen who so viciously attacked him—President Andrew Johnson cried out passionately: "And I say here tonight that if my predecessor had lived, the vials of wrath would have poured out upon *him.*"

So badgered a President as Andrew Johnson had scant time to meditate on improved relations with the populace. And now, in addition, new barriers between the President and the electorate were triumphantly being erected.

Eight

The President Becomes
a Pawn

The period of commercial expansion between the Civil War and the Spanish-American War was an exuberant one. The pulse of the nation was surging with excitement. But it was a period of such harshness that, looking back today, we can scarcely credit the stories.

Symbolic of the times was the clever stratagem of a railroad brakeman who had tired of trying to rid the cars of peregrinating hoboes. He "would try the only known method of getting a man out of the trucks without stopping the train—let down under the car on the end of a rope a heavy coupling pin that would bound viciously off the ties until the iron found its mark. Then a track walker would

106

find mangled remains for an obscure burial," records Donald L. McMurry in his treatise on Coxey's Army.

Perhaps, as Demarest Lloyd tried to establish, "Our barbarians come from above. Our great money-makers have sprung in one generation into seats of power kings do not know. . . . They are gluttons of luxury and power, rough, unsocialized, believing that mankind must be kept terrorized." But was the public conscience one whit less vulgar, one whit more humane? The men of vision and humanity were but a handful in this nation on the make. They might protest, but even the florid verbiage of the age fell, if not on deaf ears, on ears so gross there was little understanding and less effect. The robber baron and the honest pioneer were impelled by identical drives.

When industrial expansion, and the diversion of conquering a whole new continent in record time, drew all eyes west, the fascination of the Presidency ebbed. Now Congress became the hub of government as petitioners and land-seekers crowded its halls and mottled the patterned carpeting with tobacco spittle.

What is more, as the cleft between the rich and the poor widened in the newly industrialized nation, it soon became clear on which side of the cleavage the office of the President was being established—solidly on the affluent side, by a kind of individual whose rapidly swelling torso blocked all vision between populace and White House—the boss. Ever since Lincoln, burdened by military cares, had surrendered patronage to his lieutenants for disbursal, bossism had grown and proliferated. It is fairly clear that no President of this period, no matter how strong, could have maintained his authority against them; none did.

In the periodic recessions of business, in the panics and

wars and hard times, eyes turn toward Washington and the White House. But when wages shoot up and land is free for the asking, there is less need for a strong leader. Indeed, far out on a Dakota prairie, a broken plow or a dry well might easily cause a man to forget a presidential election.

And now, so engulfed by political henchmen had the President become, the people had reconciled themselves to his inaccessibility and accepted it as a matter of course. The model of the hero-god, which Washington had bequeathed to the nation and which the campaigns of Jackson and Harrison had briefly revived, had been blotted out by the smoke and din. Although these booming years were also years of unrest, the protests and petitions, as noted, were directed not toward the President, but toward the Congress. The Chief and the people were farther apart in this age than they had ever been, or were ever to be again.

The interminable struggle between the incumbent President and the Congress (particularly the Senate) continued through the age of expansionism right into the twentieth century. The experiences of "accidental" President Andrew Johnson epitomize the unpleasant story.

In addition to all the odds stacked up against him (the boss hierarchy, the lack of public mandate, the renewed sectionalism), Johnson had also to struggle against three more obstacles. The first was his own natural inclination to fortify himself with liquor before any great event or occasion of strain; the second was his quick and hot Southern temper; the third was the recently aggravated taboo, founded on the sanctity of the separation of powers, which forbade presidential intervention in congressional elections and which left him helpless to defend himself against his enemies. One can well sympathize with Andrew Johnson as he lashes out: *"Damn* the Presidency. It is not worthy of the aspirations of a man who desires to do right!"

While thousands of plain people had stood on railroad platforms in the rain to watch the Lincoln funeral train pass by, and thousands more had filed past his coffin in the cities where the sad procession halted, the rejoicing politicians had not been there. They had shut themselves behind closed doors in an orgy of gloating, smoking, drinking, and planning. The Carpetbaggers, the Union League, and the Radical Republicans were now in the saddle, and there they meant to stay. This new President could count on no loyal followers, no strong hold, as yet, on the public. The hated appeaser of the South must be discredited quickly.

History does not recount which of these shrewd and fertile minds finally discovered the key. Someone recounted having seen Johnson flush angrily when he was heckled during a speech. Then the Radicals had his measure. Every time the badgered Johnson appeared on a platform, organized hecklers and howlers drowned him out. At first the President resisted; then he lost his temper shamefully, and with it his poise. His audiences felt that he was demeaning the office of Chief Executive, and this they could not condone, whatever the provocation. Shown everywhere in his worst light, the congressional elections of 1866 went strongly against candidates who had Johnson's blessing.

Having shorn Johnson of political followers and public support, the party leaders had no difficulty in arranging an impeachment, although the only valid charge among the entire eleven was his suspension and, in 1868, removal of the disloyal Secretary of War, Edwin M. Stanton, a deed supposedly in violation of the Tenure of Office Act. A two-thirds vote was required to convict; Johnson was rescued by one vote—35 to 19. But Johnson was forever ruined. "Those whom the bosses would destroy, they first deprive of their public."

But when, like John Quincy Adams, he fled to his home constituency in Tennessee in 1869, he could nurse his wounds and rebuild his fences among old friends who not only knew of his integrity, but lovingly ignored his manners. When he returned to the Senate, after three tries at election, in the greatest "singular personal triumph" of American politics, the galleries wildly applauded the President whom the American people had come, too late, to appreciate. Shortly thereafter Johnson went to his grave, shrouded in the Stars and Stripes, his head pillowed on his worn copy of the Constitution, as he had requested, and these words carved on his stone: "His faith in the people never wavered."

It is amusing to note how the Stalwart bosses of this period insisted on identifying themselves with the public good. In his autobiography Thomas Platt wrote: "From the beginning there was not the slightest sympathy between the Johnson administration and the New York leaders. Therefore, *there could not be between it and the rank and file.*" (Emphasis ours.) He was reasoning backward. There could not possibly be sympathy between the President and the rank and file when the President was so bullied by Congress that even his authority over the removal of appointees had been stripped from him.

When General Grant, tired old warrior that he was, followed Johnson into the office, he felt he had done his share of fighting on the battlefield. Moreover, he had a full-time job trying to consume the thousands of cigars his many admirers sent him from all over the nation. He sat it out and let the party leaders carry on.

The bloody shirt, of course, was a diversionary political tactic to distract society from the cleavage in the social fabric that industrialization was bringing about. As the workers swarmed to the burgeoning cities from farm and ship, they congregated in little neighborhoods around factories and industrial centers. Economic forces were closing in on the common man, thrusting him into a state of dependency comparable to that of the serfs of ancient Europe.

"Immigration," someone has remarked, "is the sincerest form of flattery," but many of the immigrants who came to the American shore in the last half of the nineteenth century came to regret the move. Ignorant, crowded into unspeakable tenements, helpless, and often unable to read, write, or even speak English, the immigrants soon came under the protection of the political ward leader, who took them over, body and soul—and franchise. In plain words, the immigrants provided the "deliverable vote" that the many little ward bosses assured to the big boss, and this vote became a powerful bargaining item in presidential elections as well as the dominant force in control of presidential nominations themselves. When a New York Tweed, a Pennsylvania Cameron, or a California Huntington asked, "How many floaters do you want?" he was not jesting.

Nor can we place all responsibility for the boss-ridden state of the nation during this age of industrial development wholly on the forlorn urban elements. The interest-ridden, mortgage-ridden, freight-rate-gouged farmers were a despairing lot as well. First in the upper Mississippi Valley and then in the "vast insane asylum" of speculation from Kansas all through the Middle Border, the farmers, too, desperately needing help, fell like ripe fruit at the feet of the kindly local politician, the trusted henchman of the big boss.

So with the chasm between the rich and poor widening daily, what other appeal had the poor but to the protective, generous, ward or county committeeman? William Graham Sumner voiced the dominant philosophy of Carnegie and the other barons of the age when he preached at Yale: "Certain ills belong to the hardships of human life. . . . They are a part of the struggle. The fact that my neighbor has succeeded in this struggle better than I constitutes no grievance for me." When he declared that "paupers are dead-weights" who should be dropped out of society's concern, and that all that the successful man owed them was "respect, courtesy, and good will"—nothing more nourishing than that—he was merely establishing the ethic. Let the best survive; the rest rightfully perish. This was the natural law as Darwin saw it and Spencer expressed it. It was the law of the business community as well.

Yet the local *boss* did not believe that paupers were dead weights or that all that was owed to any other man was "respect, courtesy, and good will." He did not believe that all but the fittest should perish. He extended his hand to the sick and the weak and the frightened; he could find ready cash to placate an irate landlord or bail out a relative fallen into the clutches of the law. He translated, interpreted, counseled. He knew ways of doing things; he had jobs in every pocket, and much more. And he wanted only one small favor in return—the poor man's vote on election day!

Thus did the industrial cleavage of American society between the Civil War and the twentieth century proliferate bosses, big, medium, and small. And the bosses made and broke every President during that period; they imposed their ponderous bulk in the way of any possible *rapprochement* between the President and the electorate, and then cried out in shock and pain when any one of their elected puppets attempted to exercise his presidential powers.

Symbolically, perhaps, the first electric lamp in Washington, glittering like a great yellow eye over the Capitol, was lighted in 1876, the year when Rutherford Birchard Hayes was elected. "To save what they could of their tainted machine," writes historian William Miller, "the Radical politicos decided to conciliate the honest core of the business community by running as their presidential candidate the impeccable Republican reform Governor of Ohio. . . ." And in good American tradition, General Hayes had been twice wounded, had had his horse killed under him, and had been decorated for gallantry under fire.

But because he owed both his nomination and election to the Stalwart bosses in the Senate, he was doomed. Smarting at the Democratic outcry when Tilden's claim to the Presidency was rejected by the Electoral Commission, and fearful of a riotous demonstration at his inauguration, Hayes took the presidential oath in the privacy of the White House Red Room. And since Tilden had received the majority of the votes, Hayes could never punctuate his messages to the Congress with the usual prideful remarks about being the "only national officeholder chosen by the people of the whole nation."

James Abram Garfield, nominated on the thirty-sixth ballot at the Republican convention in 1884, was distinctly

113

the creation of the party bosses. During his 199 days in office they pulled at him from every direction. Yet he, like Hayes and Grant before him, was a hero of the Civil War; moreover, he had demonstrated his qualifications for leadership.

On April 15, 1865, an angry multitude of fifty thousand New Yorkers (so run the accounts) surged toward the New York *World,* shaking their fists and screaming "Vengeance! Lincoln must be avenged! Let his critics hang!" Two victims had already fallen: one was dead and the other nearly so.

At this opportune moment a visiting Congressman from Ohio mounted the steps of a building and raised his arm against the throng. "Fellow-citizens!" he shouted again and again. The booming voice carried even over the wrangling and the noise. The erect, commanding figure held the crowd's attention. "Seward is dying!" someone announced, having come from the newspaper office where a bulletin had been received, and the word traveled over the crowd, hushing it.

The young Congressman quickly took advantage of the new mood. "Clouds and darkness are round about us!" he orated. "His pavilion is dark waters and thick clouds of the skies!" Then he paused dramatically. He raised his arm to the heavens. *"Justice and judgment are the establishment of His throne!"* He let the words sink in. "Fellow-citizens . . . *God* reigns! . . . and the Government in Washington still lives!" He had tamed the beast in the crowd. In but a few moments he had quelled the riot, and he had undoubtedly saved the lives of some.

One wonders what this magnetic, handsome man "of massive and yet graceful figure, with a huge, leonine head, and a resonant voice," as Matthew Josephson describes him, might have accomplished, how much response he might have elicited from the populace, had he not been struck down by an assassin's bullet so soon after his inauguration. Once he wrote: "I do not care what others say and think about me. But there is one man's opinion which I very much value; that is the opinion of James Garfield. Others I need not think about. I can get away from them, but I have to be with him all the time. He is with me when I rise up and when I lie down; when I eat and when I talk; when I go out and come in. It makes a great difference whether he thinks well of me or not."

At once crushed under an avalanche of office-seekers, Garfield could not sleep nights. "Once or twice I felt like crying out in the agony of my soul against the greed for office and its consumption of my time," he wrote. "My services ought to be worth more to the government than to spend thus." Again, he said, "My day is frittered away by the personal seeking of people, when it ought to be given to the great problems. . . ." If only he were allowed to use his opportunities "in vital, useful activity!"

Certain it is that Garfield defied the very men who made him. Adept politician that he had been, he had the temerity to snub the bosses in the most valued appointments and made of his close friend and the greatest boss of all time—Roscoe Conkling of New York—a sworn enemy to the death. Thomas Beer, in *Mark Hanna,* dramatically describes their final confrontation: "The two men met for a last time in a lady's drawing-room, bowed to each other below a chandelier while watchers gulped, and were blocked from each other's sight by a movement of resolute friends just as Conkling got his mouth open to speak."

Not only Conkling, the overlord, but every Stalwart boss came to Garfield to excoriate him. When the President appointed Judge William A. Robertson, the Half-Breed Republican who had defied Conkling's leadership in New York, collector of the New York Custom House, he stunned the entire community of politicians. Massachusetts machine boss G. S. Boutwell wrote concerning the flouting of professional protests against this appointment (which he called "wilful and premeditated violation" of the pledge Garfield had given): "It was, however, only one instance of General Garfield's *impulsive and unreasoning submission to an expression of public opinion. That weakness* had been observed by his associates in the House of Representatives, and on that weakness was his administration wrecked."

It is strange indeed today to hear of the "weakness" of a President because he responded to the public's demands for an end to corruption. Had that "weakness" grown, might the reformed Garfield have succeeded in breaking through the tight ring of bosses to establish some contact, once more, with the people? The answer cannot be known, for an assassin's bullet accomplished what the boldest of the politicians would not have dared.

But with the advent of President Chester A. Arthur, the political managers of men and Presidents, having impeached President Johnson, bullied President Grant, battled President Hayes right out of the White House, and murdered President Garfield (for he was a victim of the excesses of the spoils system), got the gleam back in their eyes. Arthur was one of their own. Hadn't he been relieved of his position in the New York Custom House because he had been considered too corrupt to remain there?

Nobody (except the bosses) expected much of the man who had been nominated for Vice-President solely to make Boss Conkling happy. He boasted no memorable war record; no medals dangled from his chest. He had been a crony of bosses all his life. The most that historians can say in praise of the Conkling machine is that it was "never so corrupt as its Democratic counterpart of that era, the infamous Tweed Ring." Handsomely upright, with waved, silky hair, and silkier "dundrearys," always dressed like a haberdasher's model, this debonair widower had sported around with the equally handsome Conkling for many years; they were bosom friends, closer than brothers.

Although Conkling had imperiously demanded that Arthur reject the vice-presidential nomination on the Garfield ticket when he (Conkling) was in a deep sulk over Garfield's nomination, he had not reckoned with an assassination. Truly, this was "a work of Providence."

But the Stalwart bosses were soon to have impressed upon their peculiarly egocentric intelligence one fact: the assumption of the American Presidency tranforms the new President. One observer likens it to a hysteria which lasts for the first few months, never to leave its victim the same. In the late President Kennedy, young and burning with zeal, accession to the nation's highest office produced a visible elation or excitement which lasted half a year and which the television camera readily caught and transmitted.

But if the Presidency is an elixir of such heady qualities that it greatly intoxicates, it later sobers the incumbent correspondingly. It has been known to make great men out of mediocre opportunists. Both Charles Beard and Arthur Schlesinger, Sr., emphasize that to mine gold one must first have gold-bearing rock. The gold was there in Arthur, for the Presidency transformed what was once a machine cog into a brave and defiant rebel.

"Within seven months," wrote Ed Manogue in the Albany *Times-Union,* "he appointed virtually a new cabinet of his, not Conkling's choosing. In 1882 he vetoed a treaty-breaking Chinese Exclusion Bill, along with a foolishly extravagant River and Harbor Bill that called for an appropriation of 19 million. These were the actions of a statesman, and when the Civil Service Reform Act was proposed in the fall of 1882 he earnestly supported it."

The Pendleton Civil Service Bill was passed only after the murder of President Garfield so aroused the public against the spoils system that even the obdurate and haughty Senate had to bow. Civil service under the act applied to but 15,600 positions, some 12 per cent of the total, but the bill empowered the President to extend the civil service at his discretion. Today well over three fourths of all federal employees are so classified. And it was President Arthur, one-time tool and beneficiary of the most shameful spoils system the nation has ever harbored, and whose principal concern had once been the razor-edge creases in his hundred pairs of trousers, who helped to establish the reform.

It would be pleasant to say he got away with it. But the Republican bosses deserted him so quickly when the time came for his renomination, in 1884, that he was stunned. James G. Blaine's capture of the Republican nomination was the final insult to the pawn who would not remain a pawn.

Chester Arthur, casehardened in the ups and downs of machine politics, yearned for a second term, perhaps only to vindicate himself. But the majority of these battered, unhappy men who occupied the White House after the Civil War escaped from their thralldom with a sob of joy. Ever since Washington the office of President had been a "splendid misery"; the boss age carried this misery to its ultimate. No wonder the words of Garfield ring down the halls of history: "My God! What is there in this place that a man should ever want to get into it?"

Nine

The People Become
"The Mob"

When the sedate Jacob S. Coxey, horse breeder and successful businessman, pushed up his silver-rimmed spectacles on his nose and announced sonorously that he was about to launch on Washington a "petition in boots," it was understood that he was making his appeal to Congress, not to the nation's Chief. The country at that time was in one of its periodic slumps. The panic of 1893 had been followed by a depression in which unemployment was rising and wages falling. There was real and widespread suffering, and nothing at all was being done about it.

A Populist and a cheap money man, Coxey was a wellspring of panaceas (some of which were eminently sensible), and managed for a great period to command from one to six columns of copy in every issue of every newspaper of the land. His program of national financing may have been farfetched, but his public works program no longer sounds so strange. Master press agent that he was, Coxey surrounded himself with such flamboyant persons as Carl Browne, who wore a fringed buckskin coat with Mexican half dollars for buttons. Browne also wore a sombrero, high boots, and, instead of a collar, a string of amber beads rumored to be a deathbed gift of his departed wife. Others in the "army" were equally picturesque. For weeks, every freight train arriving in Marion, Ohio, had been disgorging a variety of recruits, and now, on Easter morning, 1894, as the Negro color bearer, Jasper Johnson, and Marshal Browne, on a prancing stallion, dressed the polychrome parade, the marching contingent assumed the appearance of a traveling circus. The General and Mrs. Coxey, bouncing their infant son, Legal Tender, beamed encouragingly from their phaeton as Oklahoma Sam and trumpeter "Windy" Oliver danced into line. A long horde of newspaper reporters trailed the exuberant army as it wound its way out of town.

(Interestingly enough, one of the young men who hopped off a freight noticed some construction activity in the town and learned that a new steel plant was being built. On an impulse he gave up trying to overtake Coxey, then well on his way, and asked the foreman for a job. He got it, and ultimately Benjamin Fairless became president of the United States Steel Corporation.)

The notable fact here is that a movement of discontent of such large proportions could, and did, take hold without any attempt whatever by the President to avert it by some initiative. For had Coxey's march been only the work of a handful of crackpots in Buffalo Bill uniforms, it would be symptomatic of nothing. As it was, the march on Washington turned into a national movement as the 'voiceless everywhere sought to articulate their longings. Out in Omaha "General" Kelly led his industrial army in a column half a mile long from Chautauqua ground to Chautauqua ground on the way east, camping in mud and rain on the cold spring nights while the suspicious militia eyed them from a nearby hill. They were welcomed all along their route by labor sympathizers and workers' groups. In many towns the entire population met them with food and cash offerings. The G.A.R. banqueted them and gave them clothes. Newspapermen described the conduct of these marchers as admirable and declared that they left their camp sites "as neat as a parlor floor."

So, from all sections of the West, Middle West, and South, the "petition in boots" converged on an impersonal, distant, and seemingly hardhearted government. The marchers were not treated well in all places, nor were skirmishes and rough handling unknown, since the prospect of having a few hundred or a thousand men descend on a community often terrified the citizens. In Austin, Texas, the six hundred men of "General" Fry were packed solidly and without ado into fourteen freight cars and propelled out of the state. Then in Portland, Oregon, a branch of Coxey's army five hundred strong pushed the marshal aside, evicted the general manager of the Union Pacific railroad, and stole the train. In Montana "General" Hogan's army of six hundred, fleeing eastward in a hijacked train, was pursued by federal troops. Attorney General Richard Olney was working overtime at imposing legal barriers to the great march on Washington.

Coxey reached the capital first, and on May Day his army of some five hundred unemployed met face to face with a well-fed contingent of police twice its size. While twenty thousand spectators (almost all of them sympathetic) looked on, Coxey, Browne, and Jones were summarily arrested for violations of the Capitol Grounds Act. On May 8 they were convicted of carrying banners and "walking on the grass." Of the fifty people who had been bashed and trampled by the police nothing more was said. Although the various other armies kept straggling in for some time thereafter, the "petition in boots" had been effectively crushed. Neither President nor Congress took notice!

The infiltration of cranks and radicals into Coxey's army, plus the bizarre costumes of its leaders, tended to discredit it, but thoroughgoing studies of the movement as a social phenomenon reveal sobriety and discipline, and an earnestness of purpose that is amazing. They also reveal the bewilderment and desperation of a people who, completely out of touch with their government, did not know how to make an effective appeal from their miseries.

The Forefathers had believed in the people's "right to petition," but now the most mammoth and representative petition of the people of the United States had come to a quick and disgraceful end. Coxey's march had brought nothing but more suffering. If President Cleveland on that May morning happened to hear some of the tumult drifting into his second-story window along with the scent of lilacs, he quickly closed the casement, in accordance with good presidential tradition.

123

Yet 1894 was but the climax of the alienation of the people from their President. Ever since a dominant Congress had established the Joint Committee of Fifteen (six Senators and nine Representatives, under the grim and militant Thaddeus Stevens) to oversee the Reconstruction program, every presidential utterance had been denied, every move thwarted. "Throw conscience to the Devil and stand by your Party," Stevens had ordered his Radical Republican colleagues; and his command rang continually in the ears of Grant and Johnson, drowning out their appeals for more moderate treatment of the prostrate and bleeding South.

Not only had the chasm between people and President deepened as the nineteenth century rumbled into its final quarter, but the American populace seems to have acquired a monstrous image. It was born in the minds of the machine bosses, and it carried the odor of raw fear. The exact time when "the people" became "the mob" cannot be determined—but a sensitive study of this entire period soon reveals the trend.

Admirable as Hayes had been, he seems to have had as little sympathy for the workers as he had for the political knaves who used him to "perfume" their ticket. Against the bloody and desperate Pittsburgh rioters in the great railroad strike of 1877 he dispatched General W. C. Hancock with three thousand regulars: the trains must run!

For too long a period the presidential electorate had been, not appealed to, but negotiated *for*. Mark Hanna's voters were but "cattle," Tom Platt's "rank and file" were but numbers in a machine. Almost unaware of what they were doing, journalists of the day, referring to the public, wrote: "Harrison stood aloof from the mob, avoided contact with it, despised it," and "Cleveland challenged [the mob], defied it, walked over it roughshod." The masses of the American people appear to have become synonymous with all the strikers and marchers and rioters and protestors of the age, and thus the terminology for them merged and became one of scorn not untinged with terror.

Grover Cleveland, who was elected in 1884, defeated in 1888, and then, uniquely, chosen again in 1892, appeared closer in kinship to the electorate than any President since Lincoln. The people admired this great mountain of a man, whom William Allen White describes as "candor incarnate, with a lust for iconoclasm," more for the enemies he made than for the friends he encouraged. They admired him for the kind of integrity that impelled him as sheriff of Erie County, New York, to do the hangman's work himself because it was a disagreeable job he felt he ought not to delegate. Yet there was no way of converting the good will he had won into political power; he, too, was hamstrung by the times.

The G.A.R. loathed Cleveland because it was said (rather, *they* said) that he hired a substitute during the Civil War and went fishing on Memorial Day. Courageous and robustly direct, Cleveland could raise the roof with profanity when he heard the election tales concerning his illegitimate son and, later, the less authentic stories that he had kicked his second wife downstairs. Although a combination of curious circumstances had turned the trick on the Stalwart bosses and won him a meager victory in the key state of New York, by 1,149 votes, and so had won the 1884 election, Cleveland had not forgotten who was in control. Like all the others, he had to consider the bosses before he could consider the people.

Unlike Cleveland, Benjamin Harrison owed small obligation to the people. He came to the Presidency in probably the most complicated political deal ever executed.

Senator Matthew Quay of Pennsylvania, the part-Indian politician with the droopy eyelid and the tubercular voice, whom no scandal could make blush, and who always left his opponents "clutching at empty air," was the mastermind. Combining his rare talents with those of that other political fox, Tom Platt of New York, the two master strategists were able to dispose of the Democratic incumbent and place in the presidential chair the slight, aristocratic form of their puppet, Benjamin Harrison.

Bosses are nothing if not methodical. As early as the spring of 1888 Quay and Platt plotted out the entire election, chalking the votes precinct by precinct and state by state on their big charts and planning the deployment of their lieutenants and aides. Electoral votes were what counted. They came to the conclusion that New York and Indiana were to be the key states; these, then, must be "worked over."

But as election day approached, it became disturbingly apparent that Indiana was swinging to Cleveland. Immediately the "bite" was put on the big financiers; with the help of Mr. John Wanamaker $400,000 rolled into the campaign coffers overnight. By election day an eager army of more than twenty thousand "floaters"—professional voters who would cast as many ballots as time permitted—had been purchased and put on wheels so that they might move easily from one polling place to another. Freight cars carried whole crews of Quay's bought men from Pennsylvania to Indiana.

And not only freight cars. They came by water as well.

"Steamboat coming 'round the bend;
  Goodbye, old Grover, goodbye!
  Filled up full with Harrison's men;
  Goodbye, old Grover, Goodbye!"

chanted the northern children innocently. Oddly enough, this frank mention of floaters (appropriately water-borne in the song) was not a campaign charge hurled by the Democrats, but an open gloating by the Republicans. To both parties, floaters were a recognized part of the business.

Things were moving along satisfactorily when someone discovered (or perhaps purloined) a letter which Colonel Dudley, Republican party treasurer, had written on October 4. It said, in part: "Divide the floaters into blocks of five and put a trusted man with the necessary funds in charge of these five and make him responsible that none get away and that all vote our ticket."

The papers carried the damning letter; howls of dismay rose from Republican ranks; suits of libel were filed (to be quietly withdrawn immediately after the election); voters switched one way, then another; the excitement was at fever pitch.

Then the peregrinating voters, taking advantage of their new popularity, raised the ante. Their prices rose within three days from $2 a vote to $15. In one community in Indiana more than a hundred floaters had been staked out in various buildings the night before election, and sentries were posted to guard them "against surprise by the foe." Wagons of all sizes and kinds were deployed in the surrounding countryside ready to descend, loaded, on polling places at dawn. Quay and Platt took Indiana—but only by the scant majority of 2,300 votes.

But tough as Indiana had been, sophisticated New York gave the two connivers more of a workout. Here Democratic Boss David Hill was running for the governorship, and since he knew by heart every one of a boss's tricks, he could by no means be shunted aside. But how in the world could the faithful rank and file be made to split their tickets between *Democratic* Hill for governor and *Republican* Harrison for President? How could it be got through the skulls of these not-so-bright mercenaries, the plug-uglies, drifters, and heelers, long trained to the virtue of a straight party ticket, that they were now selling their votes to *two* competing markets? How, indeed, to get them to read the ballot at all?

But the floaters rose to the occasion with uncanny astuteness. In fact, they undertook the new, more complicated service with a wide grin and a wider raise of the ante. Surely it was worth $20 a vote to have to read? The bosses, after some painful reflection, decided in the affirmative, and after a second visit to "the Street," the Stalwart coffers were weighted with another $500,000.

Every bit of effort, in New York as well as in Indiana, was necessary. By their deal with Hill and their painstaking instructions to paid henchmen, the sweating bosses scraped up a majority of some 12,000 New York votes—out of a total of 1,300,000 cast—for their man Harrison. They performed this feat while, incredibly, Hill was receiving a 19,000 majority over their own party man, Republican Warren Miller!

Thus by their clever plotting and maneuvering the bosses succeeded in canceling out the wishes of the electorate. Indeed, in spite of all this proselyting, the people of the nation rendered President Cleveland a 100,000 majority in the popular vote. But the bosses, by exerting pressure *where needed,* chalked up 233 electoral votes for their man, as against 168 for Cleveland.

If this is not bossmanship's master feat, in a period of master feats, it is at least the most clear-cut example we have of how American democratic procedures were side-stepped, and of how the bosses between the Civil War and Spanish-American War "made" every President after Lincoln. It is not surprising that there was little sympathy or understanding between the President and the citizenry. What relationship did they have to each other?

Torrential rains dampened the inauguration of Benjamin Harrison on March 4, 1889. Having learned nothing from the fate of his grandfather, William Henry Harrison, the newly elected President chose to ride in an open carriage, unprotected from the downpour, to the Capitol to deliver his inaugural address. Even then, when to regard the President as the bold champion of the common citizenry was little more than to mock him, the desire of the Chief to expose himself to the people was a sort of symbolic rite—at least on Inauguration Day.

Benjamin Harrison, that "cold, thin, white flame of aristocracy in a sordid day," was so absorbed in his dreams of the Forefathers and so dedicated in his worship of the Constitution that he hardly saw the dark deeds, and would not have credited them if he had. He had the temerity to thank God for his election, which made Quay's drooping lids widen in quick anger. Later the boss groused about it at length with his co-workers. Hadn't he tried every trick in the book to arouse the public for Harrison?

Quay was quite proud of his cleverest ruse. A letter had

been sent from one "Murchison" in California to the British ambassador requesting his opinion on who should be elected, and the ambassador, unfortunately, responded. "Cleveland," he replied. How the Irish vote shifted when, by some hook or crook, the correspondence appeared on page one of newspapers across the land! And then hadn't Quay capped it all with the brilliant deployment of his purchased voting army, which had delivered the critical votes to win the day? Yet "Benny" had no idea "how close a little band of men were compelled to approach the gates of the Penitentiary to make him President."

Harrison was a "made" President, but he at once proceeded, wrote Thomas Platt, to become just another "ingrate" like Hayes, Garfield, and Arthur! Platt groaned that he had been plagued all his life with ingrates. President Harrison, in denying him the desire of his heart, the position of Secretary of the Treasury, forfeited the New York boss's support forever. And shortly Harrison, by squabbling with Don Cameron and Matthew Quay over patronage, lost them too. They made him pay. They opposed his program and placed stumbling blocks everywhere in his path. At last the scrupulous President even managed to alienate Secretary of State James G. Blaine, and many other lesser politicos as well.

So it was that the Republican phalanx of bosses, led by Quay and Platt and tycoon W. W. Dudley, approached the 1892 presidential campaign with something less than enthusiasm. Harrison's renomination seemed inevitable, since repudiation of him at that time would be tantamount to repudiation of the party organization. Miffed and frustrated, they were caught in their own trap. They had no heart to fight the exhausting fight again for a party that had become a hollow mockery of its former delightful and profitable knavery.

As for the people, President Harrison, although conscientious, was far removed in sympathy. He had responded to the constant cries of the industrial managers and, as was the presidential custom, had sent troops to quell the "fractious and violent agitations" of the masses. At his command American soldiers leveled their rifles at miners in Idaho and at strikers in Tennessee. He had broken strikes without arbitration.

But more than the necessity of saving face damped the bosses' ardor for the 1892 campaign. Not only was the Harrison administration being condemned by the populace because of the hardships imposed by the McKinley Tariff, but—what was much more serious—it was being hissed by the bankers because of the Sherman Silver Purchase Act and other policies. Eastern capitalism, like the harlot it was, had always been quick to lie in bed with any party that promised the greatest financial advantage. And because the Republican party had consistently been at the top of the heap, capital was predominantly Republican.

The bosses knew that such moguls as Rockefeller, Havemeyer, Gould, and James Hill would shift their support from party to party where and when they saw fit. And now Wall Street was frightened. If, as the soothsayers foretold, only a Democrat could win the 1892 election, then "the boys" would produce the most solid, *conservative,* gold-standard Democrat extant. Of course, it would help, and save considerable advertising, if he were someone already well known. Thus it happened that once-liberal Grover Cleveland, who (since making a small fortune in Wall Street and ensconcing himself in all the rich financiers' clubs there) had been sounding off in acceptably conservative phrases, emerged as the best bet to win. "Cleveland will stand like a rock against financial vagaries," declared his new backers.

This was a strange campaign, the campaign of the recalcitrant bosses. With the defection of the Republican managers, Wall Street proved itself more than able and willing to mastermind the whole effort. William Whitney, Henry B. Payne, August Belmont, Henry Villard, and other glittering names rose to the challenge, and with their unlimited funds they began a massive wheeling-and-dealing campaign in an effort to unite the many dissident, boss-led factions of the Democratic party, most of which had an undying hatred for former President Cleveland.

They began by enlisting state and local politicos throughout the nation: Vilas of Wisconsin, Morse of Indiana, Stetson of New York. They implored the blunt tactless candidate to extend himself: "You can heal lots of sores by patting a fellow on the back!" They led him to a private dinner in a small, luxuriously appointed hotel dining room where, with champagne and filet mignon, they had lured bosses Sheehan, Murphy, and Croker to "talk things over." They placated Hill in some unknown manner. In the end the vast campaign chest won over the "deliverable vote" of the dissident Democratic managers.

Cleveland's victory was quite all right with most Republicans. "Let *them* take over the mess," said Theodore Roosevelt, turning on his heel. Exclaimed good old Stalwart Bill Allison: "It was God's mercy to this country that Cleveland, and not Harrison, was elected President." "Cleveland! Landslide!" exclaimed Andrew Carnegie. "We have nothing to fear. Off for Venice tomorrow." Thus

132

does Matthew Josephson, in *The Politicos,* record the reactions of these famous Republicans.

What the people said is of small moment. The nation had not switched from bossism to popular choice with the second selection of Cleveland. It had merely switched brands.

By the time Cleveland entered upon his second administration he had learned the futility of bucking the establishment. In his name Attorney General Richard Olney enjoined the workers in the grossly mismanaged Pullman strike and employed federal troops to break it up, thus allying the office of the President with the General Managers Association of the Chicago railroads. Why did Olney not use his legal power to appoint a commission of inquiry? Why did he not use his influence to compel arbitration? Why did he not sternly remind the railroads that their contracts did *not* require that they put Pullman cars on their mail trains? Only the boss-managers could answer.

The election of William McKinley climaxes this era of frustrated Presidents, men for whom no dialogue between President and electorate was possible. In the 1896 campaign the now-rested and again eager Republican politicians outdid themselves in "making a President from the ground up" in order to seat a man they could handle. They could not have chosen a finer subject for a campaign poster: a gallant captain in the Union Army during the Civil War, this handsome, clean-shaven man with the aquiline nose and honest bay window, sitting in satin lapel coat and scowling grimly over the multitude at the political rallies, was made for his role.

Sympathy provided an additional appeal: William McKinley bore the sorrow of an invalid wife, an epileptic, a fragile, gorgeous creature whose luxuriant braids of dark hair seemed almost too much for her delicate neck to sustain. That he showed himself to be a tender, solicitous husband and, in addition, was always careful to hide his cigar when his picture was taken (so as not to demoralize American youth), in no way detracted from his strength at the polls. Even McKinley proved less pliant than the bosses demanded, but all agreed that he was an enormous improvement over his predecessors. The Grand Old Party enjoyed four and a half wonderful years before the end came.

As it happened, McKinley was the last of the shackled, voiceless men. An insidious little instrument called the telephone had enabled him to call any one of thirty-two campaign managers and himself keep in touch with what was going on outside his prison. The independence he attained by this means of communication with the provinces enchanted the President. Joe Cannon grumbled that McKinley "kept his ears so close to the ground they got full of grasshoppers."

In truth, however, McKinley was listening not so much for the grasshoppers at the grass roots as for the crickets in the back room.

There had been men of high quality, comely men of intelligence and even of great potential, in the long, sad procession of Presidents after Lincoln. But no matter who had been elected to the nation's highest office in this era of politics, he could have shone no brighter on history's pages. Not only were the masses ignored; they were maligned. They had ceased to be individuals; they were statistics. They were not people; they were "mobs."

The final puppet show was on. But when the curtain fell in 1901, it was riddled with holes.

134

Part III

Developments at the Turn
of the Century:
Breakthrough

Ten

Faintly, the Leader's Voice

Between that fateful September 6, 1901, when an anarchist in a receiving line returned President McKinley's friendly handclasp with a pistol shot through a handkerchief, and the spring of 1904, something very significant occurred in the relationship between the people and the President of the United States. That something was the nation's third accidental President—a hotspur if ever there was one.

Few people disagree with the historians' consensus that McKinley's successor was one of the greatest Presidents. Those few maintain his pre-eminence was in showmanship rather than in effective reform. But it can scarcely be questioned that Theodore Roosevelt was the first people's President since the Civil War, a blustering grandstander with, as Thomas Beer describes him, "the face of a writhing mask," but a people's champion of such magnetic appeal that millions have cried, as did William Allen White, "Roosevelt bit me, and I went mad."

Here at last was the hero, the strong arm, the protector the populace had been seeking in the wilderness years after the Civil War. In the opinion of Senator Robert La Follette (who with his inflexible integrity had but little feeling for Roosevelt the dealer), this man who could not suppress a shudder at thought of the reform movement, who openly sneered at crusading journalists as "muckrakers," himself turned out to be the nation's first reformer and actually did the most to make the muckrakers effective. Moreover, Roosevelt did much to bring the people and their President together by showing the boss pre-eminent, Mark Hanna, to his place.

Senator Marcus A. Hanna of Ohio, the seasoned old President-maker, had, by 1903, tired of his role; and, fantastically enough, he had begun to covet the office himself. But Roosevelt cannily forestalled Hanna. He arranged for Senator Joseph B. Foraker—Hanna's inflexible rival boss in Ohio—to introduce a resolution in the Ohio legislature endorsing Roosevelt's nomination in 1904.

This political maneuver was something new indeed, but Hanna, exceedingly distraught, restrained his emotions. He merely wired the President that it was necessary for him to oppose the resolution. How could the President even presume to this cruelty? To cutting the very ground from under his feet in his own home territory? Perhaps, nationally, the jaded old campaigner had no chance, but to be throttled before he had had time to draw a breath? This was the kind of perfidy formerly reserved for the party bosses. Certainly the President would reconsider.

Roosevelt did not reconsider. Within twenty-four hours the wire came back. It said coldly: "Your telegram received. I have not asked any man for his support. I have had nothing whatever to do with raising the issue. Inasmuch as it has been raised of course those who favor my administration and my nomination will favor endorsing both and those who do not will oppose." In effect the President had said: "They want *me*, Mark. Either swing on the bandwagon for me or cut your own throat."

The telegram was an ultimatum; Hanna himself had uttered many such. But the significant point is that this time the ultimatum was not issued by a political manager *to a President* seeking renomination, as always in the past, but by the President to the political manager. Hanna had met his equal at last—he capitulated in tears. Another barrier between the President and the people had been shaken, its collapse foreordained. And a new relationship was in the process of developing.

The social and political ferment in the nation had been coming to a head even on that fall day when Roosevelt was recalled from his mountain climbing and thrust aboard the train that was waiting to speed him to Buffalo where the President was dying. In the words of Professor William Harbaugh, in *The Life and Times of Theodore Roosevelt:* "Crime and corruption were growing apace. Political machines based on the frustrations of the submerged lower classes or the greed of the high business order were tightening their grasp on the body politic. Nature's heritage was being ruthlessly squandered.... And worse even than that,

139

there was rising such a concentration of business power as made a mockery of the democratic process and threatened the foundations of the Republic itself."

The inevitability of reforms, the imminence of coming restraints, were clear to all but the old order. Since industrial expansion was a national phenomenon, any controls that might come had to be of national scope, too. And since the common man's supposed protector—the Congress—had encased itself in armor of the old order, armor so heavy it could not reach the sword, much less wield it—what other avenging knight did the submerged classes have but the President himself? (Lincoln Steffens quotes Roosevelt as constantly reiterating that the Congress did not represent the people: "*I* stand for the common good!") And as the effects of the closing of the frontier—that escape valve for all the restless and malcontented—began to be felt, the people's irritation with the existing conditions reached danger pitch.

A new element also added to the attention suddenly coming to bear on the office of the American President. Although "imperialism" is not a happy word today, both McKinley and Roosevelt had come to power on its iron chariot, and neither would belittle his carrier. The United States was taking its bows as a world power, a state of international importance, and its head of state was becoming the focus of newly aroused interest. The President's constitutional powers in international affairs made him the proper recipient of all foreign emissaries and communications; his actions in the international field drew the world's spotlight again and again.

Another element in the growing importance of the Presidency was the steady development at the turn of the century of ever better communications media, a faint hint of the revolution to come. "From the nation's press," says biographer Noel F. Busch, speaking of only one of many such occurrences, "—which no one in U. S. public life before or since has dominated as completely as T.R.—his arrival in New York aroused a response that would have been appropriate to the Second Coming." In spite of the staggering influx of southern European immigrants—half of them illiterate—the literacy rate of the nation as a whole was slowly climbing, and the people could thus react effectively to the President's use of the printed word.

But perhaps the most significant contributor to Roosevelt's public image and popularity was the cartoon. As Meyers, Kern, and Cawelti describe it in *Sources of the American Republic,* "At any gusty word from him, cartoons filled the air like autumn leaves in a high wind." And the President, thinking especially of the newspapers' Monday morning editions, for which he liked to time his most shocking indictments, exulted: "The White House is a bully pulpit."

These authors continue: "About the time Roosevelt became an important figure in American life there had been invented a photoengraving process which permitted the making of a chemically etched zinc block within a few minutes after completion of the artist's pen-drawing." Previously, tooling wooden blocks by hand-engraving had been a tedious business. Now, within an hour of the news, out came a cartoon about it. And President Roosevelt could coin colorful, picture-evoking phrases to make most effective use of this wonderful new weapon: "Big Stick," "the strenuous life," "the spear that knows no brother," "Square Deal." Roosevelt, unlike the dour and earnest reformers be-

141

fore him, made of his reforming a circus antic, full of high kicks and thunder, big grins and excitement. He made reform gay and spirited. In his own words, it had been "Such fun!" being President.

That a man like this should appear at so critical a moment is one of those "cropping times in the races of men" of which Aristotle speaks—when splendid men seem to spring from nowhere to seize the banner and carry it aloft. It was one of those "utterly unthinkable coincidences" that such a forceful, vital personality should be catapulted into the Presidency at exactly the time when the nation was undergoing the internal agonies of transition from rural to industrial dominance, from individualism to regimented, crowded living—a transition which imperatively called for social change.

Theodore Roosevelt's nomination for Vice-President had been arranged, as was the custom, entirely by bosses—as had McKinley's nomination for President. They had managed to prod and push him, not without considerable rough scuffling, into the dismal confines of the vice-presidential closet, and locked the door. Brushing their hands of him, they had congratulated themselves that at last this maker of small earthquakes had been removed from the principal area of their activities, and they might henceforth transgress the laws in peace.

Then in the greatest irony of American history the lock on the door was suddenly shot away by an assassin's bullet, and the door burst open to reveal, not their reluctant but gamely grinning dupe, but a hard-jawed man with the presidential diadem set squarely on his head. Belatedly, the bosses recalled that this cowboy had received, at the convention, a larger ovation than the President himself, and that the galleries had chanted that now T.R. was "not New York's son, but the nation's son!" Still, they had had as yet no intimation of how difficult he was going to be.

It is easy to see how this composite of hero-soldier, frontiersman, hunter, outdoorsman, writer, and strongman could not help but capture the imagination of the public. He had known and lived and loved the things the people had known and lived and loved. "Immediately acquainted with all sections of the country," remarks Noel F. Busch in *T.R.*, "either at first hand or by inheritance, he was equally familiar with its people on every level of wealth, education, and social status, having worked, played, and fought beside them from Island Falls to Tampa Bay and from Yellowstone to Santiago." He had friends from the highest walks of life and from the prize ring, from literature and from far western ranches, from banking and from labor.

"While I am President, I wish the laboring man to feel that he has the same right of access to me that the capitalist has; that the doors swing open as easily for the wageworker as for the head of a big corporation—*and no easier,*" he said with sincerity. He was the first President to welcome union officials—Samuel Gompers, John Mitchell, and others—into his private office. He simply loved people, all people, and he was determined to be fair to them—or at least as fair as the times permitted.

Thus when back-country farmers and ranchers and other "plain people" made the long journey to Washington to tramp their manure-caked boots into his office merely because they "wanted to shake an honest hand," Roosevelt did not think it odd. He pushed his guard away to plunge into crowds (so soon after his predecessor had been assassinated) with both hands outstretched to meet theirs, grinning and yelping greetings, while his entourage waited paralyzed with fear. He wanted to be in the midst of people; and the people felt that he liked it.

Only once did he demur at contact with the public. The President, on a speaking tour at Butte, Montana, was sitting at a scrubbed plank table in a small restaurant when his cheery host shouted to a waiter, "Pull up the shade so the people can see the President eat!" That, according to biographer Harbaugh, was too much. All the proprieties of Roosevelt's aristocratic upbringing returned at once; he begged that he might consume his dinner without having a hundred eyes hanging on his fork.

Again, his fanatic pride in the nation struck a responsive chord as the country edged self-consciously onto the international stage; it bolstered the people's confidence. His bellowings for force, his jingoism, did not sound so barbaric to ears that had so lately tuned in to a tooth-and-claw world. His personal characteristics—-ebullience, restless activity, joy, dash, great warmth, and passion—were not wasted; the crowd responded, although dumbly.

They loved the President's sense of drama. When he pranced onto a platform in an old felt campaign hat, his entrance announced by the notes of a bugle, followed proudly by seven Rough Riders in old battalion uniform, he gave a show never attained by presidential hopeful before or since. "I had to wake up people," he said, "and keep them awake. . . . If you want to wake up a hundred million people, you've got to make a big and resounding noise." He could shake sixty hands a minute and emerge from the crowds hours later untired and ready for a boxing match, a tennis game, and a swim.

Billy O'Neil, an old friend of Roosevelt's from his days in

the New York Assembly, is quoted as saying that often Roosevelt's speeches were nothing, but "the man's presence was everything. It was electrical, magnetic. . . . Perhaps my love and admiration blinded me to the real facts," he added; but ". . . as the train faded away and I saw him smiling, and waving his hat to the people, they in turn giving abundant evidence of their enthusiastic affection, my eyes filled with tears." Roosevelt ran well ahead of his ticket in 1904, and he chalked up the biggest winning margin yet: 7,623,-486 popular votes to 4,077,911 for the Democrats and some 800,000 for splinter parties. When he repeated the final words of the presidential oath on March 4, 1905, in that sun-gold, breeze-tossed day on the East Portico, his greatest moment had come. The mighty accolade that rose from the throats of two hundred thousand citizens of the Republic was equaled in fervor by only one other in history—that at Andrew Jackson's first inauguration. "Tomorrow," T.R. warned, his eyes glinting maliciously behind the gold-rimmed spectacles, "I shall come into office in my own right . . . then watch out for me!"

He spoke continually of integrity and morality, but he could connive and double back on his tracks as well as the best boss who ever lived. His friend and critic, Lincoln Steffens, repeatedly accused him of condoning derelictions in duty for a cause. "You fired crooks who would not stand with you, you kept the crooks who helped you enforce the law because it was law," he told the Chief, but Roosevelt only grinned. Writing to his lifelong friend, Cabot Lodge, Roosevelt said that the President should be a "very strong man who uses without hesitation every power that the position yields." These words were exactly what a frontier people had been waiting for.

145

When he added, "I believed that he should be sharply watched by the people," he was probably speaking with less sincerity. For Roosevelt could rant and shake his fist at the trusts one day (for the cartoonists) and then disappear into a conference room with them the next (not for the cartoonists). He did not regard this behavior as deception, although the simon-pure reformers, such as La Follette, accused him of it. He was dealing with the men with whom he had to deal as he had to deal with them, in their own devious bartering fashion, and he was wresting the best terms for the people that he could.

Strangely enough, even this conspiring with the interests did not faze the populace when it was brought to their attention by the Democrats. The people did not try to rationalize it; they simply refused to believe it. Commented the New York *Sun* in awe: "Whatever T.R. thinks, says, does, or wants, is *right.*" American business was at roaring flood stage; no dike could hold it, and the President knew it; but he was determined that business should not submerge the people and carry their rights away to the sea.

What must be remembered when judging Roosevelt and his accomplishments is that he was a transition President. Despite the ferment of the period and the terrific impact of the man, the going was all a Rough Rider might desire. Theodore Roosevelt came to power in an age of managed democracy and faced the most awesome array of political generals ever to grace the American scene. All the executive initiative once exercised by Jefferson, Jackson, and Lincoln had been usurped by the political managers, who were, of course, the agents of the business interests.

There was the Czar of the Senate, Nelson Aldrich, the handsome commercial genius who had "owned" the State of Rhode Island for decades, as crusty in his omnipotence as he was contemptuous of the people and their "rights." His expressed ideal was to see the Senate manned officially by Senators from each of the great business "constituencies"—steel, copper, railroads, banks, textiles, and the like. "In fact if not in theory this millenium had indeed been realized," comments historian William Miller.

There was the circuitous little "weasel" Thomas Platt of New York, the unsavory Matthew Quay of Pennsylvania, Benjamin Odell of New York, Mark Hanna and Joseph B. Foraker of Ohio, sometimes-high-minded Orville Platt of Connecticut, intransigent Simon Guggenheim of Colorado, and the Janus-like John Spooner of Wisconsin. There was Boies Penrose, the Pennsylvania aristocrat "whose career," says Harbaugh, "was virtually an unrelieved stench." There was that polished, ever-bubbling voice of the railroads, Chauncey Depew. There was the Democratic counterpart of Aldrich: the contriving Arthur P. Gorman of Maryland. In the House there were many lesser bosses, led by that redoubtable old rascal, "Uncle" Joe Cannon, who matter-of-factly strangled each and every reform measure.

There was also the impressive, bearded old grandee of Iowa, Senator William B. Allison, loose-frocked and straggly-haired. His army of faithful heelers, regularly augmented during the thirty-four years of his incumbency in the Senate, had made every President since Andrew Johnson cringe. It was this old Merlin of politics, through whose spell of expediency a faint hope of reform seemed once in a while to flutter like a white hand in the darkness, who would mutter, turning away his old, resigned eyes, ". . . after I'm gone . . . just wait, Dolliver, until after I'm gone." He was not gone until 1907.

So it was when Roosevelt looked about him after that first oath-taking; the brazen faces stared back at him in veiled and stony malice. And behind this massed array of seasoned bosses he saw a solid phalanx of aging men—the two dozen or more millionaires who filled the seats of the United States Senate. And behind all these politicos the new President envisioned (although they were not visible from the platform) all the mighty men of business and finance crouched and waiting to pounce at him—the moguls and the manipulators. He must outwit them all—while playing at their game.

When Carl Akeley, the famous African hunter, left on a safari, the President asked him to bring back from Africa a couple of lions to be loosed in the Senate. "But," asked Akeley, "aren't you afraid they'd make a mistake?" "No," responded Roosevelt, "not if they stay there long enough."

During Roosevelt's tenure, many of these potentates and bosses were to meet death, discredit, and Robert La Follette. Hanna succumbed, literally of heartbreak, on February 15, 1904. Quay died alone and unwept. Platt retired, being in his dotage; Allison was wavering and becoming ineffectual; Spooner was discredited. Never again would these unmatchable manipulators of men be equaled, for the times that they had mirrored were gone forever.

Bosses of various kinds lingered on, as they will always linger on when there are votes that can be bought or politics that can be rigged. But the industrial fever which had spawned these opportunists had also begotten the technological revolution which, while forming a gaping chasm between upper and lower classes, created many abuses. The abuses in turn cried out for the reforms which caused the crack-up of this greatest saturnalia of bosses in history. But on that inauguration day these formidable opponents were there to welcome the President and to form a formidable barrier between him and the public welfare.

Furthermore, although advances in the means of communication were accelerating—the telephone and the telegraph were being improved and the automobile and airplane were developing fast—technology, as an aid in bridging the gap between the Chief and his nationwide electorate, was still in its crude beginnings. It did the President little good that the Wright brothers on December 17, 1903, flew a rickety aircraft at Kitty Hawk or that on December 11, 1901, the first wireless signal was received from Europe. Roosevelt's only method of communicating with the people outside of the newspaper page was to travel about the countryside on a bumpy railroad train and from the back platform bellow at his constituents at every whistle-stop and hamlet.

From this he did not flinch. He was the first President to make an exhaustive nationwide campaign tour by train. He made the first of these tours in the McKinley campaign (the New York *Times* figured one jaunt at twenty-two thousand miles) and he reached with unaided vocal chords three million pairs of waiting ears. Returning, the indefatigable campaigner rushed to a throat specialist for relief.

Although Roosevelt could indeed bellow, his voice was only a whisper in the silences and shrieks of a continental nation, a voice lost in the vast stretches of waving grass and billowing wheat and the whine of factory sirens and sawmills. Only the press could catch those whispers in inch-high type, and in the voices of newsboys amplify them over the nation. It was a one-sided communication at best.

But the effervescent Roosevelt had not only to outwit the

bosses and bargain with the barons he had inherited from McKinley and the unillustrious past; he had other less tangible handicaps. There was the long tradition of presidential meekness voiced so unequivocally by Harrison and Buchanan—the abject denial of any consequential presidential authority. There was the traditional doctrine of the Forefathers who (understandably) had frowned upon a strong executive. Finally, there was the traditional distrust (largely fostered by the party out of power) of a strong central government or of any infringement of states' rights.

T.R., as was his rip-roaring custom, plunged exuberantly into these political briars without ado, and was instantly lacerated and made bloody. Taking no time to stanch his wounds, he leaped to the platform and showed them to the people. "I am always sure of reaching them," he exulted to John Hay. He said he actually *felt* the response of his audiences; he felt the love of the veterans surge to him across the footlights.

It is significant to note how different Theodore Roosevelt's attitude toward breaking a strike was from the attitude of any President preceding him. How differently he dealt with the Reading anthracite strike of 1902 than had Garfield with the strike of 1877 or Cleveland with the Pullman strike of 1894!

In the strike of 1902 T.R. employed a ruse as clever as it was effective in order to avoid using federal troops to subdue the strikers, as other Presidents had done without hesitation. In true Rooseveltian style, he first prevailed upon J. P. Morgan, whose properties were affected, not to oppose conciliation in any active way. This done, the President issued an ultimatum: either the management of the mines would arbitrate before a picked commission or federal troops would move in to run the mines without benefit of the management at Reading.

Loud were the grumblings. Federal troops to back up labor? "The rights and interests of the laboring man will be protected—not by labor agitators, but by the *Christian men to whom God in his infinite wisdom has given the control of the property* interests of the country," flamed corporation president George F. Baer, but the derisive hoots in the press drowned him out, and he bowed to arbitration— by management, of course.

Here was the real snag. President Baer stalwartly refused to consider the appointment of *any labor representative* whatever to the commission. The President rubbed his brow, but not for long. He sent for the labor union representative, deftly masqueraded him as "an eminent sociologist," got him accepted on the commission, and the strike was arbitrated. The workers secured an eight-hour day, a 10 per cent wage increase, and a grievance board. Related Roosevelt loudly: "Mitchell [of labor] behaved with great dignity and moderation. The operators on the contrary showed extraordinary stupidity and bad temper. . . ." And the working people rose to their feet to cheer.

President Roosevelt could use his guile on the Congress, too. When Senator C. W. Fulton, an Oregon Republican of low horizons, added to the Agricultural Appropriations Bill of 1907 an amendment forbidding any new forest preserves ever to be set aside in five western states, and the Senate passed the bill without calling the roll and handed it to the President just before the session's end, Roosevelt's foes thought they had him licked at last. If he did not sign the bill, needed appropriations for agriculture and forestry would lapse; all that Gifford Pinchot, head of the Forestry

Service, had been working for in conservation would go out the window. Yet if he did sign it, great blocks of forest preserves necessary to the establishment of a national system in the forest-rich states of Oregon, Washington, Montana, Idaho, and Wyoming would be forever lost to the commercial interests.

Roosevelt, however, was equal to the challenge. He called Pinchot to a long conference that began with "Damn!" and ended with "Bully!" Pinchot went to his files. He drew forth a great bundle of precision maps over which he and his staff had labored for many months—maps of the desired preserves in the five concerned states. In the ten days remaining before the bill must be signed, Pinchot and his men worked day and night—sometimes for forty-eight hours at a stretch, gulping black coffee from a mug in one hand while they penned specifications with the other. They drew up blueprints for twenty-one new forest reserves totaling sixteen million acres. They handed them to the President under the deadline; Roosevelt gleefully proclaimed them on March 2; *then* he signed the Agricultural Appropriations Bill into law.

This accomplishment is perhaps the master stroke of T.R.'s entire administration. He never tired of gloating over it as his senatorial foes "turned handsprings in their wrath." He had saved, he wrote later, "immense tracts of valuable timber from the hands of the lumber syndicates" and turned them to public recreation uses. This was the President at his finest.

Many who can see Roosevelt's basic morality, deep sense of public service, desire for social reform, and strong commitment to the common man deplore his wheelings and dealings with the power interests, his acceptance of their gold in his campaign chest, and his fraternization with such representatives of the old order as Senator Lodge and Senator Hanna. But would he have accomplished as much as he did in making the nation reform-conscious, in leading Wall Street toward important concessions, in gaining recognition for conservation and labor, had he been more "ethical" and unyielding? Elihu Root called Roosevelt "the greatest teacher of the essentials of popular government the world has ever known," and today many agree. Some historians believe he was also the interests' greatest friend precisely because he curtailed them just enough to ward off a revolution.

What other recourse did he have but to "deal," in an age of infant communications, with a formidable and grimly commercial Congress run by hoary professional obstructionists? Certainly Theodore Roosevelt enjoyed the benefits of a transition period when the grasp of moribund bosses was just beginning to relax. He was, as we said, a transition President, and here lay both his opportunity and his vindication.

His hobnobbing with the moguls in those brutally commercial times is not what President Hayes, for example, would have done—but while Hayes was broken on the rack, Roosevelt managed to use the tongs on his torturers. His politics was "the art of the possible," and it sometimes begged ends as an excuse for means. Over the grand tapestry of American politics this very moral agility shines forth as an attribute of his bigness as a President. It would seem that unadulterated virtue and presidential greatness are far from synonymous. Is this compromise, then, one of the prices we pay for democracy and its inherent pressures?

153

Elbert Hubbard has said with truth, "No man who expresses himself is really much ahead of his time. If he is, the times snuff him out, and quickly." Roosevelt was ahead of his times, certainly, but not so far ahead that he could not glimpse on the distant horizon a new and reformed era of greater opportunities for the President to work for the public welfare. He saw himself as an appeaser, an arbiter, a defender of peaceful adjustment who would see to it that neither capital nor labor should be too badly hurt. That he dared to strive toward this new era, raised as he had been in the venerable tradition of presidential impotence, in itself distinguishes him.

An innovator and a daredevil (he was the first President to ride in an automobile or airplane or to visit a foreign country during his tenure), he bore all the marks of greatness, even to the ordeal of being shot in the chest in a Milwaukee hotel by an insane man with hallucinations of his becoming a czar, receiving a bullet too deep to be dug for. Once he said a little sadly, "In politics we do a great many things we ought not to do!"

But the compromises and questionable alliances were not the things which made him a people's President; the populace hardly cared. What mattered to them most was that "Teddy" always seemed to know how to handle any situation, that he exuded power, and that he returned in kind their sincere, even fanatic, devotion. What mattered to them was, as biographer Hermann Hagedorn tells it, that he was common like they were. "When I visit the [Masonic] lodge," said the President, "he [the Master who was gardener on his cousin's estate] is my boss, and I must stand up when he orders me, and sit down when he tells me, and not speak unless he allows me. That's good for him and good for me."

Irvin S. Cobb said, "You had to hate the Colonel a whole lot to keep from loving him," and it was true. When, aged sixty-six, he died in his sleep, Rudyard Kipling called him "Great Heart," and Cabot Lodge, that hardened old politician of the order which Roosevelt had been fighting all his life, broke down in the Senate as he read his memorial to "Valiant-for-Truth."

Theodore Roosevelt was a President of fortune. Universal suffrage had been working for some time to make the President more directly responsible to the people. As the twentieth century shifted its Stutz Bearcats and Marmons into high gear, industry began to feel the restraint of sterner legislation. The Great Boss Age was crumbling. Reform was everywhere in the air, not only social and economic, but also political and elective. Theodore Roosevelt had reached the people more often and touched them more deeply than any President yet. But still they were half-afraid, self-conscious, and limited in their response.

155

Eleven

The Mob Evolves

Theodore Roosevelt had established a robust association with the citizens of the United States, intimate, warm, but almost wholly emotional. It was akin to the spirit that Jackson evoked, augmented considerably on his side by the development of modern means of communication. Yet it was almost entirely a one-sided dialogue; the public was still unaccustomed to such familiarity and too awkward to express itself. Certainly the exchange between President and people had little depth; it had the characteristics of a back-slapping barroom discussion—lusty, loyal, and slightly lunk-headed, with the President doing most of the talking.

Pubescence was the measure not only of communications, but of the public. A primitive and emotional response was all that could be expected of a public whose most intimate knowledge of their Chief was gained from a front-page cartoon. Roosevelt's greatness derived in part from his ability to discourse in simple, vulgarian terms and to estimate accurately the political literacy of his constituency. For a President whose chief complaint about the Presidency was its enforced inactivity ("I do but little boxing because it seems rather absurd for a President to appear with a black eye or a swollen nose or a cut lip," he said rue-fully), the histrionics, the capers, and the strutting depicted by the cartoonist were a release, and "good fun."

Indeed, the first Roosevelt must have envied George Washington, who (thanks to the iron-bound wheels of the carriage and the unyielding cobblestones of the highway) might, on inclement days, "exercise in my carriage with Mrs. Washington." John Quincy Adams complained sourly that all the exercise he could manage was early in the morning before breakfast. But Theodore Roosevelt made exercise of everything; conferences with his close advisers often became ten- or twelve-mile cross-country hikes. He always made first page.

But the age was in ferment with a new technology that would soon relieve Presidents of any need to use such tactics to attract attention. George Washington had depended on his unending line of visitors, "from breakfast to dinner and afterwards till bed time," for all his information about what was going on with the people. The table at the White House soon came to be considered a public one, and was crowded from morning till night with citizens of different degree, from visiting governors to avid trenchermen with no credentials other than a distant cousin in a governmental clerkship or a desire to bid the General good day. Washington's constant predicament was how not to lose all contact with the "valuable sources of information from the many" without being considered no better than a "maitre d'hotel."

But as the twentieth century began the nation was being bound together by wires and rails. In 1900 there were 1.33 telephones per hundred population; by 1905 the ratio rose to 4.02, and by 1915 the figure had soared to 10.09. How much this acceleration in the ability to communicate locally had to do with presidential politics is speculative, but in combination with other technological advances, it helped to change the entire character of the nation.

Certainly the nearness of the White House to the grass roots was affected as the telephone system spread and became transcontinental. As early as 1902 the first underground telephone cables had been laid, over a ten-mile stretch from Newark to New York. And on the day President Taft was inaugurated, a heavy sleet storm tore down the wires over which the event was to have been described to the people.

Of course, the fundamental inventions upon which the modern newspaper was based and upon which the political communications net was founded—the high-speed power press, the linotype, the typewriter, and the telephone—were all in existence by the turn of the century. But, like the art of the cartoon, they were all undergoing constant refinement and wider application. And it was in this new era that the wireless, the printing telegraph machine, the motor truck, and a host of devices to hasten the collection of news and speed its dissemination were added. The vast cooperative news-gathering agencies, founded in the eighteen-nineties, increased their efficiency.

A powerful sense of destiny, a mighty new confidence that man dominated his physical environment, surged through the nation. Perhaps it was overconfidence, but as the twentieth-century American viewed the pictures of his first skyscraper, the marvelous Flatiron Building created by the architect Daniel H. Burnham in 1902, he saw symbolism in the way it pointed sturdily upward.

Not only was the nation exchanging words and thoughts with more facility, but many of its leaders were voicing louder protests against existing conditions. It was a time of rising conscience, of infant humanitarianism. Then began the attacks on the slums, the challenge to the harsh exploitation of the labor of women and children in industry, the protest against the evil of liquor, the crying out against adulterated foods, the bitter indictment of the waste of life in industry.

After Frank Norris struck out at the abuses of railroads and wheat speculation in *The Octopus* (1901) and *The Pit* (1903), Upton Sinclair picked up the campaign with his damning of the packing industry in *The Jungle* (1906), and Jack London lambasted the whole system. Social novelist Winston Churchill and journalist David Graham Phillips, as well as other famous muckrakers, aroused at least the thoughtful part of the American citizenry to a new awareness of their duties as citizens. A new generation eagerly picked up the torch of Henry Bergh, who had stopped the gory pigeon-shooting and dogfights in New York and founded the Society for the Prevention of Cruelty to Animals. They followed Peter Cooper, Jane Addams, and Clara Barton, whose humanitarian foundations had helped advance civilization in the closing decades of the nineteenth century.

And as the American mind became more alive, American women grew restive. The General Federation of Women's Clubs, which claimed a membership of fifty thousand in 1898, had, by 1914, found influence even without the vote as it called the roll on a million members. Through standing committees on civics, civil service reform, conservation, education, industrial and social conditions, literature, and public health, this body reached into every sizable community through its affiliated clubs. The old idea of women surrendering their own lives and individuality to the production of large quantities of offspring was passé. Women desired broader lives, with less drudgery.

Concomitant with the women's enlarged horizons was the demand for the vote, and the antics of the National Woman Suffrage Association not only secured the attention of the nation but titillated even the crustiest editors. Everyone threw duty and work to the winds to rush to see the ladies, dressed in an eye-catching assortment of bustles, flounces, and frills, flaunt themselves on the Avenue, waving their defiant signs, answering an occasional half-hearted catcall with a tongue-lashing that made a male face burn.

On the day before his inauguration President-elect Woodrow Wilson stepped down from his train in Washington to find a nearly empty platform. "Where are the people?" he queried, wonderingly. "On the Avenue watching the suffragists parade," responded a bystander. Thus entered Washington one of the greatest crusaders of all time, of whom Herbert Hoover was moved to declare that no such evangel of peace and moral power had appeared since Christ, a leader born twenty-five years too soon.

Although the times were in ferment and reformers were

agitating on all sides, the reform movement was like a ship fitted for adventure, nosing its course, but with its anchor dragging. President Theodore Roosevelt and Woodrow Wilson both saw themselves in shepherd roles, but an underprivileged, politically inert, and doltish flock made cooperation a fickle thing. Instinctively, Roosevelt had realized that the only effective appeal was one to "Armageddon and we battle for the Lord!" They would "battle for the Lord" to the tempo of "Onward, Christian Soldiers!" but to battle for the rights of a host of small, faraway nations for which they cared not a ripe fig was furthest from their thoughts.

Indeed, most Americans were only beginning to see beyond their own bailiwicks and to raise questioning eyebrows at the spectacle of their government at Washington writhing under the heavy thumb of dominant business interests. Wrote David Graham Phillips in the October 1906 *Cosmopolitan:* "How politically careless have we been, how short-sighted, how credulous of words and neglectful of deeds, how easily tricked by cunning appeals to the prejudiced! *We have been struggling with the great thieves operating through railways and tariffs, and have not seen that it was the Senate that determined our national laws, superintended the distribution of our prosperity, and selected our national judges. We have been defeated because we have not realized that it was our Allisons and Aldriches and Lodges and Baileys in far away Washington, in the Senate, who were making our struggles futile—were making, and are!"*

All kinds of corruption involving the country's resources and hundreds of millions of dollars had seeped into the Senate and House for decades. Little of it had been noted

by the populace, and that little was garbled and vague.
Now the reformers were exposing some very raw material
in a sensational (and prejudiced) style that emptied the
city newsstands in an hour. Although President Roosevelt
publicly denounced these journalists of intemperate language as rakers of the public muck, he must secretly have
exulted in the series of exposures that were undermining
the phalanx of long-entrenched politicians who faced him
in the Senate. Even the cold blue gaze of sly old Senator
Allison of Iowa, who had stared down every President for
thirty-three years, was wavering before the muckrakers'
exposures.

And American ears were buzzing from the continuous
exposure of one after another of those famous men whose
names had been household words in their districts for a
generation or more. The reformers had caused Americans
to raise their eyes from their axes and plows, had again
helped the President to appear in focus, endowing him
with a more meaningful relationship to the masses. But the
eyes of a provincial people were as yet far from ready for so
broad and intoxicating a vision.

In 1900, although sixteen million youngsters were at-
tending elementary schools, there were six million adult
illiterates. The average child attended classes barely 68 out
of 143 school days a year. The instruction was wooden, and
the chores (largely janitorial) of running the one-room
schoolhouse fell to a young lady who was unlikely to have
had more than an elementary school education herself,
with perhaps a few months or weeks at the county normal.
This, then, was the nation's training ground for citizenship,
and it was to turn out voters with whom the President or
presidential candidate sought to discuss currency theory,

tariff policy, Senate reform, and land tenure—not to mention international affairs!

Admittedly, the schools showed continuous improvement. By 1914 the school year was fifteen days longer than in 1900, the average student attended school for 86.7 days, and the teacher's wages had been raised from starvation at thirty-eight dollars a month to bleak subsistence at sixty-six. "For every day in the calendar years between 1890 and 1919 one public high school was established," records Harold U. Faulkner in *The Quest for Social Justice,* "and between 1900 and World War I, the number of libraries boasting over 5,000 volumes had increased, thanks to Mr. Carnegie, from 1700 to nearly 3000." But there was a long way to go.

Nor was the problem of communication between President and people facilitated by the lumps of immigrants stirred into the population; much like a spoonful of flour in gravy, the immigrants refused to blend into the American society. Between 1902 and 1914 the annual immigration never fell below seven hundred thousand, and in five of those years the influx of Europeans exceeded a million. By the latter year a seventh of the total population was foreign-born, and most of these new immigrants could not speak English. Of those who came to these shores between 1899 and 1909, close to 27 per cent were illiterate. These newcomers, although outside the immediate ranks of political participants in the democratic process, were nonetheless a sizable part of the populace, and they had to be reckoned with.

Who could say what this exciting, seething new world held in store? The very technology that attracted the immigrants with its promise of opportunity revolted the re-

163

formers with its abuses. The very forces that were drawing the country together physically were at the same time enabling the intellectuals to reach a national audience.

The development of a national economic market had its impact on the sales of reading matter. Extensive advertising revenue and advances in the technique of halftone engraving combined to launch the ten-cent magazine. Pioneered by *Munsey's* in 1893, the ten-cent magazine doubled readership almost immediately and set the stage for the muckrakers. And *The Saturday Evening Post* (bought for one thousand dollars by Cyrus H. K. Curtis in 1897) increased the public's interest in reading vastly as it fed the multitude on nationalism, adoration of moneyed success, and the values of hard work and Victorian morals—all for a nickel. *Everybody's,* which thrived on controversy, saw its circulation increase from 197,000 to 735,000 in the two years between 1903 and 1905, and crusading editors like Joseph Pulitzer and Frank I. Cobb championed one cause after another in the pages of the New York *World*. Even the yellow journals accomplished one almost immediate good: they forced their stodgier competitors to loosen their style and adopt a more attractive make-up.

And so the twentieth century opened on a scene of appalling contrasts, of despair and hope, of callousness and compassion, of greed and generosity, of apathy and dedication, of ignorance and wisdom. Not many years before this same society had been quite indifferent to the manner or direction in which its tobacco juice was loosed at the ubiquitous cuspidors (the marble lobby of one of New York's finest hotels was usually covered with a sea of slime). But it had also supported the "Lyceum Course," and especially the regional circuits of the International Chautauqua

Alliance at whose encampments Americans, sitting on hard folding chairs in stuffy tents conspicuously devoid of spittoons, drank in "culture" as they listened to lecturers and educators expound their new and even shocking views. America was growing up.

It was on this scene where the advocates of change were struggling for respectability that a minority President arose and in cultured college accents began to regale the cloven land with phrases burning with new visions of "breaking away from the past." A traditionalist, he recalled them to the memory of the true American ideals in that "ancient time when America lay in every hamlet," in contrast to the class-developing society of the day. A prophet, he dared to try to impose the same ideals of fraternal justice on all the hating, bleeding, feuding world, a heretical idea of sweet shock whose darkling implications no hearer yet had begun to plumb.

Twelve

The Prophet Who Came
Too Soon

Woodrow Wilson's rise to the American Presidency is
the phenomenon of all history. On September 4, 1910, he
was an academic, a college president who had never held a
public office; on March 4, 1913, he was President of the
United States. All because the eyes of the leaders of the
"lean and scrawny" New Jersey Democratic machine,
ready to expire with years of attrition, fell upon this distinguished and somewhat disillusioned university professor
at a fateful moment in history.

But, as if the uncultured American palate was not prepared to receive such rich fare as a Theodore Roosevelt
and a Woodrow Wilson in immediate succession, fate

chose to interpose a neutral interlude. Theodore Roosevelt had elevated his protégé William Howard Taft ("You blessed old trump, you big, generous, high-minded fellow," he called him) to the Presidency, and like the popular Andrew Jackson before him, who had done the same thing for his favorite, he showed a lack of percipience shocking in a President so intuitive, so seemingly shrewd. Roosevelt never ceased to castigate himself for this deed, even, some say, plunging into a catastrophic race for the Presidency in 1912 in order to prevent his protégé's re-election.

William Howard Taft, a tall man with shortish legs and a florid chuckling face ("I am sure Theodore Roosevelt had been completely fooled by Taft's amiable gurgling obbligato when they talked," wrote William Allen White), was not, in his own legalistic fashion, a bad President. Yet his theories were absolutely inimical to those of his predecessor; he declared that the President has no constitutional authority to make himself what he sarcastically termed a "Universal Providence," and Senator Jonathan P. Dolliver quipped that when Roosevelt believed Taft would carry out his policies, he didn't think it would be "on a shutter."

That Roosevelt never detected the "serpentine glitter" in Taft's eyes when the "Aldrich crowd" was mentioned is amazing indeed. When Taft proceeded to fire the revered Gifford Pinchot and to nip in the bud many of Roosevelt's other policies, the former President's rage knew no bounds.

Taft had almost no understanding of, or association with, the people. "I have come to the conclusion that the major part of the work of the President is to increase the gate receipts of expositions and fairs and bring tourists to town," he remarked, and the statement represents a fair measure of his understanding of the office. His greatest pride in the Presidency was that it would someday make his children and children's children proud. Newsmen comment on the change in the jovial Taft once he assumed office. "How," asks Louis Brownlow, who had had some experience dealing with Presidents for the press, "could the genial and approachable Secretary of War Taft become so changed in his attitude by becoming President?" At heart Taft was a conservative jurist, not a President. The social implications and fairness of a law were not nearly so important to him as its legal phraseology.

At this period in history it may appear that the unregenerate bosses were doing a better job at President-making than was the President himself. Their choice of Professor Wilson cements this point. James Smith, the manager of the Democratic machine in New Jersey, had sniffed the fresh Progressive air spreading over the state and the nation, and he caught the new fragrance wafting from Princeton's democratized campus. Old-string bosses were dying right and left, and everywhere bossism was in disrepute; the bosses' only hope of survival was to embrace the new fad, and Wilson, although exacting dire and earnest promises of reform in those blackened hearts, succumbed to the lure of the governorship. The greatest idealist and prophet ever to take the presidential oath was on his way.

Wilson had no sooner seated himself at the governor's desk in Trenton than Smith began the boss's usual routine: he had plans. And once again the cry of "Ingrate!" rang through smoke-filled rooms, for the new governor, throwing himself heart and soul into his role as a Progressive, pushed through the direct primary, a corrupt-practices act, an employers' liability act, and the public utilities and "Seven Sisters" bills, which limited corporations so effectively that they packed up and moved to Delaware. (This last foolishness caused the machine all the bother of canceling enough reforms to woo the corporations back, once they had rid themselves of this Princeton tiger.)

That was not all. Boss Smith, who had "left the Senate under a cloud," according to historian Leland Baldwin, yearned to return to the Senate and be vindicated. "Suddenly he [ingrate Wilson] upset Smith's apple cart by announcing his support of the nonentity who had won the popular vote in the preferential primary—the people's man. Smith's comments have not been recorded for posterity; mildly put, he parted company with Wilson forever.

But the governor had gained so much support among wealthy Democratic politicians, especially from power-hungry Edward Mandell House of Texas, who saw his vote-getting possibilities, that he was urged to seek the presidential nomination. When the managers won over William Jennings Bryan's support in the Democratic convention and deadlocked favorite Champ Clark, some shrewd jockeying took place behind closed doors. Boss Charles Murphy gave in, and Woodrow Wilson won a long, drawn-out victory. Thus was a President manufactured out of whole (and 100 per cent wool) cloth. That the bosses had not chosen shoddy to begin with was another of their many fatal mistakes.

"The American people will favor nothing that savors of exclusiveness," declared "Tommy" Wilson when, as president of Princeton, he was warmly engaged in trying to oust the posh and aristocratic undergraduate clubs in favor of "democratic quadrangles." Though he failed, finally, before the onslaught of money and ancient prestige, he had found his life's goal: the establishment of what he considered an impartial justice, whether on campus or in the world.

"We are caught in a great economic system which is heartless," he said, "... and because the strong have crushed the weak, the strong dominate the industry and economic life of the country.... There has come over the land that un-American set of conditions which enables a small number of men ... to get favors from government; by those favors to exclude their fellows from equal business opportunity...."

Reforms came fast during Wilson's first administration, as they had during his two years as governor of New Jersey. There was the Underwood-Simmons tariff reduction, the Federal Reserve Act, the Federal Trade Commission Act, the Clayton Anti-Trust Act, the Newlands Act, the La Follette Seamen's Act, and there were advances in civil service coverage. The new President proved demanding, obstinate, impatient. He was "as impatient of an adverse fact as of a dissenting opinion," said biographer Robert E. Annin, who himself had no patience with the President. Ida Tarbell was confident that Wilson's "real interest in life centers around the common man," but in his absorption with goals he forgot to take the people into his confidence. This flaw was to be his undoing.

Theodore Roosevelt may take the honor of exercising the first strong presidential leadership in the legislative field, but the long, rambling annual messages through which he expressed himself left much to be desired. Mumbled in a droning monotone from the Speaker's desk by a clerk in Joint Assembly, these adjurations (one of them twenty-five thousand words in length) were scarcely heard by the legislators, much less by the public. Wilson was the first

President since Washington to go before the Congress to read his own message. Corwin and Koenig, in *The Presidency Today,* find delight in thinking how enraged "Teddy" must have been to witness this, how he must have ground his teeth in vexation because he had not thought of it himself. President Wilson was also the first President to hold a press conference.

Wilson, more conscious of the written word than any President preceding him, wrote brilliantly, understandably, and forcefully. Presidents from Lincoln through Kennedy have complained that "the President is a lonely man" or that "the Presidency is the loneliest job in the world." Wilson said, "There is a very holy and terrible isolation. . . ."

Tall, chestnut-haired, with a long, horselike face and with the added disadvantage of being clean-shaven, Wilson could not emulate Roosevelt's toothy grin any more than he could emulate Roosevelt's pyrotechnics and histrionics. When Roosevelt came whirling into a railroad station, jigging and waving a crimson bandanna "like a trainman waving a lantern," the people leaped and roared and waved red bandannas back at him. When Wilson arrived at a station in a tightly buttoned black coat, a tall silk hat, and an air of professorial dignity, the people cheered and discreetly fluttered newly laundered white kerchiefs.

Where Roosevelt slammed on his old slouch hat and went forth to set up his tent among the people, Wilson ascended to his ivory tower and gazed down upon the people and across oceans beyond them. Roosevelt had broadened the provincial public outlook to the country's borders; Wilson tried to extend it across the wide oceans to other shores. David Cushman Coyle says that Wilson "deeply longed to be loved by the people," yet succeeded in isolating himself behind "high barriers of taste and assumption of superior knowledge." "I never dreamed such loneliness and desolation of heart possible," Wilson cried out, yet it was his constant comfort that his idol, Abraham Lincoln, had also felt this supreme anguish. Wilson "loved humanity but didn't like people." Lincoln had managed to love both.

"Let House and Burleson take care of the patronage," Wilson had directed—chores which Roosevelt would not have surrendered at any price. Senator George Hoar once quoted Alexander Pope to describe Senator Roscoe Conkling: "Like the Turk, he brooked no brother near his throne"; and the consensus of historians seems to be that Wilson was like that. It was for this reason, it was said, that he surrounded himself with inferior men. He lost the front page and secured the editorial columns.

Perhaps, like almost all Presidents before him, Wilson became "insane for power." But before everything else, he was an uncompromising crusader, a zealot. His cause was a passion for brotherhood that transcended boundaries; it is doubtful whether he was as much American President as he was internationalist. His power over the American people was the same as his power over the French people and over the English people. He could take ideals of lofty grandeur and clothe them in such moving, passionate, high-minded phrases that even the crudest minds were momentarily touched. "The feelings with which we face this new age of right and opportunity sweep across our heartstrings like some air out of God's own presence," he said, and he was sincere. Such purity could not fail to impress the public.

But, as Morison and Commager note, Wilson's power

over men deserted him when he left the rostrum. Unlike Roosevelt, he had no stomach "to persuade or brow-beat Congressmen in private conversation" or to slap backs and embrace the common throng. His pen was more eloquent than his presence. He pleaded with the people: "I know you are depending on me to keep this nation out of war ... [but] You have bidden me see to it that nothing stains or impairs the honor of the United States. Do not exact of me an impossible and contradictory thing!"

Again, he said of the people: "I am sure that my heart speaks the same things that they want their hearts to speak. It is only on this impulse, in this sympathetic connection which I am sure I have with them, that I am worthy to speak for them all." Yet he fled to his yacht, the "Mayflower," during the war years "to get away from the madness ... not to stop work ... but to escape *people*, and their intolerable excitements and demands," as biographer Arthur Walworth quotes him.

Wilson's conception of the Presidency was, in keeping with modern times, one of great strength. "He must have a definite program, believe in it strongly, and then stir the people to respond either emotionally or intellectually," he said. He confessed drearily that he had only the most imperfect means of "coming to know what the people wanted." Yet possibly even if he had had the means of knowing, he would not have altered his course one whit, for he was a man committed, and his obsession was his life and, at last, his death. Like the crusading knight whose one glimpse of the Grail blinds his eyes to all else, even to the people beneath his horse's hooves, he was, as Lincoln Steffens remarked, a man who "had not sinned enough to understand sinners."

Obsessed, then, with his idea of a league of nations,

which he had advanced years before the United States even thought of entering the great European war, he could with "single eye" pursue the flame and never see that he was treading on air. Even his propagandizing, through George Creel, of the nation's half-committed, self-interested, heterogeneous people into a war-dedicated nation such as had never been known before, was only a means toward the end to which he was dedicating his life: a victoryless world united in brotherhood, and a new understanding among all nations.

When Wilson complained that he had only an imperfect way of keeping in touch with the people, he was right. In spite of the advances in communications, the facility of his pen, and the drawing together of a people in war, when the impulse is to turn to the protector-leader, no dialogue of consequence or exchange of opinion could easily take place. It is strange today to look back on that election night in 1916 when the President of the United States, up for re-election, was forced to keep telephoning the New York *World* to keep abreast of the election returns.

As Wilson's secretary, Joseph P. Tumulty, relates the story, he told the President from the *World* office that Charles Evans Hughes appeared to be elected. Instead of clutching at hope, the President quickly accepted the word that he had been "badly licked." "The only thing that I am sorry for," he said, "and that cuts me to the quick, is that the people apparently misunderstood us." Whereupon he drank a glass of milk and retired to sleep until dawn. This is by no means the attitude of a power-drunk man—rather that of a driven man, a victim who experiences genuine deliverance when it appears that fate has relieved him of his killing crusade.

At any rate, relates Tumulty, Wilson was shaving the next morning when his daughter Margaret knocked excitedly on the bathroom door to tell him that the tide had turned; he was almost surely re-elected. Retorted the President, without missing a stroke, "Tell it to the Marines." He did not *want* to believe it.

"I have made up my mind that I am more interested in the opinion that the country will have of me ten years from now than the opinion it may be willing to express today," he declared at one time. And for his Holy Grail he could ignore Cabot Lodge's vilifications ("Hopelessly cowardly at heart; wants to make himself the savior of civilization") and cruelly snub Roosevelt when that aging fire-eater begged almost on his knees to be sent to the war. He was unforgiving of friends who did not live up to his rigid moral specifications, and those who fought his "principles" were enemies to the death.

A successful politician is like a gopher. The gopher, when trapped in his burrows, is able to run backward with great speed, feeling his way with his sensitive tail. Wilson never mastered this art; he was unable to back up. True, he once said, "It is as hard to do your duty when men are sneering at you as when they are shooting at you," but he never considered retreat.

There is a President's Room close to the Senate Chamber to which a President may retire in times of real distress "to be attended by the Senators" to arbitrate privately issues most dear to the Chief. Hardly a President had resorted to it for many years. Nonetheless, Wilson, in his deep concern over the League, on one occasion retired to this room. Yet when Senators Lodge and Chamberlain entered in sudden impulsive cordiality to shake his hand, the President deliberately turned his back on them and went to stand, cold and unmoving, by the windows. Apparently, he was incapable of making even the slightest hypocritical gesture, even to save the lifeblood that was dripping from his heart.

The cheering of the people and the accolades have acclaimed Wilson as a people's President. But he was acclaimed and cheered as all saints are acclaimed and cheered. For all the fine, crystal-clear phrases, his listeners in general had no idea what he was talking about. When it came time to sign on the dotted line, his audience quietly drifted away.

Perhaps the nearest the people approached empathy with the President was in the weeks just preceding the 1916 election. The popular chant of the day was "He kept us out of war!" and this was the shibboleth which, by imputing the role of protector to Wilson, won the election for the Democrats by the scantest of margins (277 electoral votes against 254 for Charles Evans Hughes). In the end the people deserted and betrayed this leader as easily as they desert any purely intellectual concept that has not penetrated their inner being.

In 1907 Woodrow Wilson had written in his Blumenthal Lectures, given at Columbia University, of his concept of the American Presidency. Among much else he declared: "His is the only national voice in affairs. Let him once win the admiration and confidence of the country, and no other single force can withstand him, no combination of forces will easily overpower him."

Perhaps "admiration and confidence" are not enough; perhaps devotion, even rabid devotion, is needed. And to arouse such devotion it was better communications that were urgently needed in the President's desperate, last-ditch appeal to his countrymen to support the League. Using the technology of the day to the limit, the President, although suffering gravely from his fatal illness, boarded train after train and forced his tired body here, there, and everywhere over the widespread continent in an effort to bring home to the people the meaning of the League of Nations. It is averred that over half the people rose to his side.

But his efforts, though heroic, were not enough. He could not go far enough; he could not speak loud enough; he could not reach enough people to put the needed pressure on the Senate for so drastic a move. The President learned, in those weary months of campaigning for the League of Nations, rising in his limousine to speak to a crowd while his wife's hand, unseen by the onlookers, steadied him from behind, that there was indeed a "single force" that could withstand the President. It was the force of ignorant insularity—a force which it would take years of better communications to break down. On March 19, 1920, a majority of the Senate voted for the treaty, but not the necessary two thirds, and this was the deathblow. "The people were not ready," the President muttered, at the end, with tear-glistening cheeks.

There is an old Scottish ballad:

> "I am hurt," Sir Andrew Barton said,
> "I am hurt, but I am not slain;
> "I'll lie me down and bleed a while,
> "And then I'll fight again."

Somewhere back in President Wilson's tough and persistent Scottish ancestry, he had imbibed deeply of this quality of never, never giving up to the very death. He had fought with every weapon at his disposal. In between, he had lain down to bleed a while, but he had always risen to fight again for the League. There came at last a day when he could no longer rise.

Nearly twenty-five years elapsed before other men came to raise his banner and renew the struggle for international brotherhood. But by then they could cast his weapon aside for other and far sharper arms.

Part IV

The Arrival of
Modern Communications:
The Love Affair Grows

Thirteen

My Friends —

The orgy of war left a people exhausted. The outstanding work of journalist George Creel, whom Wilson had hired to rouse the uncertain nation, had created such tensions that the people's reaction was bound to be violent. They were tired of "sacrifice," tired of being grown-up, tired of having to think and suffer and be responsible, as Wilson had demanded of them. The presidential office fell to the heirs of fatigue: Harding, Coolidge, and Hoover.

Warren G. Harding, a very dark horse, had the honor of being one of the only three men since the Civil War (Franklin Roosevelt and Lyndon Johnson were the others) who received more than 60 per cent of the popular vote. But he attained even greater heights of popularity as a corpse. When he died unexpectedly in San Francisco on August 2, 1923, all the nation seemed to mourn him. The special train bearing him back to Washington could scarcely make its way through the massive crowds. It finally arrived in Washington a full day late.

Harding had never been able to make room at the poker table for any who were not his cronies. The Presidency burdened him, not with its worries, but with its restrictions. "God, what a job!" he groaned. "I am in jail." He simply lacked any feeling whatever for the people. His attraction was that he gave them, after the war's emotional binge, a kind of unthinking calm. In 1920 he had alliteratively proclaimed: "America's present need is not heroics but healing; not nostrums but normalcy; not revolution but restoration; not surgery but serenity." Normality or normalcy—whichever it was, the people wanted it!

President Calvin Coolidge also understood the temper of the nation, and he, too, dispensed soothing syrup with a lavish hand, seeing to it that the public was, as former Speaker of the House Joseph Martin expresses it in his autobiography, "free from alarums from Washington."

In his autobiography Coolidge said, "It is a great advantage to a President, and a major source of safety to the country, for him to know he is not a great man." Here was true humility, and the man who said it passed as adequate in a period that hardly needed any President at all; but when hard times or a life-or-death crisis grips the country, it is small comfort to Americans to be told that their leader is "not a great man." Bungler or no, a crisis President must *know* he is great, and communicate that confidence to the citizenry. Again Coolidge complained: "I am only in the

182

clutch of forces that are greater than I am. . . . I was not prepared for so much . . . under-cover pressure." Such a statement made by a President in the midst of a national catas-
trophe would incite a revolution.

Although the prospering public seemed complacent and
uninterested in whether or not their Chief was strong and
decisive, when the Teapot Dome scandal broke, it was another story. Congress embarked on what George Haynes
calls an "orgy of gloating denunciation," demanding instant
dismissal of the Cabinet officers involved, but President
Coolidge at his finest stood firmly against them. "The President," he declared, "is responsible *to the people* for his conduct relative to the retention or dismissal of public officials.
. . . I do not propose to sacrifice any innocent man for my
own welfare, nor do I propose to retain in office any unfit
man for my own welfare." In the face of obviously lurid
corruption on the part of the Cabinet members, the public
cheered the President's assumption of responsibility and
courage, "abundantly proved by their verdict at the polls in
the following November."

But the ardor of reform had spent itself with the war
years. Business was openly conferring at the White House
again in "deals" which Roosevelt would never have thought
of entertaining, even behind closed doors. During the
Harding administration the "trades" were scandalous. In
the twenties Presidents Coolidge and Hoover were again
openly courting the favor of economic forces already far
too bloated for health. K. Schriftgiesser, in *This Was Normalcy,* quotes Harding as remarking, "I knew this job
would be too much for me," and President Hoover, although blessed with much greater talents, concluded that
"there would never be a President who could satisfy the

press until he was twenty years dead," and went fishing. He said, philosophically, "Fishing . . . is a constant reminder of the democracy of life, of humility and human frailty— for all men are equal before fishes." But in a period of stress, the American people do not want their Chief to be equal, neither before fishes nor before the world.

Wrote Lincoln Steffens: "President Hoover, like Coolidge, honestly believed that the government should favor big business, without price. . . . One can't sneer any more that Washington is the kept woman of Wall Street. They are man and wife, and that changes everything; it makes the old wrong right."

The twenties, until it all blew up, was a time of smugness as well as of relief. America was busily engaged in building automobiles and paving its roads; the times were good for citizens and bootleggers alike. By contrast with the speakeasies the White House was a dull place and its occupants drab and unimportant.

But communications were not dull. The most spectacular role that a President was ever to play was being prepared, and the people themselves were to be invited on stage as part of the act.

President Harding had been the first President to ride to his inauguration in an automobile, the first to have his inauguration described over radio, and the first to make use of a public address system so that the assembled crowds might hear him take the oath. On November 5, 1921, he broadcast from Washington a message to twenty-eight countries in code; and his speech at the dedication of the Francis Scott Key Memorial at Fort McHenry was carried over the telephone to a Baltimore studio and broadcast from there.

In Coolidge's term—namely, on July 1, 1924—transcontinental airmail service was regularly established; in February 1927 the U.S. Radio Commission was created; and on May 20 of that same year Lindbergh flew the Atlantic solo, a feat not unconnected with presidential mobility today. Also in President Coolidge's administration, the first films of presidential candidates were made for theatre showing (September 1924) when Senator La Follette stood on the Capitol steps and waved at the cameraman. The Coolidge inaugural speech of forty minutes' duration was broadcast by twenty-five radio stations and heard by an estimated audience of twenty-three million people—a great new step indeed in bringing the people and the President into more direct communion. Yet while everything was going so splendidly, what was there to talk about?

It was during President Hoover's campaign that a candidate for the Presidency first received formal notification of his nomination under the blinding glare of the television klieg lights. Again, as with the first movie, it was not the conservative candidate who performed this daring act, but an untrammeled soul named Alfred E. Smith. Five blimps and thirty airplanes flew over the Hoover inaugural parade as the new technology flaunted its ever-growing accomplishments.

Yet when the boom collapsed and a great army of unemployed veterans marched into Washington to demand a federal bonus, the eyes of the populace left the skies and focused once more on the man in the White House. With the depression and deepening economic distress, the people's dismay increased, and the longing for the protection of a forceful chieftain became more intense than ever before.

With typical American luck, the nation discovered in this

moment of crisis a man who fully understood his role as a father-leader. No stranger to suffering, a paralytic who could not rise unaided from his wheel chair, this man could respond to the suffering of others. An instinctive leader, he had learned courage the hard way as governor of New York; knowing that strength is the first prerequisite of a leader, he had practiced long hours in drawing himself painfully erect by means of the braces on his legs and had learned how to mask the extreme pain with jokes and laughter while in the public gaze.

On one occasion, invited to dinner at the White House, he was made to wait thirty minutes for the arrival of the Hoovers. Standing in agony with braces and cane, he kept hoping that his ordeal would soon end. Twice he was offered a chair, but he dared not sit before the people who surrounded him, dared not appear a weakling in the sight of the political enemies who milled about him in carefree fashion. Only his wife knew the pain he was undergoing. For all his handicap, those around him have said they had never known a man who gave others a greater sense of security. For good or ill, from the days of the cave man to the present, strength has been the mark of the Chief.

Perhaps the second inescapable mark of the great Chief is magnetism, a personal charm that draws all manner of people to him. F.D.R. was, of course, a man of such personality as to be the despair of his opponents. Joseph E. Martin writes that although Roosevelt's receptions might be dazzling shows, nonetheless the focus of interest was the man himself as he stood there "laughing, talking, and poking the air with his long cigarette holder." The President had so much charm, insists this arch-conservative, that he easily "bamboozled" everyone around him. "As he turned on his radiance I could see the face of one of my men lighting up like the moon," relates Martin with a shudder. Quickly he acted to snatch his protégé safely away from the fatal "moon glow" and to administer the proper antidotes, which included "dire warnings."

It was to this courageous, magnetic leader that the nation turned in its plight and desperation. The brilliant hunchback Randolph Bourne, the moral dissident who died at thirty-two in the "black death" epidemic of 1918, has expressed the unending yearning for a great national father, the yearning which became so dominant in the years of the depression. Although Bourne was addressing himself in particular to the "mysterious herd-current" which rises to the surface in times of war, he would have been quick to apply his analysis to the shadow-filled days of the depression. Bourne said: "A people at war have become in the most literal sense obedient, respectful, trustful children again, full of that naïve faith in the all-wisdom and all-power of the adult who takes care of them, imposes his mild but necessary rules upon them and in whom they lose their responsibilities and anxieties. In this recrudescence of the child, there is great comfort, and a certain influx of power. On most people the strain of being an independent adult weighs heavily...." Wilson had found that as long as he whipped the people on in the unthinking momentum of war, they were his; only when he tried to re-establish them as reasoning adults did they desert him.

Yet the readiness of a distressed people to accept a protector, and the capacity of a leader to fulfill the father image, do not fully account for the development of the Roosevelt Presidency. "I have never known him [F.D.R.] to face life or any problem that came up with fear," Eleanor

Roosevelt said of her husband. Yet how could this ebullience, this confidence, this optimism, have its effect on the desolate men on the soup lines, how temper the bleak despair of the jobless?

Unless the attitude of the one could reach and impregnate the consciousness of the other, the courage could not counter the fear. How indirect and impersonal the inaugural assurances would have been, how rumor-filled those first days when the new pilot took the helm, had there been only the press to report the first hundred days of the New Deal!

But at the advent of Franklin Roosevelt there was radio. If it did not provide the living contact with the leader, it did transmit his voice, direct, alive, vital. The new President could thus convey his strength and confidence directly to the homes of the people across the nation. (For now almost every family had a radio, though it might be but some battered relic of the booming twenties.)

The effect of the President's voice was electric. He had cannily assessed the full potential of the radio microphone, and to his credit, he had pulled this Excalibur from the stone and used it to disarm his opponents. Over in Congress John Nance Garner, the crusty, old-school Vice-President, appalled at the liberal tendency of affairs, invited Joe Martin over to "strike a blow for liberty" by imbibing a few to "lift their spirits." What, Garner wondered gloomily, would happen to this sad land now that a demagogue had learned how to bypass the reasoned judgments of *rational and experienced men* (the old-time politicians)!

The inaugural speech, beamed directly to the people, so roused the country that 460,000 persons sat down to write the new President a congratulatory letter. Ever since that historic day the postman has been a vital link in the decision-making process of a President-centered democracy.

Theodore Roosevelt, a true President of the common man, received scarcely 400 letters a week. By working the headline writers hard he had, in crises such as the coal strike, worked up a correspondence of 1,000 letters a day— a peak that stood as the record right down through the Hoover administration. Ira Smith, who had been in charge of the White House mail room those many years, tallied but 200 letters a week for President Taft, and a peak of almost 1,000 a day as the Wilson high. But whereas Smith was able to care for President Hoover's mail by himself, he was obliged to take over two rooms in the State Department and hire a staff of fifty to handle the more than 5,000 letters a day that poured in on the New Deal President. On days of crisis this torrent of mail to F.D.R. rose to 25,000 a day, and on birthdays to a deluge of 150,000!

Now letter writing, however crude, is essentially a sophisticated activity. It demands not only basic literacy but a finesse and a feeling of being at home with the tools of writing, whether stubby pencil or gold-filled pen. To the little-schooled, composing a letter is a major act of creativity, a bond of communion between writer and reader, and this bond was strengthened when F.D.R. invited consultation. The outpouring of letters was the inevitable result.

With the same motive of fostering an intimate alliance with the people as a political force, Franklin D. Roosevelt invigorated the press conference. Whereas his immediate predecessors had held infrequent press conferences, wooden, lifeless affairs at which the President answered questions that had been submitted in writing, F.D.R. held two press conferences a week and answered directly the questions thrown at him by the reporters. The press conference came to life; it sparkled with humor, and the exchange between the President and the reporters provided a reasonably full account of what was going on in government and of what was planned in the future.

Thus, under F.D.R., the news conference became a forum for the initiation or advancement of policy. It appeared to be an accounting, a report to the people, somewhat akin to the question hour in the British Commons when the government answers for its alleged shortcomings. Actually, the press conference helped F.D.R. to make policy. It gave him the initiative. It offered him a chance to assess the reactions of the correspondents and, indirectly, of the people.

However, the press conference, as a political instrument, has a weakness—its freewheeling character. The assumption is generally made that the newspapermen somehow serve as a bridge between the people and their President, that they are in part spokesmen for the people. This is only partially true. For questions are often asked for their publicity value, even for their sensationalism, rather than for their significance. Moreover, the responsibility and stewardship are all on one side. The questioner need accept no political liability for the content or the tone of his query; he need not weigh his question for its quality or the possibility that it may boomerang. Nor, since most communities have but a single newspaper, is there much reason to suppose that newspapers are overly representative of their readers; their survival is not always dependent upon the readers' approval. Their future is not determined by what goes on at the press conference.

Despite these inequities, F.D.R. assembled from one hundred to two hundred newsmen twice a week for an exhibition that no other figure in the national government could match. His deft handling of the press assured him headline treatment. But, most important, it was highly productive of dialogue between the President and the people—as Professor Sidney Hyman observes, "the balance of forces rising from this new institution generally works in the President's favor."

We have noted that until the twentieth century historical circumstances, mostly a lack of efficient channels of communication, precluded the President's associating closely with the people. Now the onset of the electronic age had introduced newfangled inventions that made possible an unprecedented intimacy between them.

As this relationship was consolidated, it followed inexorably that the President would trespass on the legislative domain of the Congress. For this rapport with the voters captured their loyalty—to him and what he stood for. Surely his followers would not write one thing to him and another to their Congressman. The upshot was, inevitably, that the President could use his popular support to contend with the Congress. Although both the first Roosevelt and Wilson had dared to presume to leadership of the legislature, they had at their command no such potent servant as this new wonder of technology—the means to speak directly to the people.

The mail resulting from this phenomenon in itself raised the temperature of Congress. In the twenties a member of Congress employed only a single clerk to fuss over twenty or twenty-five letters a day. Then F.D.R. picked up an innocent looking metal object and spoke into it, and the member's correspondence leaped to between two hundred and five hundred daily missives. The "fireside chats" put a pressure on Congress never before imagined.

The grumblings began. What was happening to the treasured independence of the Congress? But—did one dare advance the doctrine that Congress should be independent *of the people?* The President had cannily married his program to the people, and there was justice and righteousness in promoting favorable action on it by the Congress.

The resentment, however, remained. And in the people themselves a peculiar development took place. When, confident of his power, their new idol overstepped the traditional bounds of presidential powers and attempted to retire certain unco-operative Senators and Representatives whom the people had elected, a strange reaction occurred. At one and the same time the voters showed themselves to be innovators on the side of presidential leadership for the New Deal *and* to be traditionalists on behalf of the preservation of an independently elected Congress! When Congressmen wailed that they were being "purged," the citizens rose up in their defense, which was equivalent to hiring a man to lock them out of their own house.

When F.D.R. branded Senator Millard Tydings a "knifer in the back of the New Deal" and sought to oust him, Tydings responded emotionally: "I will never consent to be a rubber stamp or a ventriloquist's dummy." Marylanders, who otherwise loved Roosevelt well, proclaimed their approval, and supported the "knifer" against the President's meddling. For although Americans may greatly desire a presidential program, and admire decisiveness and strength in their Chief, their champion must not be pitted again a pushover. Like the spectators at a gladiatorial combat in the Roman arena, they demand courage and skill;

they demand sweat and blood in their cause; and in true sporting style, they demand that the opponent's sword shall also bear a good edge.

Thus President Roosevelt's power over public opinion had reached its climax; it had come up against the solid walls of sectionalism and the doctrine of separation of powers. "Do you want me to exercise independent, conscientious, God-fearing judgment?" thundered Senator Walter F. George of Georgia, and the people responded with a resounding "Yea." "Shall the President *presume* to elect a Senator for North Carolina?" queried Senator E. D. Smith, and the public shouted three to one, "Never."

Without doubt, and in spite of popular gravitation toward powerful, decisive leadership, the ancient suspicion of monarchy had reared its moldering head. Such was the underlying motivation of such paradoxical events, but amusingly, the American citizenry did not recognize it. When the hue and cry over F.D.R.'s "stuffing" of the Supreme Court swept over the nation, the citizens were asked their reasons for opposing the leader whom they professed to idolize.

The wife of a businessman shook her head in distress. "I wonder," she sighed, "if the President has actually ever seen those dignified old men in their majestic black robes? If he has, how can he ever propose *such a terrible thing?*" She had been so inspired by the Court on her visit to Washington! She was sure that if only someone could prevail upon the President to "peek in on Their Honors," he would quickly "change his mind about the situation." Gravely, a Townsendite quoted the Bible: "The hoary head is a crown of glory, Proverbs XVI, 31," as a valid reason for not touching a hair of yon gray heads.

An elderly lady (who had no doubt flunked seventh-grade history) thought that "if nine justices were good enough for Washington, they were good enough for Roosevelt." A young union member was of the opinion that the whole thing might be cleared up by kicking all lawyers off the Court, and leave the President out of it. "They should never have been appointed in the first place," he declared. "If I had my way no lawyers would be judges, Senators, or Congressmen, either!"

Significantly enough, the arguments of the pro's—the minority who backed the President—were equally irrational. One young service-station operator thought that the President ought to "get rid of those old fossils" because his own uncle, at sixty-eight, lived on broth and milk toast! A young nurse was of the same opinion because she had seen a picture of the Supreme Court's dining room, which gave damning evidence of the Court's senile queerness and divergence from the norm. The judges each had different knives, forks, and dishes; and each demanded his own set of salt and pepper shakers! Wasn't this enough to convince anybody that they were too old and finicky to meddle in the government? All these reactions were gleaned by Senator Richard Neuberger in a study of 1937 opinion that was later published in *Current History*.

Thus does the ancient bugaboo of the Forefathers—the fear of the king—still lurk beneath the consciousness of Americans. "I described the American form of government as a three horse team," the President explained lamely on March 9, 1937. "Those who have intimated that the President of the United States is trying to drive that team, overlook the simple fact that the President, the Chief Executive, is himself one of the three horses." The end of the President's hopes came when salty old Vice-President John Garner shook his head and said simply, "You ain't got the votes, Chief." The upshot of the incident was a technical defeat for the President. But the defeat was only slightly damaging; from the ashes rose a voluntarily reconstituted Court that henceforth shied away from vetoing New Deal measures.

The wonder is not that Roosevelt suffered a partial reverse; it is that he carried forward so consistently and constantly. He had a flair for innovation. The moment he was nominated he ordered the delegates to await his acceptance speech; dramatically he flew from New York to Chicago to make it—a commonplace today, but on that day he shattered the hoary tradition of formal notification in which the candidate-elect, "surprised and gratified," receives in his private chambers the heralds of the happy news.

He made other innovations to capture the public imagination and eye. He was the first President to travel by plane extensively all over the globe. He endorsed the experimentation leading to the first self-sustained nuclear chain reaction at Chicago on December 2, 1942. He led in international thinking, proposing the Atlantic Charter (August 14, 1941) and its eight points, the United Nations declaration signed by twenty-six nations at Washington on January 1, 1942, and the United Nations Relief and Rehabilitation Administration signed by forty-four nations in November 1943. He daringly invited to his inauguration the electoral college that had elected him—the first time this inconspicuous, quickly forgotten body had been so honored. He was the first President to read a veto message directly to the Congress (at their rebuke he smiled wryly, and triumphed in the end). He was the first President to use an electric hotpad at an inauguration (January 20, 1937)!

Indeed, though television never developed swiftly enough to be his medium, his was the first presidential image to appear on the flickering tube, grinning into the glare at the New York World's Fair on April 30, 1939. He was the first American Chief whom the King and Queen of England deigned to cross the seas to visit, to be rewarded, alas! with barbecued hot dogs. (Himself related to eleven former Presidents by either blood or marriage, F.D.R. could embrace the most common things with dignity.) One of his greatest contributions to the nation derived from his awareness of the "frightful wastefulness of America" in both timber and soil and his many efforts to awaken the people to what they were doing to their incomparable land.

The New Deal—"rotten as an egg—yellow and it stinks," as Irvin S. Cobb described it—and its Franklin "Deficit" Roosevelt had not carried the *Literary Digest* poll of automobile owners, but it four times carried the great American public in campaigns that displayed more violent hate and fanatic love than any since those of the first Roosevelt. When F.D.R. died, calumny vied with glory to claim his memory. But the people were ill-disposed to listen to the "squeak of flying night creatures," as David Cushman Coyle calls them. "They knew that the man who had been their friend had worked himself to death in their service."

Thus it was that whereas F.D.R.'s predecessors had for over a century boasted emptily about their association with all the people, he made the boast good for the first time. He transformed the relationship of people and President and bent the technological genius of the nation to the evolution of new political instruments. Some other man, at this precise moment in history, might have succeeded in performing a like revolution; but *he was not there.*

Although the people's expectations of the Presidency were tremendously broadened during Franklin Roosevelt's incumbency, the process of political adjustment to the new reality of presidential intimacy needed more time than his three full terms provided. Although the engineers had worked a constitutional miracle destined to alter the presidential office for all time, the political ingenuity of America had not yet caught up with the implications.

Whatever the verdict on F.D.R. may be, it can scarcely be denied that this innovator exhibited a refreshing daring and the courage of the true Chief. In Mrs. Roosevelt's autobiography she gives a humorous example of her husband's need always to appear dauntless. While the President was visiting Uruguay, the Uruguayan President began to regale his guest with exciting stories of how he had been shot at (and so far, fortunately, missed) and was continually being threatened with assassination. Then he led President Roosevelt to his private car for a drive around the city. The American President, his neck no doubt prickling, seated himself in the car without flinching. As they drove off side by side, the President of Uruguay concluded his lurid tales with the reassuring comment: "But you, Mr. President, need not worry. It is only me they are after." ("Me" was one foot to F.D.R.'s right.)

President Franklin Roosevelt served through his three full terms with his neck defiantly exposed. Because he had concentrated initiative in himself in an unprecedented manner, but had not thought to create an opposition of equal stature, he was sniped at from all angles, and viciously. Technology had made it possible for the President to engineer "consent"—but no means had yet been developed for the expression of *dissent*. The President had become, not the figurehead intended by the Forefathers, but a vital agent of upheaval.

Fourteen

Electronics and the Electorate

Louis Brownlow in *The Presidents and the Presidency* reminds us that the ancient Greeks refused to permit a candidate to campaign for an office, thinking it unfair, since handsome features and superior oratory might elect a showman and defeat a less vocal, but more worthy man. The Greek candidate was underexposed, in a real sense, a dark horse. Today the American candidate is overexposed to the point of complete exhaustion. But what does overexposure do to his "image"?

"You are asking, I judge," responded James C. Hagerty to an interviewer, "whether TV permits a phony or charlatan or idiot to make an impression on the public. The answer

199

is 'no.' " (Whether this specialist in image-building has had his views altered in his new position as vice-president of the American Broadcasting Company is not at issue.)

The man who served eight years as press secretary to President Eisenhower went on: "The electric eye of the camera is a most pitiless form of communication—and insincerity or untruthfulness or downright slickness comes through forcefully in the living room of people and is spotted as such. I have seen plenty of proof of this through the years."

It is to be hoped that Hagerty's statement is true. For we must admit that television climaxes the changes in the presidential environment. It has not only made vast new demands on the occupant of the White House, but has also bestowed new privileges on him. As a result, a permanent television studio is now equipped there.

What are television and the new marvels of the electronic age doing to the role of the President? How are they altering the concept of President forged by the Forefathers? We must, in any case, expect some drastic changes. And these new developments, with what they presage for the democratic process and for the survival of the federal system, deeply concern not only Americans but the entire world.

It is hard to believe that so recent a President as Truman was elected before television. There were only 1,050,000 television sets in the United States in 1948 when "Give 'em Hell Harry" mounted the rear platform of the campaign train on a nation-circling tour that brought him victory over Thomas Dewey—and most of these sets were in bars. Truman used the radio, of course, but without the impact that Roosevelt derived from the innovation, and he certainly lacked the famous and mellifluous Roosevelt voice.

"I have never felt that popularity and glamour are fundamentals on which the Chief Executive of the government should operate," he declared. He placed greatest faith in personal campaigning, in the rough and tumble of face-to-face encounters with the electorate, abetted, however, by all that technology had to offer.

Truman later explained his position: "In my own case, communication through a press which was ninety per cent hostile was a real problem, so I had to make many long trips in order to get my message through to the people." Yet despite his feeling about the press, Harry S Truman (whose middle initial, it is said, was given him to stand either for "Shippe" or "Solomon"—according to whether his paternal or maternal grandfather was visiting the family) did not try to reverse the development of the press conference. He was unable to compete with memories of Roosevelt's radio chats; but his blunt, irreverent humor, his unquestioned courage, and his decisive manner did "get through" to the people, and they helped to make him not only a popular, but a "near-great" President.

Without the steadying and coalescing effect of television, Truman's Gallup poll ratings vacillated between an all-time high of 87 per cent and all-time low of 32 per cent. His appeal was great because, like a stern father with a sharp tongue, he scolded the people. "If you're fools enough to let the Republicans in," he shouted at an election rally, "you'll deserve all you'll get!" He said, "I'll give them hell," and he meant the people. He scrapped spiritedly with his opponents; he swore, he offered to punch people in the nose, and in general he won the warm affection of the sporting American public.

Although restricted to the press conference for most of

201

his publicity, Truman nonetheless had the honor, on September 4, 1951, of making the first transcontinental television broadcast. Television was not his forte, but he had a first requisite of the great leader: "guts." When he appeared at a public dedication ceremony less than an hour after an attempt to assassinate him—an attempt in which one White House aide was killed and two others wounded —the nation not only cheered—it rose to its feet.

President Eisenhower was also a popular President, but his administration did nothing to increase the intimacy between President and people. It didn't do much else, either.

General Eisenhower, like another reluctant dragon, General Grant, had his popularity all ready-made and waiting to put on. He came to office on a flood of good will. He was the strong man; he could command; he was comely, sincere, fatherly. And he had a grin that not only helped to win the war, but won hearts both military and civilian. Helped by a coach, he even projected a fair television image.

Why, then, did he fail greatness as well as fail to establish any understanding relationship between himself and the general public? First, he had had no political experience domestically; he favored letting the Presidency run itself, more or less, so that he might spend more time at the golf course. He did not want to ponder overmuch or think hard or read about problems. He was no politician. Because holding press conferences had become traditional, he could escape from this unhappy ordeal only when he could claim illness. Even so, the public willingly sacrificed a favorite Western to see his cheerful, inimitable grin on their television sets. For him, however, words were fortifications to climb over rather than weapons to employ. His heart wasn't in the performance.

For his official family he drew heavily on industrial management and bewildered (though even then he did not alienate) the people with a cabinet that Samuel Eliot Morison described as "eight millionaires and a plumber" (and the plumber resigned). Walter Johnson, author of numerous political treatises, quips that the general approach of "Ike" to a situation was: "What'll we refrain from doing now?"

But mostly, the General simply did not want to get involved, electronically or otherwise. He had no stomach for politics, and less for klieg lights. His administration was one of the "breather" periods the nation seems to need following such epoch-making administrations as those of Roosevelt and Truman. Everybody chanted: "We like Ike." There was no reason not to.

Elected in large part because of his high ratings in the televised debates of the 1960 campaign, John F. Kennedy eagerly explored the medium for its political potential. He used it enthusiastically and fearlessly. He staged live press conferences in the theatre-like auditorium of the new State Department building.

A long, long time had passed since (as Louis Brownlow describes a President's first recognition of the power of the press) Theodore Roosevelt "took Big Bill Price, haunting the White House gate for news, in out of the sun and rain and installed him in a tiny press room" in the West Wing of the White House. Under Kennedy in the great auditorium a couple hundred reporters vied with each other and with May Craig for the attention of the President. The result was scarcely comparable to the intimate banter of the gatherings in F.D.R.'s office, but the conferences assuredly used the new technology for the President's purposes. Kennedy was the idol of the stage; he had the lead, and the reporters were bit players. He always held the initiative, for only one question was to be asked by any newsman, and certain questions had been planted with friendly correspondents, so that the President was able to compose his own lines, spice them with humor, and play his part for a nationwide audience.

Thus the press conference departed more and more from the character of a parliamentary question hour. The television press conference, as practiced under Kennedy, was a monopoly arrangement, more or less, and it tended to demoralize the opposition. Personable, intelligent, and a master at thinking on his feet, President Kennedy won over enemies and aroused widespread admiration in these bouts.

But his greatest approach to intimacy with the people (who in general showed more awe than love in this regard) came when he entered the living rooms of the nation in "A Conversation with the President," a television program heralded even by leading Republicans as a performance more effective than the fireside chats of F.D.R. Said veteran Representative Clarence J. Brown (Republican) of Ohio enviously: "It was the cleverest piece of political public relations I have ever seen. The President handled himself very ably."

The thousand days of Kennedy prove that the Presidency by its central position in the news network cultivates overwhelming support for the incumbent. Here was a President who came to office with less than half the voters on his side, who defeated his opponent, Richard M. Nixon, by only 119,000 votes—the least of mandates. He could not drive measures through Congress on the strength of his vote-getting capabilities. To muster thin majorities for his measures he was reduced to the devices of political persuasion: military contracts, favors, patronage, and privilege.

Kennedy, acting as an honest broker, concluded most of his legislative negotiations somewhere in the middle. His depressed areas bill, for instance, had its terms badly watered down and carried with it a hundred million dollar loan fund for cotton to entice the votes of southern Congressmen. His minimum wage measure made exception of certain manual workers who most needed its protection—such as laundry workers—again to gain southern support.

But though Kennedy's legislative leadership lacked positive character because of the slender margin of his electoral victory, he rapidly became the darling of the communications media because he was an attention-getter, fervent, poised, and radiating the aura of the leader. The presidential office dominated radio, television, magazines, and newspapers. Long before his tragic death Kennedy had bolstered his Gallup ratings and lifted himself from minority to majority standing.

Thus, for good or ill, but for all time to come, presidential leadership, with the whole influence of the office, is unalterably intertwined with this modern instrument of communication. A President now must not only know what he is talking about, and how to express it well, but he must also possess the mystical ability to "project" on a television screen. It would be difficult to imagine "Silent Cal" in the role that we demand of our leader today. And how would George Washington, in his aloof and dignified impersonality, have "come across" to the waiting millions?

President Hoover once exclaimed bitterly that the people wanted dramatics, not solid values, in their leadership. Indeed, the President today is reviewed on the entertainment page as well as on the editorial page.

Superficially assessing Lyndon Johnson soon after he became President, one television critic did so, not in terms of his dedication or his knowledge, or even of what he said, but of his performance. The President seemed "stolid and at times unimaginative when compared with his predecessor. But on a few issues . . . he spoke with animation and even some verve." Typical of the reviewers' reactions was that of Warren Rogers, a writer for the Hearst newspapers: "His folksy, father-of-us-all approach spreads an aura as reassuring as a chat with one's own pastor." So, too, did the later "mood-setting" films made of the President sitting in lonely contemplation at his desk while the camera zoomed in on the bent shoulders and lined face. The President had become a "production."

Presidents suffer acutely from what Merriman Smith in *The Good New Days* calls "Potomac sunburn, a stinging allergy to printed and broadcast disapproval." Sunburn or no, there is a new pace in press coverage.

Hovering everywhere about the Chief and making news of his slightest gesture is a corps of newsmen. If he spends a weekend on a ranch, the press is on hand to identify the barbecue sauce and to count and classify the guests. If he goes to the beach, the press appears from behind an umbrella to watch him flex his muscles or to comment on his swimming form. If he flies abroad or into the next state, three planes make the trip: the President's jet, a backup airliner, and a press plane. The press plane lands first, presumably to enable the reporters to describe the chaos should the President's plane make a belly landing.

In all this there is a risk. President Franklin Roosevelt, in the years before television, worried lest people "tire of seeing the same name, day after day, [hearing] the same voice, night after night, over the radio." Overexposure is still a constant threat. President Johnson's technique has been described as "six surprises a week." When he cannot come up with these, he finds new ways of performing old but important chores. "His array of approaches to problems has been inexhaustible," says the Troy *Record*.

Like television, the jet plane and the helicopter have had a tremendous impact on the Presidency. David Lawrence, deploring the candidates' racing all around the country in the 1964 campaign, thought that the "physical presence" of a candidate on television should eliminate much of this undignified "exhibitionism." To this Johnson replied, ". . . unless the President goes to the people, unless he visits and talks with them, unless he senses how they respond . . . he cannot do the President's job. . . . The people want to see their President in person."

At any rate, the President is now completely mobile and able to project a father image wherever the magic of his presence is demanded. Let there be a flood in Ohio, and the President makes a personal appraisal as he flies over the stricken area preparatory to assigning emergency funds. Let a commonwealth of the Union celebrate an anniversary, and the President can join in the festivities, if for no longer than it takes to munch a barbecued beef rib. He now can attend the funeral of a political V.I.P., visit with an elder statesman who has a sentimental following, address a labor convention, and swoop down from the heavens on a political steak fry in less time than Jefferson took to tour Washington. Without having unduly sacrificed any of his official duties at the White House, he can say with Joe

207

Martin: "The happiest days of my life have been spent at clambakes."

As noted in considering presidential press coverage, a logistic miracle occurs every time the presidential plane rolls down the runway. A small corps of experts in security, communications, and transportation, as well as local memorabilia, must make up an advance party. When President Johnson visited the University of California in the spring of 1964, a veritable blitz struck the campus in preparation. Every spot, every detail was blueprinted. Where would the helicopter come to earth? Where should the cables be laid to keep the Chief in constant touch with critical conferences, red phones, atomic buttons, and naval fleets?

Thus all the inventions of modern times have combined to release the President from the isolation of the White House and bring him in constant touch with the people. But the Presidency is still the loneliest eminence in the world. Theodore Sorensen quoted President Kennedy as saying that the multitude of advisers is on every hand and voluble with advice, but that he alone bears the burden of decision. And when the reckoning comes, only the President can bear the blame, while the "advisers may move on to new advice." The loneliness of the President is no longer merely physical; it is spiritual as well.

As we have mentioned throughout these pages, almost every American President has either reached out toward the people or professed profound faith in them. Do not be frightened "by the alarms of the timid or the croakings of wealth against the ascendancy of the people," advised Jefferson; ". . . the people are the only sure reliance for the preservation of our liberty." Even our less effective Presidents have clung to this avowal.

208

Van Buren declared that "the second, sober thought of the people is seldom wrong, and always efficient." (Whether he held this opinion after his third unsuccessful try for re-election is not recorded.) James Buchanan, though he inclined toward states' rights to the denigration of presidential power, and is rated as a failure, stated with emotion: "Indeed, he [the President] is the only direct representative on earth of the people of all and each of the sovereign States. To them, and to them alone is he responsible whilst acting within the sphere of his constitutional duty, and not in any manner to the House of Representatives." And General Grant, hardly knowing what the words meant, opined that "the will of the people is the best law."

But now that the President is able, at last, to freely confront his people, what does he find? "The people" is an amorphous term. Politically, they, too, are affected by their environment and the technological devices at their disposal. Their competence and ability to conduct a dialogue with the President are constantly shifting. Whereas the average citizen under Wilson had not finished the sixth grade, under F.D.R. he had finished the eighth, and under Kennedy he was nearly a high school graduate. By 1960 illiteracy among persons fourteen years of age and over had been reduced to 2.2 per cent, supposedly—although the country was stunned by the rate at which the young men of the nation were being rejected by the military service for mental reasons.

Statistically, when compared to preceding generations, today's presidential constituents are an informed people. They read 59.8 million newspapers every day and scan 105 million weekly magazines as well as 185 million monthlies.

But a glance at the newsstands reveals that, if judged by the quality of their reading, the American public is better able to elect the nation's leading sexpots than to engage in a creative interchange with the occupant of the White House.

There is, however, a continuing drive from the White House to improve the conditions under which the people exercise their political authority. The story of their Chief's essential idealism is recounted by Norman Cousins in the *Saturday Review*'s obituary on John F. Kennedy two weeks after his death. Cousins wrote: "If the people looked to the President, the President looked no less to the people. He knew that on most big issues he would be helpless without them. Not that he expected public opinion to define every great question, carry it forward, move it triumphantly through the Congress, and deliver it to him for final signature. He saw his role and the role of public opinion as a process of creative interaction. He accepted the job of stating the case and giving it the proper degree of urgency. But the public also had the job to respond—one way or the other."

This is the sophisticated notion of the people. President Kennedy, although seemingly confident, doubted his ability to direct the people's responses. He was a mail-watcher.

When, for instance, more than a year before he died, his mail and that of Congress suddenly showed a flurry of opposition to the United Nations, Kennedy was troubled. With the U.N. in need of funds from Congress to underwrite its peace-keeping in the Congo and in the Suez, the ratio of fifteen "anti" letters to one "pro" letter was evidence of critical hostility. Investigating, the President discovered that the private polls of Congressmen and Senators, and the findings of a disinterested public poll, showed four-to-one support for the prospective loan to the U.N. At once Kennedy saw to it that these findings were well distributed throughout the Congress. Meanwhile, an analysis of the letters of opposition showed them to have been inspired by a common source, a hate group.

This incident shows that it is not always "the basic idealism" of the people which is demonstrated, but very often the distortions which highly organized, money-laden groups may cause to occur in the democratic process. And more and more, today, the public is becoming interest-ridden, even as it harbors stronger and more highly defined ideals in its breast. It is acting like a man who fervently organizes a revival meeting and then takes a "backhander" from the rental agent of the hall.

Theodore Sorensen, former counsel and speech writer for President Kennedy, has said that public opinion is "often erratic, inconsistent, arbitrary and unreasonable." The public is rarely concerned with the needs of the unborn or with the history of the fathers. Professor Herman Finer is even more pessimistic, declaring that the electorate today is "an inchoate mass whipped up by artificial and factitious storms only to subside into quasi-apathy."

In the black-and-white world of Harry S Truman, the people stand apart from the interests and are the pure woodland stream that feeds the muddied river of politics. Odd, then, are the results obtained on the eight occasions when Mr. Truman monopolized all the radio networks at an evening hour to reach the pure in heart on policy issues. His topics varied from price inflation and strikes to the Marshall Plan and the *coup d'état in* Czechoslovakia. As tallied by Richard E. Neustadt in *Presidential Power,* the

211

response, or Hooper ratings—roughly measuring the actual against the potential listeners in homes—were, interestingly, 43.8, 49.4, 34.4, 31.8, 57.6, 30.7, 34.3, and 31.0 per cent. (A lot of inaccuracies and variables may have affected these figures, but they are internally consistent.)

And what, you may ask, occasioned the towering peak in the ratings, 57.6 per cent, when so many conscientious Americans were avidly listening to their radio receivers? This was the occasion on which the President discussed the forthcoming decontrol of meat!

But perhaps this result is not so odd, for food is the most fundamental of human interests. One may doubt whether there will ever be a government pronouncement—except, perhaps, a declaration of war—to rival man's interest in food. Nor do these figures condemn the public as gross, but only as extremely human. President Truman insisted that "the vast majority of the people *want to do what is right* and if the President is right and can *get through to the people* he can always persuade them." Unless a President can believe this, he can never be successful, for he has nothing to build on but sand.

Again, a large part of "the people" are pre-empted by "causes"; they are enlisted in this group or that. They are thoroughly overorganized. These groups—especially those that serve self-interest—are disproportionately loud, and always so in the interests of their lowest common denominator. They discredit the public at large while adding to its fragmentation. And as more than three quarters of America's population now live in cities or on the fringes of cities, the character of "the people" is undergoing a metamorphosis. Such an uneven distribution of the nation's population alters the tone of presidential politics drastically, as we shall see. These, then, are some of the paradoxes of "the people."

As the President becomes attuned to the public, and it to him, as his lines of communication develop, a new problem arises. The President, aware that the success of his program and the verdict of history depend on the measure of his support by the public, instinctively promotes a climate of opinion that is favorable to himself and to his policies. But especially *to himself*. To do this, he must unflinchingly subscribe to the *accepted presidential image,* whose attributes we have mentioned.

President Johnson, whom Arthur Krock calls "the most political animal to occupy the White House since Andrew Jackson, if not since the creation of the Federal Government," understood this well. When he set forth, only a few days after his predecessor's assassination, to walk six blocks through streets lined with nine hundred thousand unfrisked mourners to the funeral at St. Matthew's Cathedral, his Secret Service agents stepped up to stop him. "I'd rather die than be afraid to die," he said, and strode past the agents and into the line of march of the funeral procession. Johnson knew, as surely as did William Henry Harrison and Franklin Roosevelt before him, that the President who flinches is forever lost as a leader.

And now, in addition to the preservation of this "naked eye" image, the President's television image must be enhanced. The "bully pulpit" of Theodore Roosevelt is wired for sound and for sight.

Unfortunately, the time has come when what the President says is rivaled in importance by how he looks when he says it. To what extent shall we come to choose our Presidents on their photogenic qualities and their projection of an intimate "living-room manner"? It may not be as important to be good, or even to sound good, as to look good.

The President, if he would be strong and if he would hold the initiative in making policy, must also plan the impact of his releases and his timing on his constituency. At some point this manipulation of public opinion, this culling of what is to become known from what is to stay secret, this control of the factual framework within which the political dialogue must take place, is labeled "management of the news."

Press agents Hagerty, Salinger, and Reedy have all been accused of excessive "managing," of doling out selected items of information for political ends when security was not involved and, in general, of "sweetening" the presidential image. Frankly, this "sweetening" is their job. They are employed in the White House to ward off bad publicity and to use their political light meter to decide which presidential pose and exposure will be the most flattering—as well as to inform the public of what is going on. And the public, though fully aware in most cases that the information it receives is being filtered through a rose-hued glass, shows surprisingly little resentment, for the simple reason that the masses of people want to hear from their leader, not problems, but comforting reassurances. After all, didn't they elect *him* to do the worrying?

Thus the fatuously optimistic statement, the irrational, even dangerous, glossing over of a crisis, is considered not only feasible to "maintain the national stability," but also the simplest way for a President to continue high on the popularity polls and insure his re-election. Back in 1926 H. L. Mencken observed cynically: "The man who hopes absurdly, it appears, is in some fantastic and gaseous manner a better citizen than the man who detects and exposes the truth. Bear this sweet democratic axiom clearly in mind. It is, fundamentally, what is the matter with the United States." There is, however, a violent backlash which Mencken did not mention. If the public later discovers that it has been hoodwinked in circumstances which cause repercussions, the people's condemnation can be merciless.

Mencken went on to say that "democracy, if it is anything at all, is simply one way of getting round" the various obstacles which God has interposed to the attainment of the common man's dreams. It follows that the man elected to lead that democracy must be the agent of getting round those obstacles, or he is valueless. From this viewpoint the historic concept of the President as an inspired leader who enlightens, guides, and coalesces the divergent masses, who wisely leavens the raw expression of their will with restraint in the nation's good, fades out; the Chief becomes largely a "gimme-man."

The 1964 election, in which candidates for offices of all kinds exhausted themselves in a frenzied, repetitious underlining of the appeal, "Elect me. I can do more *for you*," was a repulsive exhibition. It is painful indeed for an idealistic American who would put national and humanitarian issues before his own immediate benefit to submit to such an experience. It is even more painful for him to acknowledge that the President has developed into the chief "gimme" authority of them all. And it is just as difficult for a President to resist the development.

Nonetheless, we have had Presidents who could resist. Theodore Roosevelt did withdraw lands from the public domain and preserve them to posterity, and he was the target of violent abuse—not only from the speculative interests but from large sections of the greedy public. F.D.R., although a politician and trader of a high order, also exercised discretion of a high order. The nation's future is more dependent on the nobility of the man who occupies that highest office than on public indignation.

Norman Cousins relates that, in the space of one month, President Kennedy was urged many times by advocates of selfish interest to go before the television cameras to mobilize public opinion "like F.D.R. used to do" so successfully. As the pressure on him mounted, the President began to ask his petitioners to guess the number of fireside chats made by F.D.R. during his *thirteen years* as President. The average guess was in the vicinity of a hundred. Then the President would give the correct answer, which was *eleven*.

The hope that a Chief will resist the "gimme" pressures lies not only in the incumbent's ever-present desire to grace the history books as "one of the great," but also in his ability to recognize, as did Truman, that if his stand is honestly for the best of the people as a whole, the people as a whole, when adequately informed and appealed to, will endorse him. This is the democratic hope. And in service to this stand, television may find its highest mission.

Today the masses need no longer undertake long treks to Washington to overrun the White House in an effort just to be near, talk to, see, or hear their Chief. In Lincoln's day the corridors were often a frightful bedlam as petitioners in all conditions of travel stain and unwash milled about. With animals running wild through the Washington streets, and the streams flowing through the city choked not only with sewage but with rubbish and even dead babies (as Ann Royall has described them), the thousands of curiosity-seekers did nothing to help the problems of sanitation. In the days of Jackson the populace left its mark on the executive mansion in more ways than one. Mud-caked carpets and trampled sofas were the least of the shocks to the dignified. In Jackson's personal correspondence, a letter to Major Lewis from the Hermitage in 1834 instructs him "to have the White House rid of bed bugs" before his return!

Today the curiosity of the people as to what the President looks and sounds like, as to what he eats, reads, and does, has been satisfied. Although 1.3 million visitors passed through the public rooms of the White House in 1963, they were marched through too quickly to deposit even a gum wrapper. And they came not to speak with the President, but to see what "Jackie" had done to improve the quality of the furnishings.

So the age of technology has revolutionized the relationship of President and people by saturating the Washington scene with microphones, cameras, klieg lights, and the paraphernalia of the press. Charles Beard predicted in 1924 that "mechanical inventions may make a greater revolution in the powers of the President than a constitutional amendment." We have joined the literacy of the electorate to a tangle of communication wires. To the natural drama of the President's post there is now added an electric sense of the theatre, even a phony glitter. Distortions in the relationship are the handiwork of the public relations expert gone wild.

Historian George H. Haynes asserts flatly that if workable radio had been developed in 1919 instead of five years later, it without doubt would have saved Wilson's life. Says Haynes: "One of the most momentous decisions in America's history might have been reversed" if Wilson had been

217

able, while sitting safely at his White House desk, to project his explanations and pleas to tens of millions of his countrymen.

Today a royal retinue of reporters—they have been likened to courtiers—make up the regular White House press corps. Their hunger for news is a ready-made situation for manufacturing it. They tag after the President everywhere, even if he decides to go around the world. Their presence assures us that, should the President's plane crack up, his dying moments will be thoroughly depicted in glossy close-ups by the outstanding photographers in the field. Or if he lands safely, that his first words on debarking will be properly recorded for mankind, even though they may happen to be, "Jack, go back and see if I left my reading glasses on the seat."

Fifteen

The Dizziness in High Places

The electronic environment in which the President works enhances his influence over the minds of the voters. This we have noted. But new forces are also at work to augment the authority and prerogatives of the Chief's office, and so to multiply by many times the dominance of the President over the affairs of the nation. With these developments come the kinds of pressures that make for dizziness in high places.

During the life of the American Republic, monarchies have vanished and empires have crumbled; and with them have gone the multitudes of courtiers who whispered their importunities in the monarch's ear while they laced his doublet. Only the American Presidency has remained and been magnified; its enlargement continues apace, and with it the scores of sycophants who pander to the ego of the Chief. In 1880, when the Presidency was a mere germ of what it has become, President Hayes said: "It is no doubt well to leave the high place now. Those who are in such a place cannot escape the important influence on habit, disposition and character. In that envied position of honor and distinction, they are deferred to, flattered and supported under all circumstances, whether right or wrong, by shrewd and designing men and women who surround them. Human nature cannot stand this too long!"

Whatever the effects of this power accretion may be on the incumbent, these varied enhancements have transformed the office itself. Presumably the President still adheres to the ancient concept of the steadying leader, the symbol of national permanence, the stalwart defender of the Constitution. Actually, in response to the increased demands upon him, the Chief has unwittingly become the protagonist of constant change, a social irritant: in short, he has become an agent of upheaval. To place in the hands of a single person whom we have made an agent of upheaval an uncounted assortment of new and untried powers may not be to live dangerously. It is, however, to live quite adventurously.

The four most obvious, and most puissant, of the new forces that add so much to presidential influence might be encompassed, roughly, by four major, but not exclusive, categories: *centralization, foreign relations, "threats of crisis,"* and *"crush of injustice."*

Though few citizens have failed to note the fantastic

centralization of governmental affairs that has been taking place since World War II, not all have noted its relationship to the competence of the Presidency. Yet of those political observers who bewail the "immensity" of government, a growing number do so not only out of respect for traditional states' rights or local prerogative, but out of concern about the bigness of the Presidency. The beneficiary of centralization—if added duties are a "benefit" —is the President. The more activities the central government assumes, the bigger the executive establishment becomes in relation to the other branches of government.

Within the memory of the present generation farm programs have burgeoned, social security has become an institution, defense has become a many-splendored part of the economy, the little atom has eaten at the vitals of the budget, the exploration of space has called for billions of dollars and a vast agency, and welfare programs have multiplied. In fact, the federal outlay of funds to state and local governments increased fourfold in a decade, rising from 2.7 billion dollars in 1954 to 10.4 billion dollars in 1964! As administration increases, so does authority.

As the conservative columnist Henry J. Taylor sees it, ". . . in the planned immensity of the government as a whole, the Presidency is becoming a party of itself, autonomous and often even anonymous. That makes the American system a sick system today, a sick elephant; and a sick elephant is a formidable thing."

The fears of conservatives, whether justified or not, are extensive. Former Senator Harry S. Byrd turned slightly purple at the least suggestion that some authority be added to the President's office. When, for instance, power was requested to cut taxes by executive order and to spend for pump priming without appropriations, the venerable old watchdog sputtered: "No President in the history of the United States ever asked for such executive power.... Congress rejected all of these proposals, but the very fact that they were so openly made disturbs confidence."

The point is that the Presidency not only garners new power growing out of the centralization of governmental activities, but has become the focus of attention in budgetary and fiscal matters too. Making the economic system work is a national undertaking with international overtones. So long, therefore, as we are whipped along by the ineluctable demands for national economic growth, the chief priest conducting the ritual must be the President, attended at the altar by his Council of Economic Advisers.

By virtue of congressional act (the Employment Act of 1946) and the thoroughgoing commitment of the society to a doctrine of eternal economic expansion, the President is the guardian of the unemployed, the custodian of national productivity, and the warden of business activity. He is the archangel of good times and the Beelzebub of bad.

Henry Jones Ford in 1898 displayed such uncanny insight into the future role of the President in the tribal life of Americans that Corwin and Koenig dub him the "John the Baptist of the twentieth-century Presidency." They quote him:

"The rise of presidential authority cannot be accounted for by the intention of presidents; it is the product of political conditions which dominate all the departments of government, so that Congress itself shows an unconscious disposition to aggrandize the presidential office....

"The truth is that in the presidential office, as it has been constituted since Jackson's time, American democracy has revived the oldest political institution of the race, the elective kingship. It is all there: the precognition of the notables and the tumultuous choice of the freemen, only conformed to modern conditions. . . ."

Public opinion analyst Samuel Lubell has noted in the *Christian Science Monitor* that this tribal loyalty shifts with events. And the early position of Lyndon Johnson, which Lubell called the "Mona Lisa smile"—because everyone saw what he wanted to see—was subject to change with a change in economic circumstance. The point is that the President, in the minds of the people, is a symbol of a national outlook that he increasingly attempts to impress, even in off-year elections, on Congress, which traditionally has been so provincial.

The upshot is simply that the President assumes a quite unique and fearsome responsibility for the economic health as well as for the political and social welfare of the entire national community. But in one field, foreign relations, his role is so thoroughly dominant that it deserves special mention. In the jungle of world politics the President is truly our chieftain.

And here he must—more than in any other capacity and more than in any other field—act like a true chieftain. President Wilson, though stricken mortally ill, had to scorn the litter used by ordinary mortals, and rising dizzily to his feet, this man who had represented the United States and who symbolized its place in the world of nations had to walk without stumbling off the train and into his car, smiling gamely at the crowd in an attempt to hide the death in his eyes. When photographed with the chiefs of other nations, President Franklin D. Roosevelt had to stand in his painful braces without flinching. And President Kennedy, although suffering excruciating pains from his injured back, had to receive foreign dignitaries with the confident, unruffled manner of the leader of the world's greatest nation.

More and more, as the twentieth century has developed, we have reserved our opinion of our newly chosen President until we have tested him in international deliberations, in slugging it out with the chieftains of rival lands. Franklin D. Roosevelt displayed great spunk as he scuttled the London Conference at the beginning of his first administration. Truman did his diplomatic teething at the Potsdam Conference, and when he returned to Washington without having ceded any one of the forty-eight states to anyone, there was a feeling that he would pass muster as head of state.

Like the Israelites with their David, we early pushed the young John F. Kennedy into a confrontation with Khrushchev at Vienna, and though Goliath was not dead when the conference ended, there was exultation that the President was not dead either. Throughout the first six months of President Johnson's administration whatever uneasiness there was, stemmed from the uncertainty that foreign leaders might not heed the admonition of Isaiah: "Come, let us reason together." Our leader was still untried in foreign affairs. Only when the new Chief responded to the Tonkin Bay crisis by using force against North Vietnam did he earn eagle feathers for his headdress.

The extent of our nation's involvement with foreign affairs has grown at a breath-taking rate. As late as the nineteen-twenties the House Foreign Affairs Committee could devote one whole week, excluding all else, to discussing this single question: "Should we or should we not authorize $20,000 for an international poultry show in Tulsa?" Today, the essence of such a decision would probably be made in about fifteen minutes at the desk of a subordinate officer in the Department of State.

Our concern for our President's competence in foreign affairs has grown out of our recognition that his international role is vast and critical. "Before World War II," said Secretary of State Dean Rusk in 1964, "eight governments disposed of the continent of Africa. Now it is almost 35 and the number is growing. We do business with 112 states."

Civil wars, revolutions, border disputes, fishing wars, and assorted commotions demand constant attention. Indeed, the Department of State maintains an around-the-clock global watch and a vast network of embassies and consulates over the globe. And over all this establishment for foreign affairs, the President of the United States presides: he initiates and directs. As the Constitution provides, he alone deploys our forces to protect our national interests; he decides what ought to be done. The discretion, the timing, the pressures, the conciliations—all these legally rest with the President.

As the world has come to spill its myriad problems on our doorstep, as the United States has moved from a world power at the opening of the century to a superpower at the middle, it is the Presidency that has been highlighted. "For it is he to whom Americans and free people everywhere look for management of peace or war," says Sidney Hyman.

Thus, since the issue of war and peace overshadows all others in the mind of the electorate, the role of the President is magnified, and his relationship with his constituency becomes ever more direct, paternalistic, and close. Sander Vanocur, in the April 1964 *Harper's,* traces President Kennedy's "Voyage of Discovery" on his last barnstorming tour of the country, billed as a transcontinental trip on conservation. It was a discovery that he and the people were operating on a single wavelength. He was at Billings, Montana, when the moment of truth came:

"The crowd which welcomed him to Billings, Montana, was enormous and, considering this was Republican territory, it was enthusiastic. At the Yellowstone County Fairgrounds he . . . rose to praise the leadership of Mansfield and of minority leader Everett Dirksen in securing ratification of the test-ban treaty. When he mentioned these three words there was prolonged cheering and applause. He knew that radioactivity was a source of some concern in the West and that 150 Minuteman missile silos in the state caused anxiety. But even knowing this, he appeared to be somewhat surprised by the reaction to his reference to the test-ban treaty." This, said Vanocur, may have been the "instant of discovery," of excitement, of perfect understanding between President and people in the area of his major responsibility, foreign relations.

It is not only that the powers of government are being centralized and that the problems of world affairs are piling up in Washington; in both these areas, domestic and international, the threats of crisis are never-ending. This complex world gets out of whack so often there is no longer any relief from crises. Great crises in our history have brought forth great leaders, yet one of these leaders was perturbed even by this phenomenon. Lincoln said, "It has long been a grave question whether any government, not too strong for the liberties of its people, can be strong enough to maintain its existence in great emergencies."

As early as 1939 the Attorney General could cite ninety-nine separate statutory grants by which Congress had bestowed on the executive emergency or wartime powers. But statutes aside, the very circumstances of modern politics generate crises. Woodrow Wilson once noted that a President is free "to be as big a man as he can." But nowadays, comments Richard Neustadt, he *cannot* be as *small* as he might like.

This constant pressure may exact its price. The three-foot ocean sunfish, who is at all times under great pressure because of the ocean depths, has had its spinal cord shrunk to a fraction of an inch, and its skeleton, according to authority C. M. Breder, Jr., is "degenerate to the consistency of cheese." Whether the new pressures cause a moral degeneracy or a spiritual toughening of the presidential character will depend on a host of intangibles, both within and without the man himself.

In the face of such pressures and emergencies, the call is to the bold as well as to the strong. Livy said, "In great straits, and when hope is small, the boldest counsels are the safest." Boldness of action itself becomes a policy apart from what one is being bold about. This makes large headlines, but it does not necessarily lead to wise solutions. One of the hazards of the Presidency is the working conditions; it is uncomfortable to carry on with a historian looking over your shoulder. True, constant observation may inspire, it may awaken slumbering courage and nobility, as it did in Polk, Garfield, and Arthur; but it may also encourage rashness in pursuit of an heroic image.

Up to now students of the Presidency have customarily viewed presidential powers largely as a constitutional response to opportunity. A crisis occurs, and the answer is one of national unity in which the leader vastly enlarges and exploits his strengths. Then, the crisis met, in a spate of fatigue partisan views reappear, and the Presidency returns to normal.

But today there is little ebb in the political affairs of men, scant relief. And like a tiring muscle, the public responds less and less vigorously to each new crisis. What we witness is not so much an electorate less sensitive to an emergency, or even a people grown suddenly apathetic; rather, the people are increasingly, and aggressively, rejecting the heavy responsibility that the current continuing crises impose. The minds of men have been overwhelmed, and are pushing aside the issues as impossible of solution.

Thus all the self-indulgence and frantic seeking for entertainment are not mere indicators of surrender; they are gestures of positive dismissal. And in such a process the leader does not shrink, but grows. A terrified child needs a father's legs to hide behind to shut out the sight that appalls him.

Back in 1884 Henry C. Lockwood commented on the passionate hero-worship that prevailed among the American people. "Under our form of government we do not think so much of what Congress may do. A great multitude declared: 'Give us President Grant! We know him. He is strong! He will rule!'" A hundred years after Grant, when any two-bit sovereign may kick up an international sandstorm, and the alarm bell rings without ceasing, the cry is ever louder for a man of force and action. So dependent on the Chief have we become that we avidly scan his every movement on television for signs of his physical condition. Should he inadvertently reach to loosen the collar that the laundry has shrunk or fail to suppress a grimace as the lights strike his eyes, the stock market may plunge.

Yet we gloat over the duties we have piled on the President. Remarked Lyndon B. Johnson even while he was still viewing the Presidency from the Vice-President's chair: "The President carries heavier burdens than I ever envisioned. You feel little goose pimples coming up on your back because it's such a frightening, terrifying responsibility." That he now works sixteen hours a day and sleeps only five and "feels fine" gives the people a sense of gratification in the stamina and consecration he shows (not unmixed, however, with sharp pangs of concern). Said President Eisenhower in counseling his young, untried successor, John F. Kennedy: "You'll find that you won't have any little troubles to worry about. All the little troubles are solved below—you just get the big ones."

Finally, the President is cast irrevocably in the role of protector of the people against injustice, a role which has developed into that of indulgent father-giver. Intimacy with the public calls forth a wealth of promises, sometimes exaggerated beyond all reason by the competitive seeking of office. And as he makes promises of more and more to more and more groups of the society, he becomes a reformer, wedded to transformation. In the business of molding the wedges of population into an arc of support he is profligate with fatuous avowals.

He will banish the cyclical ups and downs of the capitalist system. He will eliminate the pockets of poverty, which private enterprise has so far tolerated. He will open the floodgates to new immigration, which will alter the face of the nation. He will seek stronger international alliances, which will mean some loss of the ancient national sovereignty. He will alter the tariffs. He will endorse great new outlays of the public moneys. He will promote social welfare in the form of more social security benefits.

In short, by advancing himself as the champion of many causes, he has become the apostle of change, of innovation —*an agent, in fact, of upheaval.* By presenting himself as the champion of the common man against the crush of injustice, he has become the antagonist of the *status quo.* If all his overzealous promises were to be summarily realized, we would experience a social upheaval little short of revolution.

Again, the role of champion of the people, in addition to fostering support of the President, tends to kindle strong emotions, including an awe and respect for the office quite out of proportion to man's human limitations. President Truman once said to Eric Sevareid, "What you do not understand is the power of a president to hurt." The President has such emotional effect upon the people, said Mr. Truman, that once, after chiding a college student at a lecture for referring to the state governor as a "local yokel," he felt impelled, after the meeting, to seek out the pale and stricken lad to reassure him and reduce his chagrin. "Mr. Truman went on to observe that a word, a harsh glance, a peremptory motion by a President of the United States could so injure another man's pride that it would remain a scar in his emotional system all his life," concludes Sevareid.

To be so many things to so many people the President

truly needs to possess empathy, that common denominator of which William Ellery Channing spoke so long ago when he said: "That great men and the multitude of minds are of one family is apparent, I think, in the admiration which the great inspire into the multitude. A sincere, enlightened admiration always springs from something congenial in him who feels it with him who inspires it.... The germ is in him."

In the nearness to which the Chief has come vis-à-vis the people at large, and in the immense powers accruing to him, the President has reached a position of influence unequaled in all of American history, certainly never dreamed of by the Founding Fathers. A mediocre man could no longer survive in this dizzying atmosphere.

Yet all through civilized history men have tended to avoid choosing the outstanding candidate, the best-known and most forceful leader, simply because he is controversial and has acquired so many enemies. Since the oft-repeated instance in which the Greek generals, voting to decide who among them had excelled in the war again Xerxes, gave each the first vote to himself and the second to Themistocles, it has been a maxim of politics (reiterated by James Madison) that if any gathering of society is unanimous in the choice of the *second best,* that man is in truth the *first.*

Charles Judah and George Winston Smith, in *The Unchosen,* bring out that "when the choice [of President] lies between a brilliant man and a safe man, the safe man is preferred" by the parties. As examples of outstanding (but assailable) Senators who were denied the nomination by their parties they list William H. Seward, Lyndon

Johnson, Estes Kefauver, Robert A. Taft, William Gibbs McAdoo, Benjamin Bristow, and Champ Clark. There are many others, including Robert La Follette, Sr.

How long, now that the Chief has assumed all these new responsibilities, all this power, in an age demanding instant but careful decisions, when one misstep may be calamitous, dare we go on arbitrarily casting aside our biggest man for a compromise? There is no "safe" man today.

When John F. Kennedy said he wanted to be President "because that's where the power is," he knew whereof he spoke. When President Truman reminded us that the Constitution, regarding the powers of the Chief Executive, was a "flexible instrument," he also was merely pointing out a fact of which every President is keenly aware.

Perhaps in the future we shall always be blessed with Chiefs of superhuman humility, levelheadedness, and wisdom. But it seems almost too much of a risk to take. Arthur M. Schlesinger, Jr., when asked recently whether it took a genius to operate the complicated system, responded: "It takes a man of immense intelligence, energy, discipline, retentiveness of mind, perseverance, will, intellectual curiosity, judgment and vitality—it takes all these qualities to make it work. Whether that constitutes genius I don't know."

Part V

Our Strange New Problem:
"Instant Democracy"

Sixteen

In the Shadow of
the Skyscrapers

On January 8, 1964, a new and untried President, Lyndon B. Johnson, standing before the backdrop of the American flag, gave his first "State of the Union" message before the full Congress assembled in the House of Representatives. Conscious of the sober faces before him, of the steady eyes of the pro-tem President of the Senate Carl Hayden and Speaker of the House John McCormack at his back, and of the scribbling of the scribes at the desks below him, the new President enunciated his program—in good, solid political platitudes designed to ingratiate all, and offend as few as possible.

He accomplished his aim. But this warm, friendly giant,

this perfectionist, this consummate politician of "total recall," was not alone in displaying canny motivations. His attractive wife Ladybird took this occasion, too, to make political hay. She invited four special guests to sit with her in the executive gallery to hear the address—a signal honor. Who were these honored gentlemen?

Two were Governor Carl Sanders of Georgia, symbolic of the prodigal South which the Democrats wish to return to the fold, and David Lawrence, the former governor and leading Democratic politician of the state of Pennsylvania, renowned for its decisive big-city vote and for its fickle political allegiance. The other two gentlemen were the mayors of the nation's two greatest cities: Mayor Robert Wagner of New York and Mayor Richard Daley of Chicago.

This guest list is of special significance to the political analyst. It is heavily weighted in favor of the big cities, and with reason. The year 1964 saw the country become (according to the formula given in the *Statistical Abstract*) 80 per cent "urban," a new record in a seemingly irreversible trend. This percentage, of course, includes all the many smaller cities and larger towns spread over the nation that, in truth, are not "big city" at all; but they are *nonrural* —they do not appear on the open countryside but lie in clusters and layers, usually, around larger cities.

The percentage, however, indicates the trend. These smaller cities and towns are growing apace, and are fast being absorbed into the fringes of the nearby great cities. We are inevitably becoming a nation dominated by the skyscrapers and their denizens, a political power bloc that looks trustingly toward the White House. It is a power bloc that cannot be hypocritically ignored much longer.

It is *the* power bloc that in the future will choose and elect the President of the United States, and he will be beholden to it. He will be the President of the Cities.

Although political analysts so far minimize the political importance of the big cities, the Presidents quite evidently do not.

American urbanization is proceeding so fast one cannot keep up with the statistics. Many who did not go to the city now find the city creeping to them. As Stewart Udall has reminded us, "The city reaches out into the country, but the country doesn't reach out into the city." New England is 69.9 per cent urban (generally speaking, concentrations of 2,500 persons or over, the urban fringe, and places with a density of 1,500 persons per square mile are considered urban and partake of urban problems); and of the individual New England states, Rhode Island is 86.4 per cent urban, Massachusetts 83.6 per cent, and all but Vermont have well over 50 per cent categorized as urban dwellers.

The Middle Atlantic is the most heavily urban—81.4 per cent—of all the regions of the nation, closely pressed by the Pacific states. Indeed, the only Mountain state that boasts more cowboys and ranchers than city folk is Idaho. It is a commentary on the times that the many men of the open spaces who portray the Old West and gallop authentically across our television screens themselves live in millionaire's mansions in Beverly Hills and neighboring cities.

As for the East North Central states—Ohio, Indiana, Michigan, Illinois, and Wisconsin—where once the pitchfork was the badge of distinction and where no presidential candidate could make an impression without first showing his pitching prowess—these states are now three-quarters urban. Indeed, the South is the last outpost of what was once a nation of farmers; and with Florida and Texas already three-quarters urban, and more and more industrialization on the way, this stronghold is bound to collapse.

But as cities burgeon and spread, so do the problems. The senior Senator from New Jersey, Clifford Case, lists them as education, employment, housing, recreation, discriminatory practices, open spaces, sewage disposal, urban sprawl, health services, transportation, crime prevention, water and air pollution, slum clearance, and taxation. In fact, there are few imaginable problems which do not occur in "these obscene hives," as Cleveland Amory terms the sprawling decay of the great metropolises. All are facets of unplanned growth, of a disorganization so chaotic as to stun the mind of man.

Collectively, our metropolitan regions are floundering for want of direction and support; individually, a new kind of environmental insecurity presses on a population that is contending with the machine for living space and struggling against complete anonymity. Collectively and individually, the urban society has desperate need for a beneficent protector. Because of their abject dependency, city people are more susceptible to the paternalistic aura cast by the Presidency.

The attack on transportation problems, on urban decay, on slums—these and many others find no dynamic champions in state legislatures. Too often the members of the legislature are, as a result of gerrymandering, unsympathetic to the cities. But even though the governors may be conscious of urban interests, the states are, of course, not nearly as richly endowed with tax resources as is the federal government.

In these critical circumstances, and in spite of the traditional American belief that municipalities should shoulder their own burdens, the cities have in their very real plight bypassed the state governments. And increasingly the President has identified himself with their interests. As Howard Penniman expresses it in *American Political Process,* "As the Solid South breaks up (it has been doing so since 1948 so far as the Democratic candidate goes) the temptation to pitch his appeal to the big cities becomes irresistible to a Democratic incumbent or hopeful."

When Oswald Spengler wrote of Rome, "A great part of the *cives Romani* for whom *panem et circenses* constituted all existence, possessed no more than a high price sleeping-berth in one of the swarming anthills called insulae," he was emphasizing the utter dependence of the city populace on the rulers. Today city dwellers are demanding a great deal more than bread and circuses, but the dependence is the same. At this juncture in history, we find the Presidency, of all the branches of government, best able to respond to the desperate cries of the urbanites with political proposals tailored to metropolitan needs.

It is to be expected that as city voters increase, the "President of all the people" will pitch his appeal more and more to the city interests. We again take note that the statistics given of urban growth are misleading, in that they include so many thousands of communities of "small towns" that have not yet grown big enough to partake of the true city's distresses. Statistics aside, the political facts tend more and more to bolster dominance by the cities in the real sense—a dominance in politics by the great metropolises *alone.*

But how truthful—or misleading—are the statistics now being quoted, statistics which state that 75 to 80 per cent of our people are living in the shadow of the skyscrapers?

We find in the 1960 census that 58,004,334 persons were living within the limits of the great cities and that another 54,880,844 persons were living within the immediate environs of these greater metropolises, a total of 112,885,178 authentic urban dwellers, or almost 63 per cent of the entire 179,983,000 souls living (as of 1960) within the borders of the United States.

This is an amazing increase of 26 per cent in urbanites over the 1950 census. (It is extremely revealing to note, also, that out of the total of 538 electoral votes, only sixty-seven represent states with a population more than half of which is listed as "rural" by the United States Bureau of the Census.)

Sweeping aside all geographical, regional, and sentimental interests, and considering only the principle of "one man, one vote," it might appear that the urban 63 per cent of the nation has full claim to the choice of the Chief Executive and to the program he adopts. There are, however, political hazards in the potential control of national affairs by twelve urban centers. Although these twelve metropolises account for little more than 50 million people, they are able to elect the President and overwhelm the rest of the nation because the electoral college system is gerrymandered in favor of the *big* urban centers.

An examination of the "general ticket" system of choosing presidential electors is revealing. American election lore abounds with stories of apparent distortions in this system in which *all* of the electors allotted to a state go to the candidate who wins a simple majority of the state's popular vote. For instance, Charles Evans Hughs in 1916 carried Minnesota by a popular plurality of only 359, but he received all twelve electoral votes of the state. In 1960 Kennedy received 1,385 415 and Nixon 1,363,324 of the ballots cast in New Jersey; nonetheless, Kennedy was awarded New Jersey's sixteen electoral college votes, and Nixon got none. On a national scale, in the election of 1924, John W. Davis received six million popular votes that brought him no electoral votes at all, whereas two million others brought him 138 electoral votes.

Another quirk of the electoral procedure, a quirk which —considering our dedication to the virtue of numbers—is of vast interest, is that it may produce a minority President. A minority President, of course, is a man who receives an electoral college majority but falls short of a popular majority in the nation. Among the Presidents who thus squeaked into office were John F. Kennedy in 1960, Harry S Truman in 1948, Woodrow Wilson in 1912, Benjamin Harrison in 1888, and Abraham Lincoln in 1860. In the light of this history, a committee of the House once sweepingly condemned the system as "not fair, honest, accurate, certain, or democratic."

A very crude picture of how these inequities arise may be drawn as follows: State A, with seventeen million voters, commands forty electoral votes. State B, with five million voters, commands fourteen electoral votes. Suppose that:

	Popular Vote		*Electoral Votes*	
	Republican	*Democrat*	*Rep.*	*Dem.*
State A votes	9,000,000	8,000,000	40	0
State B votes	1,000,000	4,000,000	0	14
Result:	10,000,000	12,000,000	40	14

In other words, with a popular *minority* of two million votes, the Republicans come up with an electoral *majority* of twenty-six. This is how a minority President is made.

Returning to our premise that the electoral college is

gerrymandered in favor of the big urban centers, we note that when a state is even slightly urban, an urban-interest vote can register the whole of the state's electoral delegation for its candidate, making the rural vote count for zero. Moreover, when one or two large cities constitute a majority or even a plurality of the ballots cast in that state, then that city, or cities, command all of the state's electoral ballots. All the most populous states, those which command an electoral college majority, are so dominated. That is why political analysts concede that a candidate who carries twelve states will be elected President; in each of these highly populated states the big-city vote decides the issue.

In the olden days, when Matt Quay and Mark Hanna fought to control a presidential election by managing the big-city vote of a few key states, they figured on a complementary rural vote, a fairly predictable party support that the big-city vote would cap. Today, for the first time, the big cities alone can do the electing.

Richard L. Strout, in the May 2, 1964, *Christian Science Monitor,* presents some eye-opening facts regarding the 1960 presidential election. "Republicans lost, it appeared, ... because they lost the big states with big cities," he wrote. "President Kennedy carried the seven large states: New York, Pennsylvania, New Jersey, Massachusetts, Michigan, Illinois, and Texas." The Republican party, looking toward the 1964 election, had "noted that 'in 1964 11 states will have 268 electoral votes, two less than required to elect a president. In most of these states there is a concentration of population in metropolitan areas.'"

The Hearst commentator Henry J. Taylor adds some interesting statistics concerning the metropolitan control of President-making. Observing that "our country has only slightly more than 100 cities exceeding 100,000 population," he says, speaking of the Democratic party, "in fact, if the South is held, nine big cities alone—it takes only nine—can turn out enough votes for the party to win a Democratic majority in the Electoral College. These nine are Boston, Chicago, Cleveland, Detroit, Los Angeles, Milwaukee, Philadelphia, New York and St. Louis."

He then goes on to state that although Truman lost much of the South to the "Dixiecrats," his victories in the *five largest cities* took him to the White House. As for Kennedy, "Three wards in the single city of Chicago alone exceeded Mr. Kennedy's total national majority." Philadelphia and Pittsburgh have repeatedly swung Pennsylvania's thirty-two votes; Los Angeles and San Francisco have delivered all of California's thirty-two, and St. Louis and Kansas City have controlled Missouri's thirteen—to mention only a few examples. (These electoral votes have been somewhat altered since 1960.)

These facts are of great and increasing significance as state after state falls into the column of "city-controlled" commonwealths.

Granted, no vote, no segment of a democratic society is ever solid. A variety of interests constitute the urban vote —some quite rural in character (like the dealer in farm machinery). But the vote of any single segment of the population need not be "solid" to elect. Any erosion occurring in the "solid vote" may be offset by erosion in other segments of the population. To be politically significant—even decisive—a voting bloc need only have a "strong tendency" in some direction. The city of Albany, New York, is not "solid," but for forty-two years a ten-to-one ratio of Democrats to Republicans in the main city districts has made elections fairly predictable.

And a people whose main roots or interests are cement-bound will, in general, pursue other interests in government from a people whose roots are in the soil. Looking down from the fortieth floor of his skyscraper (which sways a trifle in the wind anyway), the city voter's view of the threat of enemy missiles is quite different from that of a Nebraska farmer lost in a boundless sea of tossing wheat. It is bootless to argue that a city apartment dweller, gazing out daily upon an adjoining rat-infested slum, does not have different ideas about the governmental funds needed for urban renewal from the ideas of dwellers in a tidy little seacoast town.

Governmental largesse for clean air is regarded as a crass waste by the Montana cowboy culling his herd in the fresh breezes of the Rockies, and the state capital's yearning for a center for the arts (financed by a federal subsidy) leaves the small-town tax-conscious banker not cold, but exceedingly hot.

Thus, however unrefined the statistical process and however crude the generalizations, the implications of this review are clear. Presidential politics are today essentially urban politics. There is a definite "big-city vote"—and it is deliverable under the proper circumstances. In "the velocity of history," the trend toward the city is apparently irreversible. Small wonder that presidential election calculations and strategy already revolve with dizzying concentration around the big-city vote.

The first clear-cut and unabashed indicators of the strong link between the White House and city hall came with President Kennedy, himself a rather direct offshoot of the big-city system. Kennedy's power was built on the close association of his organization with city leaders. The association paid off in the way he carried Philadelphia two to one, and by a margin that more than accounted for his state-wide majority. It was New York City that put the state of New York in his column, and it was Chicago that made him the presidential choice of Illinois. His two-to-one ratio in St. Louis gave him his victory in Missouri.

Since the first proposal for the creation of a Department of Urban Affairs and Housing in 1963 to the actual adoption of this plan in 1965 (as a cabinet agency now termed a Department of Housing and Urban Development), the misgivings have been closely related to the election statistics. The temptation for a President to concentrate pressure for political support in an agency with billions of dollars at its disposal would be difficult to withstand. There was some recollection of the Freedman's Bureau of 1865, through which northern radicals gave forty acres and a mule to former slaves in return for political support. Were we now to substitute three rooms and a bath as the bait for the building of a vast new federal political machine?

Could the new intimacy between Washington and the cities, and their growing dependence on federal appropriations for water, transportation, air pollution control, harbors, urban renewal, hospitals, schools, and welfare, culminate in anything other than a political alliance? How long can any President, now in control of instantaneous communication with the people, rural as well as urban, and equipped to fly in on a moment's notice for a parade or a visit whenever local zest for his party is flagging, fail to misuse such a powerful alliance? In the past, when more decorous conduct was demanded, Presidents without number were rebuffed none too gently for intervening in state elections, yet in 1963 President Kennedy did a soapbox stint in a Philadelphia *city election* to save the day for the Democratic mayor, and without undue editorial comment! Thus the new partnership has been made inescapably evident. The possibilities, of course, are dynamite.

There are no inherent virtues in rural citizens superior to the virtues of the denizens of the city. The record of bucolic political chicanery is too disillusioning to support such a conclusion. But whether a circumscribed urban viewpoint —perhaps working to the detriment of the country at large and to the neglect of the countryside—is desirable, or even endurable, is another, more debatable matter.

There are other very real dangers in this affinity of the President and the cities. The conditions of city life, with its interwoven physical dependencies, its masses ready to be mobilized into demonstrations and mobs, make it a more efficiently and economically organized element of the population. In plain words, the congestion, centralized authorities, and thorough organization of city life make the city a perfect setting for the rigid control of a political dynasty, a rock-ribbed machine.

We need not dwell here on what happens to the citizenry, rural and urban, when government handouts are the order of the day. History has already demonstrated that any large outpouring of government wealth is too heady a draught for our shaky moral values to withstand. The public land peccancies, the pension racket after the Civil War, the canal binge, the patronage excesses, right up to the modern agricultural scandals, are sad evidence of the results of mixing privilege and politics.

Should, then, some President's organization (personal

or party) get its teeth so securely into the people's neck (aided amply by federal largesse) that they can never be pried loose, the Republic is at an end. State-wide machines were rampant in the nineteenth century; the "Cameron-Quay Dynasty" ruled Pennsylvania absolutely for sixty years; Tom Platt in New York and Nelson Aldrich in Rhode Island tyrannized those states for a full generation; for decades every word of Simon Guggenheim in Colorado and Marcus Hanna in Ohio was a command. This, also, is American history. It can happen nationally, fifty times worse.

Such contingency aside, however, the difficulty lies in the constricting of the President's constituency. With his election and re-election depending on a narrower and ever narrower cross section of the electorate, inducing him not only to cultivate the favor of the cities exclusively but to hitch grants and aids directly to the presidential vote, an essential quality of the Presidency as traditionally conceived and enshrined is endangered.

On the one hand the President stands for all those values, concepts, and understandings that draw us together as a people. He is the Chief of Consensus. He performs those ceremonies which bind us together as a people. He presumably seeks to array the whole of the citizenry in support of goals that are beyond controversy. It is much more than the art of peddling crumbs from a political feast; it is not a case of balancing favors and patronage: it is a matter of articulating the common commitment of the whole society.

On the other hand the father of all the people must repeatedly act the role of political advocate and leader of one segment of the population. This, too, is an honorable role. But there cannot be a gross imbalance in his attentions, if

247

he would retain his larger office, his accepted constitutional role. The frequent exercise of such partisan advocacy by the titular leader not only seriously tarnishes the glitter of his chieftainship but also, among many other things, weakens his stature in international affairs.

If, then, the arithmetic of presidential elections causes the President to emphasize his partisan character as a champion of cities at the expense of his larger unifying function as father of all the people, we are, indeed, in the throes of a revolutionary adjustment. During all American history, the avowed desideratum of all Presidents has been to be President of all the people. Will urbanization cancel out what technology has at last brought within reach?

Truly, the character of the Presidency is changing before our eyes. The timeworn constitutional notions about presidential restrictions, checks, and counterchecks are being shaken, indeed, torn up by the roots. Do we want to retain Truman's picture of the Chief as one who "alone has no sectional, no occupational, no economic ties. If anyone is to speak for the people it has to be the President." What is happening to that old-fashioned leader, the President of Jackson, Lincoln, Garfield, Cleveland, Wilson, and the Roosevelts—the President, indeed, of Kennedy and Johnson as well—who felt such empathy with the far-flung hamlets and the millions living in the nation's hinterlands? Will he become a forgotten stranger in an ever stranger land?

Seventeen

Our Crumbling Checks
and Balances

And so we have progressed from the remote, almost legendary leader to one who has almost instant access to the ears, eyes, and minds of the populace. In this still pluralistic society, tugged this way and that, affected by mass lethargy, it seems implausible to envision some unscrupulous demagogue of the future, gifted to "play upon the passions and ill humors of the masses," who might influence them overnight to act unwisely, even tragically, for the Republic. Isaiah's warning to his people that an errant leader would "destroy the way of thy paths" has an archaic ring in this sophisticated age.

Yet technology has flung wide the door to the rabble-rouser; once he is established, it will be too late to set up a counterforce. And truly the insane pressures and demands of the age will tempt the most prudent President to resort to Madison Avenue tactics to win a vital victory.

Today any man who can surmount the killing hurdles of state primaries, the bartering of selfish interests, the snappy repartee of the press conference, and the cruel and soulless glare of the television lights, must perforce possess a high-gloss finish of incredible toughness. When the candidate is at last through slugging, dealing, undercutting, and buying his way to a party's nomination, we may well cherish whatever shreds of virtue he may still retain.

That the qualities which brought him to success will magically vanish in the redeeming effulgence of the Presidency can happen. It has happened, as with President Arthur ("Where are these good men who will stand up with me to the fight?" he burst out in despair when his old cronies sneered at his reformation). But for the nation to depend on magic of this kind in a Chief of such vast powers is too much of a risk to take in this hair-trigger world.

Professor Herman Finer has recently reminded us that ". . . for many fatal decisions, the President of the United States is not compelled to seek the assent of anyone." The growth of presidential influence may be seen in the field of civil and military appointments; whereas in 1796 President Washington submitted 85 nominations to the Senate, in 1958 President Eisenhower submitted 59,079! "How formidable a weapon of presidential will this power has become!" comments Finer.

Yet the power to appoint is very secondary today to such presidential power as that over the budget, foreign aid, and emergency, renewal, and disaster allocations, to mention but a handful. "In the American political system," writes Richard Neustadt, "the President sits in a unique seat and works within a unique frame of reference. The things he personally has to do are no respecters of the lines between 'civil' and 'military,' or 'foreign' and 'domestic,' or 'legislative' and 'executive,' or 'administrative' and 'political.' At his desk—and there alone—distinctions of these sorts lose their last shred of meaning. The expectations centered in his person converge upon no other individual; nobody else feels pressure from all five of *his* constituencies; no one else takes pressure in the consciousness that *he* has been elected 'by the Nation.'"

That a post already unexcelled in power is gathering, with the proliferation of governmental functions, more and more power to itself can hardly be questioned. And not only does the office absorb power from every spillover in every direction, but the incumbent himself is in the process of shifting his own sources of power.

William G. Carleton, writing in the December 1961 issue of *Harper's,* describes how President Eisenhower, by his great military popularity, and President Kennedy, by his elaborate personal organization, made themselves President quite over the heads of the political managers. Their personal glamorization outshone all other considerations. Thus Kennedy was able to surround himself "by satellites rather than political equals or competitors." There is no evidence that the "personality cult" has suffered any setback under President Lyndon B. Johnson.

Dr. Carleton goes so far as to suggest that the American President no longer needs the support of his party, as has been the case all through history. He can flout the managers and get elected; they are no longer the intermediary be-

251

tween him and the electorate. It might be more realistic to say that, rather than being in a position to flout the party machinery, the Chief is now in a position to manage it. He no longer needs to knuckle under as every earlier President has done, but he still needs an organization to support him throughout the land.

Spectacularly, then, our new presidential "personality" finds himself the center of a dazzling spotlight which withers political rivals and drives them into his shadow. More and more the Chief, released at last from any necessity to bow overdeeply to the old and tried counsels of his peer group, finds himself the radiant center of government, drawing ever greater power to itself. He has been given a magic carpet: "We interrupt this program to bring you a special broadcast. Ladies and Gentlemen, the President of the United States!" The moment is electric. The development bears watching.

The President, many have noted, is at the zenith of his earthly ambitions. Once in office he is headed only for the history books. How can he ensure that he will be listed among the "great"?

Looking behind him, the Chief notes the standards by which his predecessors have been measured. He sees that the Presidents who do most, who live in crises (many of their own making), who conduct great wars, who dare most, are loved most, and also hated most—it is these, and these only, who make the grade. The old proponents of a "weak Presidency" are forgotten along with the Presidents of uneventful, peaceful reigns. He sees that, more and more, the great politician triumphs over the great statesman. And he has become aware that a President must be able to look a people in the face and lie. The question is not one of ethics, if he considers the safety of the Republic at stake, but one of judgment.

With such temptations—or rather, "facts of life"—before him, and such instant power to arouse public support at his fingertips, the fears expressed by James Fenimore Cooper hardly seem valid: "As a rule, there is far more danger that the President of the United States will render the office less efficient than was intended, than that he will exercise an authority dangerous to the liberties of the country."

The Founding Fathers were fanatic in their insistence on "checks and balances" against the excessive accumulation of power by any arm of the federal government. Influenced by Montesquieu and William Blackstone, they were convinced that excesses in government could be avoided only by compartmentalizing it and then setting off one branch against the other. John Adams, with great satisfaction, listed no less than eight such checks:

States and territories against the central government
The House of Representatives against the Senate
The President against the Congress
The Judiciary against Congress
The Senate against the President in matters of appointments and treaties
The people against their Representatives
The state legislature against the Senate
The Electoral College against the people

Adams' list actually contains but two checks on the President: those of states' rights and of the Congress. To these might be added (for what it may be worth) the ex post facto check of the Supreme Court, or Judiciary, on the President.

Corwin and Koenig assume that adequate safeguards automatically come into play to counteract a too ambitious Chief Executive. They list these additional checks on the President: the undeniable pressure of public opinion, biennial elections, an alert press, freedom of legislators to criticize, and the vast number of vocal, private interest groups, all of whom avidly watch the President for any misstep. But in any consideration of countervailing powers there must loom, overshadowing all else, the great lethargic bulk of the Congress of the United States.

Between Andrew Johnson and Lyndon Johnson a century-long river of history flows. When Thaddeus Stevens pointed his scrawny finger in the direction of the White House and announced a hundred years ago, "He [the President] is the servant of the people *as they shall speak through Congress,*" Andrew Johnson bristled. The subordination of the Presidency to the Congress, he decided, was insupportable; it was the most flagrant sort of distortion of constitutional doctrine. Recalling Alexander Hamilton's declaration that "Congress forgets itself when it tries to play the executive," Johnson truly strove to be a "strong Chief," but he was a hundred years in advance of his times. Alone in his constitutional trenches, unable to summon any logistic aid from the grass roots, bereft of public backing, he was forced to surrender to the Congress, more ignominiously than anyone before or after.

Yet today the party leaders gather amiably in the White House every Tuesday morning for bacon and eggs. Three times a week the Senate majority leader and the Senate whip (being of the President's party) pay their political

Chief a special visit. How different this camaraderie from the day not only of Andrew Johnson, but of most of our Presidents. Are there underlying causes (more basic and of longer duration than the new presidential powers) which have brought all this about?

The history of our government has been one of constant strife between the Congress and the Chief. When the Senate cabal conspired to meddle with Lincoln's cabinet, he rose in angry defiance, declaring unequivocally, "I AM MASTER, and *they shall not do that.*" Only the powers conferred by the emergency supported him. Andrew Johnson called the Senate "the damned scoundrels," and cared not who heard him. And President Cleveland in 1895 complained bitterly: "Think of it! Not a man in the Senate with whom I can be on terms of absolute confidence. . . . Not one of them comes to me on public business unless sent for, and then full of reservations and doubt. We are very far apart in feeling and, it seems to me, in purpose."

But the lordly and pre-eminent Senate is not alone in badgering the Chief; the attitude of the House may be discerned in the words of eighty-year-old, tobacco-chewing "Uncle Carl" Vinson when a member of the press accosted him as he was impatiently awaiting the eight o'clock opening of the House cafeteria. Bill Surface asked the old Georgian, who had an unequaled record of service in the House (since 1914), if it was true that he had served under nine Presidents? "I didn't serve *under* nine. . . . I served *with* nine. I don't serve *under* anybody," returned the venerable gentleman, with some acerbity. Presidents all down the corridors of time have learned this disillusioning fact about the Congress of the United States.

The cordial relations that exist today between the Chief

and congressional leaders have developed not because the President has at last adopted more tact, but because during all the long years of conflict, when the Congress was energetically trying to crush the President's independence, it was failing, increasingly, to meet the nation's legislative needs. The Congress failed to offer integrated leadership, satisfactory response to the exigencies of time, to sift out the important measures sorely demanded. It spent most of its time in agitating, in Finer's words, "for those hundreds of small (often private) bills which confer benefits on individuals and pork-barrel tidbits on cities, counties and states, and bills which cater to pressure groups, of which no congressman need be proud."

Thus the President, on Congress's default, has moved in to become the chief legislator. He must work through Congress, but he does so with ever more assurance, using his new pressures and public backing to make whatever deals he must perforce make to put his program into effect.

We have already noted that it was F.D.R. who fashioned his intimacy with the electorate into the telling weapon which today's Presidents use to challenge the Congress. That new leadership persisted even through Eisenhower, although the General had no great personal taste for the role. Under Lyndon Johnson, it is at its peak. We hear no denials of legislative authority from the Chief today! Instead, it is his set of proposals that gives unity to the actions of Congress. More and more we tend to grade the Congress by the President's assignments. If the lawmakers measure up to what he expected of them, we applaud them as diligent; if they fall short, we stamp the Congress as "do-nothing."

President Johnson was refreshingly frank about his relationship to the lawmakers. Just before a big lawn party for the Eighty-eighth Congress and their families, even as he bemoaned what the preparations were doing to the White House lawn, he said: "You don't think I'd be having 1,000 of them down here if their record had not been very good. This is one of the best Congresses in history. Out of 50 bills I submitted, they passed most of them." And following on Johnson's landslide election in 1964, the heavily Democratic Eighty-ninth Congress passed such a series of landmark laws as to alarm some observers by the lawmakers' docility.

In view of this co-operation it is hard to believe that only a few years ago the traditional interpretation of separation of powers still persisted. Mr. Justice Douglas, in his concurring opinion in *Youngstown Sheet & Tube Co.* v. *Sawyer* (1952), while acknowledging the President's unique power to "formulate policies and mould opinions," adds that, nonetheless, "the impact of the man and the philosophy he represents may at times be thwarted by the Congress. Stalemates may occur. . . ." Then the famed Justice, weighing a proposal to allow some legislative authority to the President, concludes that to do so would distort the constitutional pattern. Today it is not likely that the *fait accompli* could longer be ignored. The President is openly exercising the proscribed authority. One cannot depend on the phrase "separation of powers," hallowed though it may be, to serve as countervailing power when in reality it has come to lack both force and full meaning.

We have considered at some length the Chief's newly acquired ability to sway the people to exert pressure upon the Congress. But for a considerable period the President has been developing many other, though lesser, weapons of congressional control. For example, there is tremendous significance in the way in which the President today shares his popular standing with those legislators who commit themselves to his legislative program. It is they who are privileged to have their campaign photos taken in the company of the Chief. When a new project is undertaken by any federal agency in such a Congressman's district, the announcement is made through the lawmaker's office, thus implying that he may share the credit.

A cold shoulder by executive agencies to the importunities of a Congressman for local recognition could, if prolonged, be a devastating blow to his standing in his home district. There are many occasions when community leaders *must* be ushered into the presence of the Chief Executive, when a study group *must* hear the head of the Peace Corps, when the Queen of the Great Lakes or "Miss Distilled Turpentine of 1966" *must* be greeted with full White House ceremony by the President's lady herself. A Congressman who is locked out will cut a sorry figure with his constituents.

What a President gives, he demands payment for. The Chief is a horse trader. The interminable conferences, phone calls, breakfasts, messages, the sending of trusted Cabinet members to the congressional lobbies, the caucuses, information leaks, the providing of friends with the drafts of favorite bills, the explanatory briefings, the jockeying, the secret "understandings," the "reasoning together," the backslapping and coddling of visiting constituents, the quietly applied thumbscrews—all these are old and tried techniques of the protector of all the people. Patronage, too, is never dead or out of style. The President, although losing much to civil service, has thousands of favors to grant, funds to dispense, jobs to give or to take, contracts to allocate.

Moreover, the very reasons why Congress has lost, or is losing, its pre-eminence in legislating—its recalcitrance, provincial orientation, absorption with minor matters, and blocking tactics carried too far—confound it once more when it would present a rival national leadership to that of the President. The opposition of the House often deteriorates into a sniping action in which the shots are fired from committees by chairmen who, although they ignore the party label, are chosen because they have been returned to Congress many times by a "safe" constituency. Because, therefore, they tend to be ultraconservative, their opposition is often described as mere obstructionism.

By an incredible stroke of luck, both Johnson and Humphrey are born conciliators, artists unexcelled at compromise and persuasion. By exercising their amazing talents to soften harsh opposition, they not only strengthen the Chief's leadership, but actually tend to preserve congressional authority from the imposition of too angry and drastic reform.

However, because of this congressional irresponsibility, the House in particular continually discredits itself as a center of sensible countervailing power to a possibly overbearing Chief Executive. The Congress *should* be such a countervail. Such was the intention of the Constitution. But provincial attitudes and often senseless opposition have in recent times prevented its playing such a role.

That the Founding Fathers did not foresee the corrosions of history is unfortunate. Or perhaps some of them did foresee the provincialism but, fatigued with arguments and compromise, surrendered to Hamilton's contention

259

that our government was "as good as could be devised," and that if its vices were corrected it would no doubt be rendered impractical.

Those who propose the "streamlining" of the Congress might resolve certain questions before outlining their plans. Can a government be made to function "too smoothly for wisdom"? Is, as former Governor Edmund S. Muskie of Maine contends, the stability of our government (which astonishes Europeans and Asians alike) dependent in great part on our very deliberation, our "counterbalanced and constitutionally inhibited" institutions? How much do we want to restrain the opposition in order to get quick action? How may we strike a good balance between too cumbersome a democracy and too autocratic a one? Past dalliance must be corrected; but can powers once wrested from the Congress ever be restored to it? When we decide we are getting too much "instant democracy" from the President, will the restoration of former checks be possible?

But what of the other checks against the President mentioned earlier? Much has been made of our "pluralistic society." The question now arises, How long can we preserve a pluralistic society, with its great variety of opinions, when the centers of mass communications blanket the entire nation with conformist "news"—news that very often follows the "line" of a federal bureau or agency? The news on insecticides has long been doctored by the Department of Agriculture. The news on the effects of atomic fallout was long belittled by the Atomic Energy Commission as it sought to reduce the public's opposition to its atomic testing program. (Today the government's position is reversed, since it wants public support for the test-ban treaty, and the executive gives us the facts about the amounts of strontium 90 in the bones of babies.) It so happens that heretofore the A.E.C. was engaging in deception and that now the President is giving the nation the truth.

But the duplicity of federal agencies is not at issue here. The question is, How much of a countervail is the much-touted "pressure of public opinion" going to be against a magnetic, persuasive President who has greater television "projection" than scruples? It would seem that such a President's appeal would be able to overwhelm, for example, a states' rights issue, whatever the principle involved. What will "public opinion" of the future be if not the opinion of the authoritative, ever-present leader? The President will make public opinion.

There are those, then, who put much store in corporations and private interest groups as counterforces to the Chief. The great American corporation emerged from World War II as the characteristic institution of American society; Professor Andrew Hacker of Cornell University, quoted in *Current* in December 1963, declared that "all signs are that the future lies with the great corporate institution" with its ever agglomerating masses of wealth and power. As far as a counterforce is concerned, it is unlikely that ever again will we be blessed with a poor man in the White House; to reach the pinnacle the Chief is becoming daily more dependent on millions of dollars in campaign contributions or from his own fortune. Whatever quietus he has made with big business and its cause, the President of the future is not exactly its "man on the spot." Too many of these corporations have their destinies influenced by a regulatory commission he controls or by government contracts he approves or by the government investment and tax policy he directs.

One must recognize that in itself the great bulk of America is a protection against excessive domination. The dissident press can still be influential, but the journalistic forces of opposition to presidential policies tend to have no place to focus their efforts. The President, on the other hand, personalizes *his* policy.

There is still the Supreme Court as a restraint on an overambitious President. The Supreme Court has been making its power felt so much in the last decade that it is being accused of usurping the constitutional roles of both the Congress and the Chief Executive by continually amending the Constitution. Arthur Krock of the New York *Times* notes that the Justices have attained so much supremacy that "the President automatically enforces the decrees of the Supreme Court, and . . . appeals to Congress to use its limited power to vacate them get nowhere." It proclaims "revolutions in the American political process," and the "revolutions are immediately accomplished."

Friction between the Chief Executive and the Supreme Court, like friction between the Chief Executive and the Congress, is in good American tradition. As early as 1832 Andrew Jackson, enraged at a Court pronouncement, said angrily of Chief Justice Marshall: "He has made his decision: *now let him enforce it!*" With that one sentence, he cleaved to the heart of the Supreme Court's weakness. While the lovely black robes and dignified surroundings bemuse the populace, and reverence clings to its dictums like lint on velvet, the Supreme Court is hopelessly handicapped against any President of the future who may not display the conscientious, Constitution-respecting attitudes to which it is accustomed. The Supreme Court may pontificate and hand down its honored decisions. But what does it mean? Federal troops must be called out to enforce the really important ones. The Supreme Court cannot execute its decisions. And who must call forth the federal agencies of enforcement? None other than the President of the United States—*if, and when, he so chooses.*

An entirely different counterforce to the Chief's dominance has not yet been mentioned. Like the corporation, it is neither crumbling nor desirable as an offset. This institution is quite modern, is endowed with massive power, has large sums of independent funds, and has no responsibility to speak of to the people. It is beyond their control. It is also, for the most part, beyond the control of Presidents, who come and go while it remains. It is the federal bureaucracy.

Because the bureaucracy is a mammoth, headless "thing," because it is becoming daily a greater political force, which must be reckoned with, it cannot be ignored in any discussion of presidential stumbling blocks. Bureaucracies that go on and on with the same personnel decade after decade, becoming ever more hidebound and inflexible, can seriously impede even the most persuasive executive. Marriner S. Eccles, in *Beckoning Frontiers,* offers us a picture of what was encountered by one of our most ingratiating Presidents, Franklin D. Roosevelt. He quotes the President:

"The Treasury is so large and far-flung and ingrained in its practices that I find it almost impossible to get the action and results I want—even with Henry [Morgenthau] there. But the Treasury is not to be compared with the

263

State Department. You should go through the experience of trying to get any changes in the thinking, policy, and action of the career diplomats and then you'd know what a real problem was. But the Treasury and the State Department put together are nothing compared with the Na-a-vy. The admirals are really something. . . . To change anything in the Na-a-vy is like punching a feather bed. You punch it with your right and you punch it with your left until you are finally exhausted, and then you find the damn bed just as it was before you started punching."

It is true that bureaucrats bow more to congressional sentiment and cater more to it than to either public opinion or the President. It is to the Congress that they must look for their appropriations, for their daily bread. Bureaucrats, like many a Congressman, were there before the incumbent Chief, and they expect to be there long after he is gone.

But even the bureaucrats may be brought into line by the Chief Executive. Equal representation, which is surely coming to the House, will tend more and more to align House members with the President as their constituencies become one and the same. Bureaucratic snubbing of the Chief will disappear. Exactly how? We have already noted that the electoral college is gerrymandered to give dominance to the urban vote and urban viewpoint, thus imposing an urban outlook upon the President himself. Reapportionment and redistricting of the House will, of course, alter that body drastically, imposing on it, also, an urban outlook. When the interests of both President and House are joined, foolhardy indeed will be the bureaucrat who fails to bow deeply to both.

What is true of the executive departments is true also of the many independent commissions that depend so heavily on congressional appropriations. But even if certain of these independent, irresponsible nuclei of concentrated power were to continue for some time in their errant, irritating ways, they would not be counterforces, but mere stumbling blocks. One-purposed, narrow-horizoned entities, each pursuing its small and special goal, they could oppose little of reference or relevance to the national welfare as a whole. The heads of departments and commissions are often large-souled and earnest men, even self-sacrificing men. But they are caught in a bureaucratic net toughened by the decades. It is the bureaucracy that rules itself. As for the nation, the leadership of the most daring and whimsical President would be infinitely preferable to the leadership of one of these "things."

The old order, the ancient pattern of checks and balances, is crumbling. Restraints upon the President by the great new forces rising in our society—the bureaucracies, the departments, and the massive new corporate entities which Professor Hacker so greatly fears—are unthinkable and must be circumvented. Yet ought we not give some thought to reconstructing and modernizing the political devices of restraint that are at hand?

Eighteen

Reinforcing Our
Constitutional Restraints

Some eighty years ago Henry Brooks Adams said, "Power is poison. Its effect on Presidents has always been tragic, chiefly in an almost insane excitement at first, and a worse reaction afterwards; but also because no mind is so well balanced as to bear the strain of seizing unlimited force without habit or knowledge of it; and finding it disputed with him by hungry packs of wolves and hounds whose lives depend on snatching the carrion."

This metaphor of wolves and hounds has, perhaps, but shrunken relevance to the President of our day. There is, however, an underlying truth in the concern here expressed over the concentration of executive power, potential or immediate. It bids us pause before we pull the teeth of whatever "wolves and hounds" remain.

There are, broadly, two approaches to the problem of restraining the power of an office and its occupant. Following tradition, we can bolster the institutional countervail of competitive power centers such as the Senate and House. We can, simply, limit power by defending the apportioning of it.

Such an approach, however, is no longer a simple constitutional exercise. It cannot be merely decreed that an arm of government, be it Congress or any other, henceforth must share more responsibly in decision-making. The obvious way to increase resistance to undue power in one arm is to fortify an opposing arm with new robustness. By sharpening the responsibility of the opposing unit, by reinforcing the President's rivals for public favor, we would set up a countervail.

All countervail does not exist in the Congress, but the most important is there. (It is worth recalling that, when Charles de Gaulle sought to impose his will on France and eyed the American system to decide how best to do it, he concluded by stripping the legislature of nearly all its authority to challenge his decisions.)

Without doubt, congressional recalcitrance both fetters and exasperates the President. Kennedy remarked laughingly: "It is much easier in many ways for me—and for other Presidents who felt the same way—when Congress is not in town." T.R. clenched his fist and shouted: "Sometimes I wish I could be President and Congress, too!" Concerning which remark, F.D.R. said: "Well, I suppose if the truth were told, he is not the only President that has had that idea."

The more confidently the President can look to a popular mandate for justification of what he is proposing, the more vital it is that pockets of opposition be able to organize their protest. For this reason and for the obvious advantages of deliberation (and without considering other consequences), we can hardly discredit the ancient checks and balances or give serious thought to discarding the tried and proven doctrine. It may be of interest here to recount the most renowned example of a republic which abandoned the idea of checks and balances, as the political scientist Leslie Lipson describes it in his *Great Issues of Politics*.

For half a millennium Rome was a republic, rich in achievement and power, and embodying principles that were essentially democratic. "Wanting to avoid a repetition of the tyranny they had suffered under some of their kings, the Romans adopted the device of a distribution and separation of powers and relied upon the various agencies and authorities to balance, and thereby check, each other," he writes.

But crises, wars, and the supervision of its expanding provinces demanded a stronger central authority. "Only one institution attempted to fill the need: the Senate," says Lipson. The Senate was a strong and noble body, but there came a succession of ambitious men who tried to undermine it. "The last century of the republic's existence (133–31 B.C.) comprised a dismal catalogue of revolution, counter-revolution, and coup d'etat." At length the Roman Senate was brought to its knees; and autocracy followed with all power in the person of the emperor. That the ruler was beholden to the people for his power lingered only in ceremony "as a perfumed memory of the past ... deference to an ancient form."

It would probably amuse a President, harassed by Congress as he sometimes is, to be measured for imperial robes by any pedant. But, the validity of historical analogy aside, we ought, out of the logic of our situation and our awareness of political realities, to seek not so much to curb Congress as to find a legitimate manner for it to express its opposition in a responsible way. We need within the Congress a counterforce which will not only sniff out the weaknesses in presidential proposals, but do so on the basis of national guidelines and with an alternative program in mind.

Such an opposition cannot be bred from the local blood lines represented in the House, even though that body is the most representative of the people. Someone with a national pedigree must be joined to this body to raise the opposition to the same national level at which the President himself operates. There ought, in fact, be an Opposition Leader whose roots of leadership will be somewhat deeper than the shallow roots of the minority leader.

The sole member of the opposition party who has heretofore conducted a dialogue with the people at all comparable to the President's—and the only man who has the stature to command the networks with any degree of the President's authority—is the man who was defeated for the post of Chief. We ought therefore to find a key place in the internal organization of the House for this leader of the opposition. His very eminence would compel him to lift the sights of his party colleagues and challenge presidential policies constructively.

It is revealing that former Presidents of the minority party have set up their oracular headquarters for periodic pronouncements on public issues. Although a stabilizing force, this procedure fails to provide responsible opposition. Although revered, their peak of power has passed, their lance blunted. But the current defeated leader of the opposition is a future threat and a power to be respected.

Political commentators and students of political science have long deplored the complete collapse of a working opposition in national affairs between elections. Except on the state and local level the defeated party goes to pieces for three years. In general, the parties have not matured to the point where they select a man who can lead them, not simply as the candidate of the hour, but, possibly, for four years more in the wilderness—a man of solid, enduring qualities and appeal. Comments Eric Sevareid: "Conventions do not deliberately vote for caretakers and there is no real 'party machinery' to control. Not on the national scale. Parties out of power have no national leader save in the meaningless 'titular' sense. The party 'machinery' is entirely state and local."

He adds that even the state and local party machinery becomes more fragmented and quarrelsome "and therefore in all probability even more unprepared for a national fight" when the next election year rolls around. Though his remarks alluded to the 1964 contest in particular, they apply to any election period.

To suggest the creation of an Opposition Leader of influence and purpose is not to propose that we adopt a parliamentary form of government. We ought not, for it probably would not flourish in this alien soil. We ought not to subject the President to a vote of no confidence or end his tenure on defeat in the House—these are the key elements in parliamentary government.

Yet the post would be far from a vapid one. Some of the

consequences of elevating the presidential candidate of the losing party to this permanent post would be these: Greater care should be given to the choice of a candidate if the party had to put up with him not only in raising money all over the country but also in the halls of Congress. The campaign itself would take on dignity if each candidate knew that he would be facing his opponent in one capacity or another for four years. *Most important,* such a man would provide a focus of attention for the opposition, a responsible spokesman, somebody to challenge the President for the headlines and for the analysis of national affairs—in short, someone to share a portion of the glaring spotlight, perhaps even a faint aura of the Chief's glamor.

It is a mark of political sophistication that we have, at least until now, conducted our public affairs through a two-party system. First one party, then the other, is in power. We do not, as was the custom in England until the time of Queen Anne, cruelly thrust our defeated party leaders into exile. We do not even impeach them.

But neither do we urge them to organize for a constructive assignment. Instead, the members of the defeated party settle down to a grumbling acquiescence under a loose association of legislative leaders. The years of opposition are punctuated by destructive criticism and loud cries of woe. How much more energizing to the Republic if they could rally an alert, critical, conscientious citizenry around a program symbolized by the respected man of their choice —the defeated candidate for President and Opposition Leader.

In times of national emergency the Opposition Leader might well lift the Congress from narrow, partisan meanness or piddling hindrances to an understanding, but independent, co-operation. His role would challenge the President to show himself a statesman. Already, however hesitantly, some preparation has been made for such a part. The late Adlai Stevenson, in particular, undertook to interpret the opposition stand in the off-year elections; but he had no political base. He would have been able to make himself widely heard had he had an office in the Capitol.

So far, in our consideration of the Congress as a countervail, we have concentrated in most part on the House. This is because the Senate, while sharing many of the House's faults regarding sectional attitudes and often senseless obstructionism, has a rather special mission and make-up. The Senate of the United States is theoretically the stronghold of federalism, and the essence of federalism is the division of authority, the limitation of power, a limitation which can be enforced by either component part. Here, then, is the *constitutional* basis of a true countervail against the possibility that a too dominant Chief and a handful of urban managers will run the nation. The Senate promises to be the last bulwark of the balance of powers on which the government of the United States was constructed.

Certainly the Senate, like the House, is responsive to the will of the People, but in a more deliberate, less excited way. And because the Senate's membership is limited, and Senators have longer tenure and an elder-statesman character, they play a vital role in the public forum. Next only to the President, they guide public thinking; they are capable of commanding attention in the press and on television. And they are keenly conscious of their role as a countervail to the Chief. Consider Senator Robert Taft, whose constituents elected him time after time as a sort of neutralizer, an anchor to windward, a brake, long after most of them had abandoned his ultraconservatism. Consider, too, Senator Everett Dirksen, that craggy, rumple-haired reactionary whose opposition has of late become historic and sometimes statesmanlike.

Admittedly the Senate, because of its power, has been able to perfect the art of obstructionism. But although senatorial filibusters enrage the public on many occasions, they amuse and even reassure them on others. It is to be remembered, as Senator Maurine Neuberger reminds us, that the filibuster may fairly often be a delaying action with the sole purpose of giving the public time to catch up on the issue and make itself heard.

But senatorial recalcitrance, no matter what its origin, has a deeper significance of which we often lose sight. Since the Senate is the stronghold of federalism, the very backbone of our form of government, the delaying tactics of the Senate are in fact the *most potent defense of federalism anywhere in the nation.* Whether we approve of the actions of the Senate depends, then, on how sensitive we are to the need for decentralization. If we wish to preserve a measure of regional power, the protection of senatorial waywardness is basic.

The problem is how to trim the abuses of procedure in the Senate while not injuring the federal principle; how to "reform" the Senate without hamstringing its proper function as champion of the states, which is the essence of federalism.

However, the very notion of countervailing power is under attack when we adopt the slogan "One Man, One Vote" as our measure of democracy. The exact dimensions of the problem are still somewhat cloudy as the nation hastens to adjust its political life to the June 1964 decrees of the Supreme Court. In a decision hailed as a "bomb-shell," "a major political earthquake," and a "knockout," the Court decreed an end to geographical representation in the upper chambers of state legislatures. Henceforth, membership in both houses will be apportioned by population.

What are the implications of the "one man, one vote" principle on the national level? Is it an enthronement of the idea of majority rule to the exclusion of minorities? Is it total abandonment of John Adams' sage advice on checks and balances: "There is, in short, no possible way of defending the minority . . . from the tyranny of the majority, but by giving the former a negative on the latter. . . ."

The Supreme Court decision, comments Dan Button, editor of the Albany *Times-Union,* has "implications which are tremendous . . . the questions already being raised are vital, basic ones, affecting the entire structure of governments of all levels throughout the United States." Indeed, these very "tremendous implications" of the decision of the Supreme Court (whose own selection, incidentally, falls quite outside the "majority choice" doctrine) on the future of Congress itself are disturbing. Will the self-righteousness of the doctrine, which Justice Harlan in his minority decision said "flies in the face of American history," overwhelm not only the state governments but the federal government as well?

But all questions of democratic dogma and minority representation aside, strictly mathematical apportionment of the House will, as suggested earlier, give the President of the United States and the House of Representatives *identical constituencies*—the constituency of numbers.

This, of course, will tend to make the House the weakest sort of countervail to an unduly domineering and ambitious Chief Executive.

This leaves the Senate as the only legislative arm which will depend on geographical and other considerations besides numbers for its selection. In a society dominated by metropolitan forces as a consequence of the enshrinement of the politics of arithmetic, we may dearly need such a counterforce. For in contrast to a majority juggernaut which could ram through precipitate decisions, the Senate acts to compel the kind of political reasoning and compromise that constructs workable solutions without fatal alienation or undue bitterness.

Here, then, is the value of the Senate. The fact that the collective constituency of the Senate *does not match* that of the President, either in time or space, endows the Senators, on numerous issues, with the capacity to stand up against the Chief without fear of political reprisal and defeat. The fact is that the Constitution of the United States guarantees that the Senate's constituency be an inviolable guarantee of its independence. To change that one part of the Constitution which says that we *cannot* change that part of the Constitution would be "Constitution-smashing" with a vengeance.

There is a strong custodial tradition in the Senate—a commitment to statesmanship. This, coupled with the presidential ambitions of most prominent Senators, invests Senate action with a strong undercurrent of responsibility. It is daily impelling more of them to blend their regional biases with some conscientious understanding of the national welfare.

Much ridicule is being heaped upon the "mossy old

routine" of the Senate, its peculiarities, its tedious hearings, its aristocratic posturings, its senseless delays. Bernard Schwartz has compared the senior members of the two houses to a group of feudal chieftains, and the major committees to their own baronial fiefs. But could not the chieftains be rotated and the fiefs modernized? It is well to recall that wherever and whenever in history the feudal chieftains are disarmed and scattered, the absolute king takes over all.

There is one more point in this defense of the Senate: raw majority rule overthrows the most vital tenet Americans possess, that the highest virtue of the democratic process lies *not* in the majority's unopposed, thundering power, but in its awareness and concern for the minority. The virtue of majority rule lies in its restraint, in its capacity to withhold the whip of power and to concede the rights of what seems like an obdurate minority. To remove this sophisticated principle of restraint is a backward step in civilized politics.

The New York *Herald-Tribune* commented editorially, on November 29, 1964: "While the Executive Branch grows and multiplies, amassing its arsenal of computers, marshaling its troops, deploying its departments and bureaus and agencies, Congress slogs along in its time-tattered way, never quite catching up with where it ought to be. In the words of Oklahoma Senator Monroney, 'We who are the comptrollers of the world's biggest business are literally using a high, slant-top desk, an old-fashioned revolving stool, a big thick ledger and a quill pen.' "

That the Congress is aware of its failings is the important consideration. A major study under the tutelage of a congressional committee is now under way to work out a program of reforms such as cutting the workloads of major committees, modernizing the seniority system, computerizing whatever is susceptible to such short-cutting, and bolstering the professional staff of consultants upon whom Congressmen can rely for advice. Thus the unwieldy Congress is in line for both procedural and structural streamlining.

There is a danger that the tremendous current productivity of Congress, under the expert manipulations of a tactful President such as Lyndon Johnson, may blind us to the requirements of the age. Our satisfaction over one Congress's lawmaking record should not sidetrack long-needed reforms. Instead, we should evaluate Congress qualitatively: Is it organized to give mature and *responsible* thought to proposals before it? Is it weighing measures on a scale that gives weight to national as well as sectional interest? Is it bringing to public policy the considerations that a White House staff might overlook? These are the more important requirements of the future in which the Presidency becomes overworked and overemphasized.

We need the Congress. But we need it as responsible countervail and not as unreasonable obstructionism.

Nineteen

Countervail: Men To
Match the Hour

Imperative to the survival of the Republic are two conditions: the power of the President, while great, must be responsible, and his role as Chief of all the people, and not of the cities alone, must be maintained. No counterforce in the House or Senate can be effective if it is not mirrored in the electorate. It is an axiom that, in a democracy, power is not imposed from above, but rises from below. In a democracy, it is the people who are the valid repository of its strength and continuance.

The people of the future are city people. It will, however, not matter so gravely that the President cues his program

278

for the large urban centers if the people in those cities can rise to the nobility of stewardship over the nation. Is there such a hope?

Thomas Jefferson once wrote: "The mobs of great cities add just so much to the support of pure government as sores do to the strength of the human body." There was yeoman's prejudice here, but the view accords with the disdain for the masses exhibited by the most prominent of the philosopher Forefathers of ours. James Madison was convinced that only "prudence, respect for character, and religion" can restrain the masses from abusing the minorities, and that in a great mass of people these virtues quickly diminish. "In a multitude," he said, "[their] efficacy is diminished in proportion to the number which is to share the praise or blame."

There is relevance in these comments on the masses, but they are not the whole story. We shall turn to James Madison again for the other side of it. The true hope of the Republic, he believed, was to "extract from the mass of the society the purest and noblest characters which it contains, such as will at once feel most strongly the proper motives to pursue the end of their appointment, and be most capable to devise the proper means of attaining it." In short, what we urgently need has long been the backbone of England, a chivalric caretaker elite—but an elite of talent and intellect, not of birth, and devoid of the trappings and the abuses of English aristocracy.

Nor is this a fatuous dream. In those very cities of giant size where exists the severest threat of political manipulation is assembled the talent of the ages, of our entire civilization. Never has a civilization provided such a wealth of intellectual experience and training to such a large segment of its people, and never have talented people gathered in such numbers.

Moreover, the cities have given strong evidence of proper motivation and varied leadership. Where are more people giving more time, thought, and money to more worthwhile projects? Where will one find more zealous workers for national and individual welfare? The cities, the centers of culture and sensibility, are also the centers of conscience. Our great philanthropies and humanitarian movements are there headquartered. The city is the spawning bed of ideas and the hotbed of causes.

As the big cities take over the making of policy for the nation, both because of their critical role in President-making and the composition of the House of Representatives, the welfare of the Republic finds itself dependent on the quality of that urban citizenry. We can scarcely reverse or even slow down the process of communication between President and people and the pattern of vote solicitation by favors which it encourages. But it is essential that the broader interests of the advantaged elements find expression through inspired leadership. If, as has been hammered home by many a cynic, we have no "elite" which is able to take over this caretaker role, *we shall have to create one.*

Yet it is the myopic observer who denies to America its noble class. Several years ago we visited in Washington, D.C., the offices of the Wilderness Society, a national organization that has been fighting a back-to-the-wall action for many years to preserve the last 2 per cent of America's spectacular wild country. There in a crowded, dim cubbyhole of an office, far from the untrammeled wilderness where he would have liked to be, a man in shirtsleeves sat in the stifling heat, hunched over a desk piled with letters, reports, and copies of the hundreds of exploitative bills that annually fill the congressional hoppers. The man was Howard Zahniser, executive secretary of the Society and editor of *The Living Wilderness*.

Howard Zahniser worshipped the wilderness, its mountains, lakes, and open skies. Yet he had chosen to chain himself to a city desk, season in and season out, not because he received a large salary (he didn't), but because he was fired with an inner consecration to the saving of America's natural beauty. The drive to protect the remnants of the wilderness was so strong in him that he relinquished his own enjoyment so that others who came after him might have a chance to experience what he consistently denied himself.

In 1964, at the age of fifty-six, this dedicated man died. His last effort was a stirring plea for the passage of the Wilderness Bill, whose benefits he had for some time known he would never see. Five months after his death the Wilderness Bill, after eighteen hearings and eight years of rejection, was passed because public demand had grown loud enough to outshout the selfish minorities. Watered down, imperfect, "just a beginning," it gives the American people ten years from passage to save all the wild country that will ever be saved; but were it not for Zahniser and others of his kind, there would be no such opportunity.

There are many such dedicated men in our great cities; every benevolent institution is, as Emerson once said, "but the lengthened shadow of a man." The individual urge toward self-giving exists strongly, even passionately, if we can only create the community climate in which it can express itself. In these city people lies the "best Remedy"

281

upon which Jefferson relied to correct the whims and mis-judgments of a democratic populace—the good sense of the "aristoi," the "wheat," as Jefferson distinguished it from the "pseudo-aristoi," or "the chaff." It is to this "natural elite of mind and selfless purpose" that we must turn for our most dependable, and truest, countervail to lopsided democracy and its follies.

Here, however, we encounter a problem of tragic signif-icance. Most of the leaders who should provide direction for the cities do not dwell there. They have fled to the outly-ing suburbs where they have established their homes and fealty; sociologically and politically they have abandoned the great city proper to a handful of politicians and to what has become, essentially, the rule of the jungle.

As a consequence, the core cities have decayed, and the leaders have cast off the responsibility not only to renew them but to direct their vast political power. In 1960 the expert participants in the Goucher College symposium on "Human Values in the Emerging American City" be-wailed the "flight of the burghers" because of the cultural bankruptcy it brought about. We must be even more dis-heartened at the loss of potential leaders, the decimation of all but self-motivated or machine authority, the rot at the heart of what is to be our national future. If the great city's political power is to be dominant in the nation, it is at present a frightening portent.

Thus the reconstruction of cities and their spiritual re-newal, the return of leaders to the helm, have become matters of national concern and perhaps survival. Unless we revive the cities, we cannot put much store in a quali-tative direction to the power of the Presidency.

In short, our urgent need is that the leadership in the city shall become as dedicated to a broad conception of public affairs as it now is to minor public health measures and organized charity. The kind of intellectual elite that will revive our cities, clean up our politics, and raise the sights of the presidential constituency must, however, be rooted in the community it speaks for, and committed as a viable political force.

Are large segments of the commercial, banking, and manufacturing communities foreclosed from participation in government because they are either footloose, dogmatized, or socially fettered, or simply because participation is "against corporate policy"? Does an outmoded folklore prevent many persons of character, intelligence, and personality from participating in an uplifted metropolitan society? Then let commerce reconsider the stakes at issue and reshape its folklore. Already many corporations are permitting their best talent to move into the government bureaucracy, into the management area. The corporations have much to give.

The cities of the nation are bursting with persons yearning to give their spare time to national and local causes. There are men and women of good will to be enlisted from labor unions, financial circles, humanitarian and conservation organizations, women's groups, communications, publishing, the arts, and elsewhere.

Frankly, the moment has come in our civilized culture when it is imperative to create an entirely new set of values for the nation, not only for Americans to emulate, but for foreigners to see. Exploitation and predation may have been excusable in a hungry young pioneer nation on the make; today they are little more than obscene, the despicable relics of a primitive philosophy. The time is ripe to

283

replace our historic interest in *private* concern with a greater interest in *public* concern, even though it means some sacrifice financially and personally—*and it will.*

Again, the ability to sort out the significant facts and issues of the day from the trivia and trash, to assign priorities to public projects, to weigh the local advantage against the national or international need—this is hardly the characteristic of the mass! These tasks require leadership of a high order, a leadership that will discuss the issues, educate the people, and guide the thinking of the public while carrying on a dialogue with the Chief Executive. When will our best talent cease sublimating their good impulses? When, instead of sending a youngster to a fresh-air camp for one week of the year, will they face up to the real problem—the *removal* of poisonous gases from the city's atmosphere—so that the youngster need not be sent back to live, with all his family, in these noxious vapors for the remaining *fifty-one weeks?* The shirking of such responsibility can no longer be condoned.

> Ye prate of patterns and the web of doom,
> Is God then tangled in a warp and woof?
> Is not the Weaver at the Weaver's place?
> Go seat you at the loom.
> Create the goodness that is heaven's proof.
> Work with God if you would see His face.

These ringing words were quoted by the late Dr. Arthur Compton, renowned scientist and Nobel Prize winner, as an expression of responsible citizenship. The entreaty is doubly significant today. It is important that the dialogue between the President and the cities be maintained as something more than an echo!

In 1956 the Duke University symposium on "The Presidential Office" came to the conclusion that the office has blossomed because of the expectations people the world over harbor of the Presidency. "Because of these heightened expectations," says J. Francis Paschall in the Foreword, "we hear little nowadays... of the ancient cry of presidential autocracy. Rather, the fear now is that the power of the President will prove unequal to the task of satisfying the expectations centering on him."

A decade has passed since the symposium was held, but the presidential outlook has changed amazingly in that brief period. Yet political observers have not realized that their campaign for increased presidential authority, now almost a doctrinal article of faith, has, almost overnight, become obsolete. The demand for a more powerful Chief has been answered by an expansion of the office the magnitude of which we have not yet had time to assess.

Mr. Gallup announced recently that the public expresses itself as being strongly in favor of electoral college reform wherein, instead of "winner take all," each state's electoral votes would be apportioned to the candidates according to their statewide voting strength. The votes given the losing candidate in any state would not simply be cast out; they would result in electoral strength and be added to his *national* total. Such a process would indeed be a countervail against any future President's addressing himself only to the dozen or so greatest cities and ignoring the rest of the nation, the small cities, towns, and farms. Sadly, however, because of the understandable opposition of the big states, electoral college reform is unlikely to be adopted in the foreseeable future. The big states, furnishing the bulk of presidential nominees simply because they swing

285

the electoral votes, are not likely to relinquish such favor readily.

Finally, there is one more check on any President who, in the exuberance of his new-found power over the people, might become unwisely motivated. It is the man himself. It is his yearning for a favorable verdict from the generations yet to come, his desire that his name be added to the short list of six or seven Presidents already inscribed on the scroll of "Great." Respect for the verdict of history may prove to be the most effective curb of all.

In another chapter we saw that the President, casting a cynical eye back over history, may note that discord, wars, violence, and opportunism have characterized the administrations of those men we now call "great." But if he is keen, he may also note more important indices. Presidents Washington, Jefferson, Jackson, Lincoln, the Roosevelts, and Wilson, without exception, were men who had the strength to oppose selfish interests. They were preponderately moral men who emphasized moral and human values, discerning men who looked far ahead to future welfare, valiant men who dared to oppose the exploitation of the nation's resources.

The elbow-jostlers and personal-favor-seekers who surround the President will not determine whether he has been great, near-great, fair, or a pitiful failure. (Indeed, they are the very ones who will earn him a lesser rating— in direct proportion to his surrender to their greedy pleas. Jackson's "greatness" has been seriously imperiled because of this very weakness, in spite of his monumental service in democratizing the presidential office and linking it to the people.) The sycophants will not judge the Chief. *Posterity will judge the President.*

President Polk, although harassed by bosses and accorded only one term, is now dubbed "near-great" because he hewed to his convictions without faltering. President Grant was a failure, or near-failure, because he amiably let the favor-seekers take over. When F.D.R. exclaimed angrily, "Any President who gives over to selfish interests is a washout," he showed in this one sentence that he understood the true basis of greatness. Where would the "great" Theodore Roosevelt stand today if he had not struck out so boldly for conservation and business reform?

Thus the principled Wilson, though he failed, succeeded. Harding, though shallowly "popular" throughout his incumbency, is today considered a total "failure." The posterity that will judge today's President will care not a fig that every heeler loved him; it will judge him solely on what kind of an America he left *to them*.

In writing of the ambitions of American Presidents for both great achievement and universal love, Kenneth Crawford, in the November 23, 1964, issue of *Newsweek,* writes that "none has ever had both." Lincoln was hated and despised by many millions. Eisenhower was universally loved, but "it is doubted that history will refer to him as great." Then he continues: "Like his predecessors, Mr. Johnson will have to choose between popularity and history. His friends think he will opt for history, but they may be wrong."

But "popularity" is a hollow, meaningless word. Even so, "popularity" (as used in common parlance) and "greatness" (as defined by the historians) are far from being mutually exclusive. No American President in the historians' "first seven" was without a large and passionately devoted following among the populace. In an uncanny way,

287

the people "smell out" greatness in a leader. But his acts and daring make not only many fervent friends, but also many fanatic enemies. (Recall that the common people loved Cleveland for the enemies he made.) *Universal* love is never the fate of great men. They would hardly want it.

Wilson said that he had to hold back the declaration of war that he knew was inevitable until his people were ready, not merely to follow him, but "to do so with a whoop!" With modern technology and a modern George Creel to write his script, that whoop might be excited by a real presidential "performer" within days, perhaps within hours. Today the interrelationship between the President and the people—the dialogue and understanding that exists between them—has become so close with the development of modern communications that it has distorted the relationship of all the branches of government and has altered the nature of the Presidency.

The quality of our civilization, insofar as political decisions mold it, rests, then, on this new and relatively untried power alliance between the President and the people. But how far does the President really dominate it? He can influence and sway citizens in a flash decision. But the most pervading influences in our society are commercial; selfish interest is the only organized interest we have heretofore recognized. Our mores are steeped in commercialism and self-advantage, and in generations of applying the philosophy of self-gain as the first criterion, the ingrained tendencies have hardened to custom.

Thus the President, no matter what his own idealism, perforce launches his side of a dialogue and dominates it only within the framework of our material social goals.

Normally the subject matter of the dialogue is confined to the materialistic program of the various interest groups. This is the imprisoning factor in our elective kingship— our docile acceptance that the constituency can be rallied most effectively by a crass appeal to self-interest. Yet when Winston Churchill, in a supreme moment, offered the British people nothing but blood, tears, toil, and sweat, he received the most heartening response in all history. Are the American people of weaker fiber than those of the political homeland?

Certainly the Presidency as an institution is thin. There is a brittleness to a political system that entrusts the perpetuation of its enduring values to an institution as superimposed as the Presidency. Power elites such as a medieval clergy or nobility enveloped the whole of a society and thus penetrated to where values are formed. In our society the President has, too often, been forced to operate or channel his appeals through commercial wavelengths, without dilution. Thus it is to be expected that in this instant democracy of ours the danger of an unprincipled demagogue— the kind of Chief who would encourage unwise and opportunistic decisions, because of the inbred philosophy of his followers—is heightened.

But there is another, and a far brighter, side to the American character, steeped though it has been during our period of industrial development in the pursuit of crass goals. There is an underlying common sense and a wholesomeness, even a latent denial of self, in the American citizenry, traits that have cropped up in times of crisis. The ancient ideals of the Republic die hard. The vast but suppressed yearning (of which we have spoken) toward

289

sacrifices and self-giving, best epitomized today by the Peace Corps and by the valor of our men on a remote and terrifying battlefield, is a relic of the old ideals.

Here, then, is where our need for a "natural elite," in whose code of service our Forefathers laid so much store, makes itself vitally evident, this time not as a countervail but as an agent that will give social depth and resonance to the President's constituency. It can bring to the surface the long-submerged, old-fashioned virtues of which we have so long been ashamed, strip them of ridicule, and make them viable again.

The establishment of such leadership, which, ideally, would shepherd all society, would infuse it with benign purposes and stamp a new element of nobility on the philosophy of the nation. Sir James Frazer's warning in *The Golden Bough* that "the world cannot live at the level of its great men" does not mean that it cannot live at a much higher level than it is now.

So while an unprincipled President who appeals solely to material gain may have the winds with him at the moment, there is no doubt that a strong, responsible President can rouse the American people with far finer visions of community life—arouse and excite them. John F. Kennedy struck an idealistic chord that vibrated throughout American youth. Lyndon B. Johnson has committed his administration to a new and more civilized concept of living—to greater compassion, to an awakened pride in a clean nation, to the saving of wild beauty and the fostering of man-made beauty, to an Athenian concern for cultural advancement. He and the First Lady (who gave spark and sparkle to the campaign) have already aroused unparalleled enthusiasm among the masses.

But people in the mass—whatever their desires—are unorganized and woefully inarticulate when compared to the interest groups that instantly spring into action to forestall every public-spirited move. A nationwide elite could guide and mobilize the public enthusiasm which the Chief arouses. Either the President must find backing for his idealism in positions of strength—or he will be forced to fashion his support from elements motivated by self-interest. Clearly the story of presidential leadership has only begun. This is the challenge of the lonely quest.

Bibliography

Adams, Charles Francis (ed.). *Memoirs of John Quincy Adams, Comprising Portions of His Diary from 1797 to 1848*. 12 vols. Philadelphia, 1874–77.

————. *The Works of John Adams*. 10 vols. Boston, 1850–56.

Agar, Herbert. *The People's Choice from Washington to Harding*. Boston, 1933.

Angle, Paul M. (ed.). *The American Reader*. Chicago, 1958.

————. *The Lincoln Reader*. New Brunswick, N.J., 1947.

Armbruster, Maxim Ethan. *The Presidents of the United States, a New Appraisal*. New York, 1963.

Bailey, Stephen K. *Ethics and the Politician*. Santa Barbara, 1960.

Baker, Ray S., and William E. Dodd (eds.). *The Public Papers of Woodrow Wilson*. New York, 1925–27.

Baldwin, Roger N., and Clarence B. Randall. *Civil Liberties and Industrial Conflict*. Cambridge, Mass., 1938.

Barry, David S. *Forty Years in Washington*. Boston, 1924.

Bassett, John S. *Life of Andrew Jackson*. 2 vols. Garden City, N.Y., 1911.

Beard, Charles A. *The Presidents in American History*. New York, 1948.

Beer, Thomas. *Hanna*. New York, 1929.

Bendiner, Robert. *Obstacle Course on Capitol Hill*. New York, 1964.

———. *White House Fever*. New York, 1960.

Benson, Lee. *The Concept of Jacksonian Democracy: New York as a Test Case*. New York, 1961.

Benton, Thomas Hart. *Thirty Years' View, or a History of the Working of the American Government for Thirty Years from 1820 to 1850*. 2 vols. New York, 1854–56.

Berman, Edward. *Labor Disputes and the President of the United States*. New York, 1924.

Binkley, Wilfred E. *The Man in the White House: His Powers and Duties,* rev. ed. New York, 1964.

———. *The President and Congress*. New York, 1946.

Borden, Morton. *America's Ten Greatest Presidents*. Chicago, 1961.

Bourne, Randolph. "Unfinished Fragment on the State, 1918," *Untimely Papers*. New York, 1947.

Bowen, Catherine Drinker. *John Adams and the American Revolution*. Philadelphia, 1949.

Bradley, Duane. *Electing a President*. Princeton, N.J., 1963.

Brant, Irving. *James Madison*. Indianapolis, 1941.

Brownlow, Louis. *The President and the Presidency*. Chicago, 1949.

Buckingham, J. S. *The Eastern and Western States of America,* vol. I. London, 1842.

Buehrig, Edward H. *Woodrow Wilson and the Balance of Power*. Bloomington, Ind., 1955.

Burr, S. J. *The Life and Times of William Henry Harrison*. New York, 1840.

Busch, Noel F. *T.R., The Story of Theodore Roosevelt and His Influence on Our Times*. New York, 1963.

Carroll, E. Malcolm. *Origins of the Whig Party*. Durham, N.C., 1925.

Case, Clifford, "A Cure for Sick Cities," *Saturday Review,* February 9, 1963.

Cavaioli, Frank J. *West Point and the Presidency; the Voter's Attitude Toward the Military Elite*. New York, 1962.

Chamberlain, Ivory. *Biography of Millard Fillmore*. Buffalo, N.Y., 1856.

Cole, Arthur Charles. *The Whig Party in the South, an Essay*. Washington, 1913.

Coleman, Mrs. Chapman (ed.). *The Life of John J. Crittenden*. 2 vols. Philadelphia, 1871.

Colton, Calvin. *Life, Correspondence and Speeches of Henry Clay*. 6 vols. New York, 1864. See particularly volumes I, II, and III.

Colyar, A. S. *Life and Times of Andrew Jackson, Soldier, Statesman, President.* 2 vols. Nashville, 1904.

Corwin, Edward S. *The President, Office and Powers, 1789–1957,* 4th rev. ed. New York, 1957.

———, and Louis W. Koenig. *The Presidency Today*. New York, 1956.

Cotter, Cornelius P., and J. Malcolm Smith. *Powers of the President during National Crises*. Washington, D.C., 1960.

Coyle, David Cushman. *Ordeal of the Presidency*. Washington, 1960.

Curtis, George Ticknor. *Life of James Buchanan*. New York, 1883.

Davidowicz, Lucy S., and Leon J. Goldstein. *Politics in a Pluralist Democracy*. New York, 1963.

Dietz, August. *Presidents of the United States of America, Portraits and Biographies,* 3d ed. Richmond, 1963.

Dougherty, J. Hampden. *Constitutional History of the State of New York*. New York, 1915.

Duer, John. "A Discourse on the Life, Character, and Public Services of James Kent" in *Proceedings of the Convention of the State of New York, 1821*. New York, 1848.

Eaton, Herbert. *Presidential Timber: A History of Nominating Conventions, 1868–1960*. New York, 1964.

Eaton, John Henry. *The Complete Memoirs of Andrew Jackson*. New York, 1878.

Eckenrode, H. J. *Rutherford B. Hayes, Statesman of Reunion*. New York, 1930.

Egger, Roland Andrews, and Joseph P. Harris. *The President and Congress*. New York, 1963.

Faulkner, Harold U. *From Versailles to the New Deal*. New Haven, 1950.

Fincher, Ernest B. *The President of the United States*. New York, 1955.

Finer, Herman. *The Presidency: Crisis and Regeneration*. Chicago, 1960.

Ford, Paul (ed.). *The Works of Thomas Jefferson*. 12 vols. New York, 1904-1905.

Foulke, William D. *Life of Oliver P. Morton*. Indianapolis, 1899.

Fried, Albert, and Gerald E. Stern (eds.). *The Essential Lincoln, Selected Writings*. New York, 1962.

Goebel, Dorothy Burne. *William Henry Harrison, a Political Biography.* Indianapolis, 1926.

Goldman, Eric F. *The Crucial Decade.* New York, 1956.

Greeley, Horace. *Why I Am a Whig: Reply to an Inquiring Friend.* New York, n.d.

Gunderson, Robert G. *The Log Cabin Campaign.* Lexington, Ky., 1957.

Gunther, John. *Eisenhower, the Man and the Symbol.* New York, 1951.

Gutkind, E. A. *The Twilight of the Cities.* New York, 1962.

Hacker, Andrew. *Political Theory: Philosophy, Ideology, Science.* New York, 1961.

Hagedorn, Hermann. *The Roosevelt Family of Sagamore Hill.* New York, 1954.

——— (ed.). *The Works of Theodore Roosevelt.* New York, 1923–26. (Memorial Edition.)

Hamilton, Howard D. *Political Institutions.* Boston, 1962.

Harbaugh, William Henry. *Power and Responsibility: The Life and Times of Theodore Roosevelt.* New York, 1961.

Hathaway, Esse V. *The Book of American Presidents.* New York, 1931.

Hay, John, and J. G. Nicolay (eds.). *Complete Works of Abraham Lincoln.* 12 vols. New York, 1894–1905.

Haynes, George H. *The Senate of the United States.* 2 vols. New York, 1938 and 1960.

Heller, Francis Howard. *The Presidency: A Modern Perspective.* New York, 1964.

Henry, Laurin L. *Presidential Transitions.* Washington, D.C., 1960.

Herring, Edward Pendleton. *Presidential Leadership: The Political Relation of Congress and the Chief Executive.* New York, 1940.

Hobbs, Edward H. *Behind the President.* Washington, D.C., 1954.

Hoover, Herbert. *American Ideals Versus the New Deal.* New York, 1936.

Howe, George Frederick. *Chester A. Arthur: A Quarter Century of Machine Politics.* New York, 1934.

Hoyt, Edwin P., Jr. *Jumbos and Jackasses: A Popular History of the Political Wars.* Garden City, N.Y., 1960.

Hyman, Sidney. *The American President.* New York, 1954.

—— (ed.). *The Office of the American Presidency in Annals of the American Academy of Political and Social Science,* Vol. 307, September 1956.

James, Marquis. *Andrew Jackson, Portrait of a President.* New York, 1937.

Johnson, Gerald W. *American Heroes and Hero-Worship.* New York, 1943.

Johnson, Julia E. *Increasing the President's Power, a Compilation.* New York, 1933.

Johnson, Walter. *1600 Pennsylvania Avenue; Presidents and the People, 1929–1959.* Boston, 1960.

Josephson, Matthew. *The Politicos.* New York, 1938.

Judah, Charles, and George Winston Smith. *The Unchosen.* New York, 1962.

Kane, Joseph Nathan. *Facts about the Presidents.* New York, 1959.

Kennedy, John F. *Profiles in Courage.* New York, 1955.

Koenig, Louis W. *The Chief Executive.* New York, 1964.

——. *The Invisible Presidency.* New York, 1960.

Lamon, Ward H. *Recollections of Abraham Lincoln, 1847–1865.* Chicago, 1895.

Laski, Harold J. *The American Presidency, an Interpretation.* New York, 1940.

Levin, Peter R. *Seven by Chance: The Accidental Presidents.* New York, 1948.

Lewis, Lloyd. *Myths after Lincoln.* New York, 1929.

Link, Arthur S. *Woodrow Wilson and the Progressive Era.* New York, 1954.

Lipson, Leslie. *The Great Issues of Politics,* 2d ed. Englewood Cliffs, N.J., 1960.

Lomaski, Milton. *Andrew Johnson, President on Trial.* New York, 1960.

Lonaker, Richard P. *The Presidency and Individual Liberties.* Ithaca, N.Y., 1961. See especially Chapter 5, "Public Opinion and Persuasion."

Lorant, Stefan. *The Presidency.* New York, 1951.

Lossing, Benson J. *Diary of George Washington from 1789–1791.* Richmond, 1861.

McClure, Alexander K. *Our Presidents and How We Make Them.* New York, 1900.

Maclay, William. *The Journal of William Maclay: United States Senator from Pennsylvania, 1789–1791.* New York, 1927.

McMurry, Donald L. *Coxey's Army.* Boston, 1929.

Marshall, John. *Life of George Washington.* Philadelphia, 1804–07.

Mason, Alpheus T. *Free Government in the Making; Readings in American Political Thought.* New York, 1949.

Meyers, Marvin, Alexander Kern, and John C. Cawelti. *Sources of the American Republic; A Documentary History of Politics, Society and Thought.* Chicago, 1961.

Michener, James A. *Report of the County Chairman.* New York, 1961.

Miller, William. *A New History of the United States.* New York, 1958.

Milton, George F. *The Use of Presidential Power, 1789–1943*. Boston, 1944.

Moore, Joseph West. *The American Congress, 1774–1895*. London, 1895.

Morison, Elting Elmore (ed.). *The Letters of Theodore Roosevelt*. 8 vols. Cambridge, Mass., 1951–54.

Morris, Richard B. (ed.). *Encyclopedia of American History*, New York, 1953.

Moos, Malcolm. *Politics, Presidents, and Coattails*. Baltimore, 1952.

———— and Stephen Hess. *Hats in the Ring*. New York, 1960.

Neustadt, Richard E. *Presidential Power, the Politics of Leadership*. New York, 1960.

Nevins, Allan. *Grover Cleveland: A Study in Courage*. New York, 1932.

———— and Henry Steele Commager. *A Short History of the United States*. New York, 1945.

———— and Frank Weitenkampf. *A Century of Political Cartoons*. New York, 1944.

Norton, A. B. *Reminiscences of the Log Cabin and Hard Cider Campaign*. Mount Vernon, O., 1888.

Parton, James. *A Life of Andrew Jackson*. 3 vols. New York, 1861. (Revised one-volume edition, 1863.)

Penniman, Howard R. *American Political Process*. Princeton, N.J., 1962.

Pollard, James E. *The Presidents and the Press*. New York, 1947.

The Presidential Office in *Law and Contemporary Problems*, Vol. 21, No. 4, 1956.

Rauch, Basil (ed.). *Franklin D. Roosevelt: Selected Speeches, Messages, Press Conferences and Letters*. New York, 1957.

Remini, Robert V. *The Election of Andrew Jackson.* Philadelphia, 1963.

Rosenman, Samuel I. (ed.). *The Public Papers and Addresses of Franklin D. Roosevelt.* 13 vols. New York, 1938-50.

Roosevelt, Anna Eleanor. *Eleanor Roosevelt, an Autobiography.* New York, 1958.

Roosevelt, Theodore. *An Autobiography.* New York, 1913.

———. *State Papers as Governor and President, 1899–1909.* New York. 1925.

Rossiter, Clinton. *The American Presidency Today.* New York, 1956.

Sevareid, Arnold Eric. *Candidates 1960: Behind the Headlines in the Presidential Race.* New York, 1959.

Schlesinger, Arthur M., Jr. *The Age of Jackson.* Philadelphia, 1945.

———. *The Age of Roosevelt.* Boston, 1951.

Schwartz, Bernard. *The Reins of Power: A Constitutional History of the United States.* New York, 1963.

Smith, Charles Page. *James Wilson, Founding Father, 1742-1798.* Chapel Hill, N. C., 1956.

Smith, Theodore Clark. *James Abram Garfield: Life and Letters.* New Haven, 1925.

Stanwood, Edward. *A History of the Presidency,* vol. I. Boston and New York, 1916.

Stimpson, George. *A Book about American Politics.* New York, 1952.

Sussman, Leila A. "F.D.R. and White House Mail," *Public Opinion Quarterly,* Vol. 20, No. 1, 1956.

Tebbel, John. "Presidents and the Press," *Saturday Review,* September 14, 1963.

Thomas, Elbert D. *Thomas Jefferson, World Citizen.* New York, 1942.

Thomson, Charles A. H. *Television and Presidential Politics: The Experience in 1962, and the Problems Ahead.* Washington, 1956.

Tobin, Richard Lardner. *Decisions of Destiny.* New York, 1961.

Tourtellot, Arthur B. *The Presidents on the Presidency.* Garden City, N.Y., 1964.

Truman, Harry S. *Memoirs.* 2 vols. Volume I: *Years of Decisions.* Volume II: *Years of Trial and Hope.* New York, 1956.

Tugwell, Rexford Guy. *The Enlargement of the Presidency.* New York, 1960.

Ullman, Morris B., and others. *Statistical Abstract of the United States.* Washington, D.C., annually.

Walworth, Arthur. *Woodrow Wilson.* New York, 1958.

Weingast, David E. *We Elect a President.* New York, 1962.

White, Theodore H. *The Making of the President, 1960.* New York, 1961.

White, William Allen. *Autobiography.* New York, 1946.

White, William S. *The Professional: Lyndon B. Johnson.* Boston, 1964.

Williamson, Chilton. *American Suffrage from Property to Democracy, 1760–1860.* Princeton, N.J., 1960.

Wilmerding, Lucius, Jr. *The Electoral College.* New Brunswick, N.J., 1958.

Wilson, Woodrow. *Constitutional Government of the United States.* New York, 1961. (Columbia University Press Edition)

———. *The New Freedom.* New York, 1913.

Wister, Owen. *Roosevelt, the Story of a True Friendship, 1880–1919.* New York, 1930.

Yellen, Samuel. *American Labor Struggles.* New York, 1936.

Index

303